AMERICAN SCREAM

The Bill Hicks Story

AMERICAN SCREAM

The Bill Hicks Story

CYNTHIA TRUE

Sidgwick & Jackson

First published 2002 by Sidgwick & Jackson
an imprint of Pan Macmillan Ltd
Pan Macmillan, 20 New Wharf Road, London N1 9RR
Basingstoke and Oxford
Associated companies throughout the world
www.panmacmillan.com

ISBN 0 283 06353 X

3 5 7 9 8 6 4 2

A CIP catalogue record for this book is available from
the British Library.

Typeset by SetSystems Ltd, Saffron Walden, Essex
Printed and bound in Great Britain by
Mackays of Chatham plc, Chatham, Kent

To Colleen McGarr &
Duncan Strauss

What I feel most moved to write, that is banned – it will not pay.
Yet, altogether, write the *other* way I cannot.

Herman Melville

ACKNOWLEDGMENTS

I never met Bill Hicks and I relied on the voices of his friends and colleagues to bring him closer to me. Each person interviewed revealed a facet of this complex man and I am greatly indebted to: Rick Ashton, Len Austrevich, Brent Ballard, Dave Becky, Kevin Booth, Chris Bould, Charles Brand, Peter Casperson, Seamus Cassidy, Robin Chambers, Linda Corke, David Cotton, Randy Credico, Terry DiMonte, Sandy DiPerna, James Dixon, William Donovan, Stephen Doster, Rupert Edwards, Garth Ennis, Robert Fiorella, Jeff Foxworthy, Frank Gannon, Janeane Garofalo, Bob Gold, Ed Hammell, Mike Hedge, Bruce Hills, Caroline Hirsch, Sean Hughes, Bruce Hyman, Dom Irrera, Pamela Johnson, Andy Kindler, Paul Krassner, Matt Labov, Carl LaBove, Jay Leno, John Magnuson, Paul Mayhew-Archer, Joyce Mango, Frank Mango, Marc Maron, Bill McGathy, Rose McGathy, Rick Messina, Jimmy Miller, Jack Mondrus, Robert Morton, Monique Moss, Harry Nichandros, Peter Noble, Michael O'Brien, Jim Patterson, Paul Provenza, Ron Robertson, Tom Ryan, Earl Saltzman, Steven Saporta, Bill Scheft, T. Sean Shannon, Bob Shea, Dia Stein, Jon Stewart, Matthew Tilton, Johnny Torres, James Vernon, Tony Visic, Dan Vitale, Mark Wilkes, Geof Wills and Chris Young.

Without the guidance and support of Colleen McGarr and Duncan Strauss I wouldn't have had the courage to take on this project. They lovingly discussed Bill for hours and answered intrusive questions with grace and good humour for over three years. While running a busy management company, they introduced me to sources, read drafts, searched their memories for the tiniest of details and cheerfully corrected my mistakes. (My sincere apologies to their cat Otis, whom I erroneously called 'fat' in the last draft.)

Dwight Slade recreated Bill's youth for me in astonishing detail and sent me beautifully written stories about their childhood adventures together. Through Dwight, Bill the boy came alive and the sweet little character who stored his jokes in a secret place moved me.

In Austin, David Johndrow gave up many Saturday afternoons to share his memories, letters and photos of Bill and was not only an essential source, but also a true friend. Charlie Sotelo is another Austin friend who generously helped with research for this book, shared his considerable knowledge of stand-up comedy and made my time in Texas memorable.

Bill's Houston friends John Farneti, Riley Barber, Steve Epstein, Andy Huggins, Ron Shock and Tracey Wright are tremendous storytellers and interviewing them can hardly be called work. A special thanks to Farneti, who was a gracious host every time I came to town. His thoroughly and vividly recalled the Outlaw years and played me the best stuff from his extensive comedy record collection.

Laurie Mango shared many personal moments and letters that laid bare Bill's tender spirit. Fallon Woodland provided my with unique insight into Bill's later years and freely shared the wonderful phone messages Hicks left for him.

Sarah Thyre, Andy Richter, Randy Sklar and Jason Sklar were gracious in helping me out with key research.

Thanks to the journalists who were on to Bill Hicks first: Len Belzer, Michael Barnes, Jack Boulware, Bill Brownstein, Lawrence Christon, Michael Corcoran, Bob Daily, Frank DiGiacomo, Robert Faires, Allan Johnson, Gerald Nachman, Mike Sager, Edith Sorenson, Michael Spies, Ernest Tucker and Rick Vanderknyff. Their reviews and interviews were key in piecing together the trajectory of Bill's material and his thoughts about his career over the years.

I am particularly grateful to John Lahr, whose influential *New Yorker* profile of Bill, 'The Goat Boy Rises', was a constant resource and whose book *Light Fantastic* is an inspiration. John offered me great advice about beginning the biography process, and sent me priceless letters Bill wrote to him.

I thank my editor Gordon Scott-Wise for his creativity and patience with a first-time author. Thanks also to Charlie Mounter for her enthusiasm and attention to detail, and to copy-editor Richard Collins, who rescued countless sentences.

Will Kaufman read the first and second drafts with the sharp eye of a scholar and the patience of a committed professor. His fascinating book, *The Comedian as Confidence Man*, was never far from my desk and I appreciate how much he taught me about the art and science of irony.

Claudette Sutherland is an unequaled editor and teacher. She meticulously reviewed this book at several stages and was crucial in shaping the final result. I am a better writer because of her work.

A special thanks to Cyndi Stivers, who taught me a great deal about good reporting and got this project rolling when she ran my story on Hicks in *Time Out NY* in 1997.

Daryle Conners, Strawberry Saroyan, Trista Delamere, Tulis McCall and Emily Schlaeger read chapters and gave incisive notes when I was too close to the whole thing. Moon Zappa was in the ring with me from the start as we both faced writing a first book. Our working afternoons, typing, laughing, griping and escaping to lunch made the process a lot less scary.

Carrie Camillo, Amy Poehler, Elizabeth Goodman, Jennifer Waldburger, Farai Chideya, Nisa Ahmed, Jonny Cragg, Dennis Golonka, Lizzy Disney and Ray Wright kept me going when I was in Texas, feeling very far from my own life. Heather Willihnganz, Matthew Huffman, Asa Soltan Rahmati, Sean Shayan, James Milnes, Janel Moloney, Jamie Denbo, George Schreiber, Tom Ryan, Judith Shelton, Waylon Dobson, Beth Littleford, Rob Fox, Bradley Cooper, Kelly White and Maria Bartolotta made Los Angeles feel like home in a matter of months.

I was able to relish this incredible experience because of my parents, Robert and Nancy Young, who have given me aid, encouragement and love every step of the way.

AUTHOR'S NOTE

Bill Hicks is most known, particularly in America, for being unknown. He's the comedian whose entire act was axed by producers at *The Late Show with David Letterman*, in October 1993, partly because he made fun of pro-life and the Pope. He's the guy who died four months later from pancreatic cancer at thirty-two years old.

It is tempting to read his story as a tragedy. The bare facts are harsh: a genius often overlooked and taken before his time. But that misses the point. The life of Bill Hicks is the definition of a life fulfilled. Bill believed he was here for a reason. He created a body of work rich enough for the most prolific of careers and he packed in enough adventure for three lifetimes: getting onstage at fourteen, skipping college, gobbling up books, philosophies, films, music, carrying on hundreds of intense friendships, inspiring his peers, making his first appearance on *Letterman* at twenty-two, searching for UFOs, eating passionately, going vegan, drinking, smoking, tripping, getting sober at twenty-six, playing guitar, singing the blues, writing movies and, through it all, crossing the country hundreds of times telling his truth. 'I'm not here to blow time away,' he told a friend at twenty-five, when he was frustrated with his lack of progress. '[I'm] running out of time.'

When Bill was diagnosed in June 1993, he redoubled his efforts. He added dates to his road schedule, recorded more than ample material for a fourth comedy album (*Rant in E-Minor*), began writing a book, finished a script, developed a television show for Channel Four in the UK and wrote a forty-page essay about his censorship experience on *The Late Show*.

His keen attention to his legacy was not in vain. Almost eight years later, Bill's voice resonates and his material is more relevant with each day. When Bill, circa 1991, riffs on America's 'cultural

dungheap', the glut of toothy-top-of-the-pop-chart-sitcom mediocrity meant to distract us from the 'totalitarian mind-control government', he could easily be reacting to 2001. Even the players basically
remain the same: Debbie Gibson is Britney Spears; George Michael
is Ricky Martin; George Bush is George Bush.

(What I wouldn't give, though, to hear him do twenty minutes
on Katherine Harris.)

In his last year, Bill wrote a great deal about his vision of heaven,
a smoky den where all his 'dead heroes' were hanging out. His
favorite bit was about Jimi Hendrix. Bill explained the singer's early
death as a reclaiming by Hendrix's alien brothers, who had dropped
baby Hendrix off in a ship. 'We'll pick you up in twenty-eight years,'
they told him. 'Jimi, show 'em how it's done.' I mention that line
because I thought of it almost every time I sat down to write about
the short life of Bill Hicks.

CT
Los Angeles
June 2001

FOREWORD

I'm at the Melbourne comedy festival. Just finished a show and I'm feeling pretty good about myself. The promoter says there's an American comic on next door. He's not selling any tickets. They've had to paper the audience. Did I want to check him out? I'm thinking I'll have a quick look but didn't hold out much hope. I'd tired of your pat Americans asking the audience where they were from and asking what they did for a living. On swaggers Bill Hicks dressed in black. He looked so uncool. He reminded me of my older brother. This didn't bode too well as the most profound thing he ever uttered was, 'Give us 50 pence or I'll tell Ma you've been smoking.' Hicks grabbed the microphone and stared at the audience as if he was about to go into the boxing ring with them. It should be pointed out that all comics need to be loved. It is why we tread the boards to a bunch of strangers every night. The comic will start with his good material, get the audience on his side, much like a first date. The room is suddenly filled with an odd tension. A flat, soft drawl emits from the speaker's 'Thank you, thank you. You know to go out with a comedian it takes a very special lady . . . or a bunch of average ones. How you doin'?' A small section of the audience laughed louder than they ever had before. Some men with partners tried to stifle their laugh. A few women walked out. I fell in love.

That night I saw the future, past and present of stand-up comedy. He took comedy on a higher plain. A place the rest of us can only dream of. I didn't agree with some of the things he said but, by Christ, I'm glad he was saying it. He paid a heavy price for his honest opinions. They killed him. Not in a dramatic way, but in the way he passionately lived his life. Being a genius is a heavy burden and he's the only one I'm ever likely to meet.

I still miss you, Bill.

Sean Hughes

PROLOGUE

Los Angeles, 17 November 1993

It's late on a Wednesday night and Bill Hicks stands onstage at Igby's, a small out-of-the-way comedy club in West Los Angeles. 'Folks, I appreciate you coming out,' the thirty-one-year-old comedian says into the microphone. 'It's a very sentimental evening for me and a very exciting one.'

He scans the sold-out crowd, crammed around tiny cocktail tables, sipping beers. He runs his hand lightly over his stomach. 'This is my final live performance I am ever going to do, stand-up comedy wise.'

Nervous laughter and a soft chorus of *no*s float through the room. *What?* someone blurts.

He can't be serious. As many of the staunch fans and close friends in the club tonight know, Hicks has made empty threats to retire from stand-up almost every year since he began performing professionally in 1980. And at this moment, after 'sixteen years of virtual anonymity in the country I love', as he puts it, the tide is rapidly turning in America. Hicks is already a hot name in the UK and Ireland, has been for two years, selling out 2,000-seat theaters in London, Dublin and Glasgow. Now with the publication, two weeks ago, of a *New Yorker* profile in which renowned drama critic John Lahr calls Hicks 'an exhilarating comic thinker in a renegade class all his own,' his profile at home has never been higher.

'It's almost as though I've been lifted out of a ten-year rut and placed in a position where the offers finally match my long-held and deeply cherished creative aspirations,' Bill has just written Lahr in a note thanking him. 'Somehow people are listening in a new light. Somehow the possibilities (creatively) seem limitless.'

And tonight, at Igby's, there is a change in him. Trimmer than he's ever been, the typically husky six-foot-two Bill has abandoned his signature head-to-toe black for an ensemble in earth tones: 'delightful fall colors', as Bill calls them. No more 'angry comic', he's been telling friends. His brown tweed jacket, khaki pants and olive button-down shirt hang on his lanky frame. The hair he usually slicks back is longish, also thinned out, and hangs just over the rim of his round granny glasses. His dark brown eyes are as piercing as ever though they look a bit larger on a face that has suddenly lost its pudge. The effect, in front of the beige stage curtain, is anti-hip, almost professorial.

Quitting the stage, he assures the audience, has come about because incredible things are happening to him. He has another big announcement.

'I found out today I got my own TV show on CBS coming out in '94.' Bill grins beneath his patchy reddish beard.

He raises his hand, interrupting the cheers. The half-hour show that CBS is about to put on the air every week starring host Bill Hicks is called – he pauses here – *Let's Hunt and Kill Billy Ray Cyrus*.

The crowd roars.

Bill nods proudly and, encouraged by the show of support, he paces the stage, one hand in his jacket pocket, while he details how he plans to catch Cyrus, that 'no-talent cracker asshole', by his 'fruity ponytail', pull him to his knees and put a gun in his mouth. He punctuates his point by shoving his fist in his own mouth and emitting a ferocious gun blast.

His reference to a deal with CBS is a note of typical Hicks irony. 'Let's Hunt and Kill Billy Ray Cyrus' is one of the jokes the producers of the new CBS program *The Late Show with David Letterman* called a 'hot point' when they censored Bill four weeks earlier. (Even though on air, Bill called Cyrus a 'no-talent cracker *idiot*'.)

On Friday 1 October, Bill had taped a six-minute set for *Letterman* in its much-heralded new 11.30 time slot. About two hours after the taping, around 7 p.m., the show decided to pull Hicks's performance: *Unsuitable for broadcast* Bill was told when he got the call in his suite at the Mayflower Hotel that evening. 'Certain things you don't talk about,' CBS spokesperson Rosemary Keenan sniffed to the *New York Post* in the wake of Bill's banning. 'Religion is one. Blowing somebody away is another.'

But the rumor was that it was Bill's pro-life jokes – 'If you're so pro-life, do me a favor: don't lock arms and block medical clinics. Lock arms and block cemeteries' – that made the show especially nervous.

The producers tried at first to say it was the CBS Standards and Practices department who pulled Bill's appearance. *Standards and Practices*, Bill snorted to anyone who would listen. 'Isn't this the same network that shows *Full House*? What are your standards exactly? Stupid to retarded?'

But Bill knew the truth now. It was *Late Show* producers under the helm of executive producer Robert Morton and David Letterman – not CBS – who had decided to strike his entire set; a set which had been *approved* by those same producers, information that Bill reminded nearly every one of the roughly twenty reporters he'd talked to in the month that followed. He had played by their rules for ten years, performed all twelve *Letterman* appearances with a gag in his mouth until he barely recognized his own act and it wasn't enough for them. They were *still* afraid of some stupid jokes.

Still, the censorship furor had provided the perfect news hook for the *New Yorker* piece, which detailed the shutting up of America's secret boy genius by the nation's reigning cool comedian. Even Bill half joked to Lahr that the *non*-appearance had earned him 'more attention than my other eleven appearances on *Letterman* times one hundred'.

There will be a *Let's Hunt and Kill* Christmas special, Bill tells the Igby's audience, stretching the bit out to three minutes. In that one he'll crossbow Marky Mark in the 'abs' and watch the model/rapper disappear into the melting blood-soaked snow. Hicks merrily skips across the stage as he describes a perfect Marky-free universe where birds chirp in harmony and everyone walks with a spring in their step. 'All I'm tryin' to do, folks, is rid the world of all these fevered egos that are tainting our collective unconscious and making us pay a higher psychic price than we can fucking imagine.'

That, Bill says, is precisely how he pitched the show to CBS. And all the development executive wanted to know was, 'Will there be titty?' Bill had agreed there would be, and the executive had pronounced him a genius. But the guy was curious about something. *Where had Bill Hicks been all these years?*

'Ohhhh, at the Comedy Pouch in Possum Ridge, Arkansas, you *fuck.*'

ONE

Beep. *Hey Fallon, this is Willy. Explain to me what this fucking fascination with family values is that people are espousing out of their fucking rectums in all the goddamn newspapers.* Family values. *They apparently didn't know* my *family. It's all a bunch of horseshit.*

West Texas, Summer 1976

'Ladies and gentleman, I had a rough upbringing. I was breast-fed.'

The boy stood on the little stage with both his hands stuffed in the pockets of his dungaree cut-offs. The kids stared at him. He said *breast.*

'On falsies.'

Bill shifted nervously. He had done fourteen minutes. Seven minutes his, seven minutes Woody Allen's. Like anyone here at Baptist church camp would know the difference.

Wait until Dwight heard about this. He, William Melvin Hicks, aged fourteen, had gotten stage time.

Everyone knew all about it soon enough. Some of the ladies in Mrs Hicks's Sunday school class asked if she had heard about her son Bill's performance. 'Well, Mary, he is very funny,' the head pastor said. 'But you may want to look at how you raised him.'

Now there would be a long conversation with a million questions. His mother in her chair, his father in his. What was with this joke telling? What about baseball? They had no idea that their youngest child was upstairs carefully typing one-liners and locking them up in a scuffed briefcase underneath his bed. Bill was a serious kid. If anything, his older brother Steve was the clown.

Bill didn't get his parents either. William *Melvin* Hicks. It was bad enough that the universe had foisted upon him – son of two Baptists born in tiny Mississippi towns – the surname *Hicks*, without adding *Melvin* to the mix. The fact that it was his father's middle name, too, made no difference; all it represented to Bill was the gulf between him and his parents.

James Melvin Hicks, born in 1923, was the son of a railroad agent and had grown up on the family farm in Leakesville, Mississippi, a two-square-mile town in the south-east corner of the state. A tall robust man, Jim Hicks fought in World War II and when he came home he got a job as a traveling salesman for General Motors in Covington, Louisiana. There he met his wife-to-be, Mary Geneva Reese, a petite schoolteacher six years his junior with brown hair and dark eyes. Mary was born in Magnolia, Mississippi, about 140 miles west of Leakesville, and raised in Farmington, Louisiana, one of six children, all born at home. As a young girl she tap-danced and once even sang on the radio. When Bill asked her why she had never gotten on television, she said, 'Honey, we didn't have TV back then.' In 1950, Mary received a BA in Education from the University of Southwestern Louisiana in Lafayette and after she'd settled in nearby Covington, a sorority sister with a husband who worked at GM introduced her to Jim Hicks, who had an apartment in their building.

Jim and Mary Hicks already had two children, a seven-year-old daughter, Lynn, and five-year-old Steve, when they welcomed eight-pound two-ounce baby Bill in the early hours of 16 December 1961 at Pineview General Hospital in Valdosta, Georgia. As Bill described it in his 1992 television special, *Revelations*, on the day of his birth 'the world turned upside down and inside and out and I was born, screaming in America'. It was an interesting choice of words because the South that Jim and Mary brought their boy into was nothing like the one in which they had grown up. As the Civil Rights movement played out in cities all around Valdosta the South was rupturing. Hardly a day went by without bullwhips, tear gas and fire hoses being used on protesters calling for desegregation and almost every morning international headlines screamed about a fresh horror in Atlanta, Nashville, Raleigh, Biloxi, Mobile, Birmingham or Jackson: another bombed church, mass arrest or midnight lynching. In May, the historic Freedom Ride bus carrying black and white activists set out on a tour of the South and at almost every stop mobs of angry whites beat its passengers and attempted to torch the bus. The attack in Montgomery, Alabama, was so brutal that 600 Federal troops were sent in to restore order.

This was the Southern legacy that was Bill's great shame, the one he would come to mock relentlessly onstage: the lumbering, stupidly cruel Ku Klux Klan South. *Burl Hicks*, he called his redneck alter ego. Oh, there were a few things that made Bill proud. He read every word Mark Twain ever wrote, including *The Adventures of Huckleberry Finn*, about twenty-five times. And then there was Elvis Aaron Presley, born in Tupelo, Mississippi, just 240 miles north of the Hicks family farm. Bill's friend John Farneti used to joke that if it were true that you only had to go back eight generations to find everyone related to George Washington, you'd only have to go back about three to see the Hickses' chromosomes cross paths with the Presleys'. At any rate, from the age of five, all Bill wanted for Christmas and birthdays was Elvis records – which wouldn't have been so notable if he were a decade younger. In first grade, for show and tell, Bill stood on his teacher's desk and lip-synced 'All Shook Up'.

By the time Bill was a precocious tow-headed, brown-eyed one-year-old President Kennedy had sent 400 Green Berets to Vietnam, which he said he hoped would prevent further direct American military involvement. The screaming was just starting.

But all of this turmoil hardly ruffled the day-to-day lives of young white suburban families like the Hickses. Mr Hicks climbed the corporate ladder at General Motors and Mrs Hicks set up house, found a new church and made friends with the neighbors in each place the company transferred them: Florida, Alabama, New Jersey and, when Bill was seven, Houston, Texas.

In the late 1960s, corporations like Learjet, Greyhound and Shell Oil, drawn by low wages and, believe it or not, the luxury of air conditioning, were relocating to the Sun Belt and spurring a major white-collar migration to the South. So it was that when the Hickses settled into a five-bedroom brick colonial on Chadbourne Drive in the upscale Memorial area west of downtown Houston, it seemed as if almost all the young families were from somewhere else, too. The new arrivals, eager to fit in, and without much common history, found a bond in their prosperity. Most of the fathers in Memorial held executive positions at Exxon, Texaco or Shell in an era when the price of gasoline jumped from $2 to $40 a barrel. Home to NASA (no small thanks to the efforts of President Johnson) and the world's first indoor sports arena, the brand new Astrodome, Houston was a gleaming meritocracy where social access was available to anyone with enough cash. And in Texas, where even Pee-Wee leagues are carefully ranked, being big on sports and belonging to the right church helped a lot, too.

The Hickses' new neighborhood, its sprawling trees, neo-Tudors and Taras evenly spaced on manicured quarter-acre lots, was so pristine its planners had succumbed to Anglophilia and named the subdivision Nottingham Forest. The streets crossing Bill's had names like Dairy Ashford Road, Avon Street and Briar Knoll Drive. (More like Oil Spill Way and Unleaded Lane, Bill and his best friend, Dwight Slade, snickered.)

Bill's family fit perfectly into this scenario. Mr Hicks was the kind of gardener who divided his lawn into watering zones and kept track of the number of squirrels he caught annually in his trap. After Bill mowed, Mr Hicks measured the grass with a yardstick to make sure it was the right height. The Hickses won Yard of the Year so many times in a row the neighborhood association finally left the sign in their lawn permanently.

At first glance, Bill fit in, too. At twelve, he was a tall good-looking kid and an exceptional athlete. When he wasn't snake-hunting and massacring ants with his buddies down at the Buffalo Bayou, which edged Nottingham Forest, he was at sports practice. He was a star running back in football, one of the fastest sprinters on the Spring Forest Junior High track team and he had a killer right pitch, breaking several of the baseball records set by his older brother Steve. 'In Little League Bill played six-inning games and he would strike out sixteen of the eighteen outs,' Dwight Slade said. 'Not once or twice, but routinely.' Everyone assumed Bill would eventually win a full baseball scholarship, even go on to the majors if he wanted.

Bill might have been accepted, but he felt like an alien. He was uncomfortable in his own skin, ill at ease in his own home. 'It was weird, man,' Bill said years later. 'My family's always been like strangers to me.' He didn't feel that he and his parents ever talked about anything but what they expected out of him. Bill's two dogs, Chico and Sam, were never allowed indoors. The master bedroom, on the first floor, was locked at all times. Children were not allowed in the formal dining room or living room. (Even Mr Hicks only entered the living room every so often to play 'Kitten On The Keys' on the piano.) When one of his friends left a footprint on the wall-to-wall carpeting, Bill stopped playing immediately and got out the vacuum. And there was absolutely no swearing on the property. When a friend of Bill's was overheard exclaiming 'I swear!', he was sent home.

Bill felt like they were all slowly going crazy, their brains choked by rules and routine. It was as if they were hanging on for dear life to a framework, trying to contain something rotten. It wasn't as if his parents had big fights or anything; on the contrary they were WASPs who swept unseemly problems under the pink floral daven-port. But there was this unsettling silence, this quiet tension in the house. His father sometimes sat in his reclining chair in the dark, staring out the window for hours, not saying a word. Other days, he was chatty, munching on sunflower seeds, peppering Bill and his friends with questions about school and espousing the virtues of American-made cars.

By the time he was thirteen, Bill was trying to exit the family as much as possible while still living under the same roof. His room was his one cell of sanity where he could think his own thoughts, his only relief from the matchy-matchy order of the house. After school, Bill came through the back door into the kitchen, downed a bowl of Golden Grahams, and bounded up to his bedroom. He turned on his revolving fan, blew off his homework, and read – his little room overflowed with Danny Dunn and Hardy Boys mysteries, *The Hobbit*, the dog-eared *Huckleberry Finn* – or just put on a record.

He'd listen to KISS and Rory Gallagher until his mother called him down to dinner. He played Gallagher's *Deuce* so much he wore it out and had to buy a new one.

Bill saw no reason why dinner with the family should interrupt his reading and he invariably arrived at the table with a book. As his parents and brother made small talk (his sister Lynn had gone off to the University of Texas), Bill buried his nose in his book and tried to answer his father's questions with one word. *Heavenly days!* Didn't Bill have anything to report? *I'm sure your mother would like you to talk to her once in a while instead of hibernating in your room.* Bill was sure *he* would like it if his mother wasn't a dreaded substitute teacher in his own school ('God, your mom's a bitch!' kids told him as they passed in the hall) and if his father didn't mow the front lawn in a Bermuda jumpsuit. What the hell was he supposed to say to people who didn't want him to go see KISS in concert because the group wore make-up? His parents, in turn, were flummoxed. What were they supposed to do with a kid like this? Sending him to his room wasn't exactly punishment.

Sunday mornings were a different story. No matter how vehemently he protested, Bill was going to church with the rest of the family and to Sunday school after that. Every week it was the same routine: Bill burrowed under his bed covers while his parents pounded on his door and, finally, just before 8 a.m., one of them would burst in and demand that he get dressed before they were all late.

'I don't want to go to church,' Bill hollered at his father as Mr Hicks tore his covers off and dragged him out of bed. 'Give me one good reason.'

'When you get your own place and you're paying your own bills, you can do as you mighty well hoo-ha please!' Mr Hicks yelled back.

'You make me sick! Just leave me alone.'

But to Mr and Mrs Hicks, Depression babies raised in Southern Baptist congregations, not attending church was unthinkable. It wasn't a matter of religious fervor as much as reflex. Though they may have seemed Bible-thumping by Yankee standards, they didn't consider themselves particularly so and in Texas, where the Christian fish symbol turned up in the Yellow Pages, on bumper stickers and tiled in the bottom of fish-shaped swimming pools, they weren't.

'We were Yuppie Baptists,' Bill joked to the *Houston Post* in 1987. 'We worried about things like, "If you scratch your neighbor's Subaru should you leave a note?"'

Bill tried to lose himself in his thoughts as the pastor's voice boomed. He hated all the fire and brimstone stuff, the save yourself scare tactics. Did all these people really believe the Bible was the *literal* word of God? Three hours later, Bill was the first one in the Cadillac and by noon he was back in his bed, pulling the shades, trying to catch a few more hours of sleep.

His exhaustion, ironically, stemmed from a gift his parents gave him. It wasn't dramatic, but looking back everyone agreed that when Mr and Mrs Hicks gave Bill a small black and white television for his own room, it was a turning point.

Until he got that little TV, Bill thought there were only two comedians: Bob Hope and Johnny Carson. Now he was staying up way past his bedtime every night, stretched out in the dark, watching *The Tonight Show*, the volume on low, and he was getting to see comedians like George Miller, Freddie Prinze, Steve Landesberg and Robert Klein. He laughed quietly into his covers, the laughter of recognition. These guys were much older than him, of course, Easterners and mostly Jewish, but he soaked up their every clever word, every irony and sarcasm. It cut the syrupy nonsense he had to endure all day, the teacher who yelled, 'Goodbye! Go to church! Have a good weekend! Go to church!' on his way out the door. It was more than funny. It was a possibility. You could make a living doing this.

Maybe there was a way out after all.

Bill memorized their routines and bought a couple of books on stand-up comedy. When his new hero Woody Allen, star of late-night bedroom features such as *Casino Royale* and *Bananas*, said in an interview that he liked Robert Benchley and Charlie Chaplin, Bill began to collect bits of information about them, too. He wanted to buy Allen's book *Without Feathers*, but Mrs Hicks wouldn't let him have it; one of the chapters was called 'The Whore of Mensa'.

Bill quickly discovered that since he was only fourteen, had never been married and wasn't worried about mortality, stealing jokes from the *Tonight Show* guys didn't always go over at school the next day. He typed up as many of his own Allen-inspired one-liners as he could – *My girlfriend is very petite. She's a stewardess on a paper airplane* – and when he finished one he'd slide it under Steve's bedroom door for his review. Steve, the one person in his family Bill respected immensely, would critique them and hand them back. 'Keep it up,' he told Bill. 'You're really good at this.'

Sitting around the Spring Forest Junior High locker room in football pads one autumn afternoon, some of the guys were trading jokes when Bill decided to test-drive one of his own. 'My father was a mortician and he was fired from his job,' he said. 'He was accused of having an intimate relationship with a corpse. We were shocked.'

Bill paused.

'It was purely platonic.'

His teammates looked at him blankly. No one knew what *platonic* meant.

TWO

Beep. *These fucking whore-like pieces of shit goddamn fascist fundamentalist scumbags. Anyway, I'm at home and I'm playing Mario. I guess I'm gonna put it on Pause 'cause I'm going all the way tonight. I'm going all the way. And all the tricks are going to be known to me. So I'm going to put it on hold a minute and go rent a film with a woman takin' a shit in another woman's mouth. And, uh, just try to feel good about myself. Hahahahahaha. Later.*

There was only one other person Bill knew who got comedy like he did and that was his friend Dwight Slade. Dwight's family had moved to Houston from Marietta, Georgia, when his father took an upper-level management job with Shell and they lived a few miles away in Nottingham II. The boys had met in the seventh grade during a neighborhood game of Commando Tag. Dwight, the youngest of four boys, was a quiet kid, and a perpetual outsider because his family moved around so much. Dwight's parents drove him crazy, too. The Slades, though interfering, were actually more relaxed than the Hickses. 'But here was my friend who I aligned myself with, who had a TV in his room and told his parents in no uncertain terms to basically fuck off,' Dwight said. 'And I felt obliged to do that, too.'

Throughout junior high, Commando Tag was Bill's favorite game after baseball. Most evenings after supper a gang of neighborhood boys met at Nottingham Elementary, which provided any number of excellent places to hide amidst the low classroom buildings and playground equipment. Once everyone had hidden, two It commandos roamed around trying to hunt the others. Once you tagged a guy, he too became a commando. Bill loved being outdoors at dusk, with the fireflies flashing and the cicadas screeching. The game got really interesting when the sun went down just after nine o'clock and huge packs of boys roamed around in the dark trying to trap each other.

Bill and Dwight paired off as an It team most of the time, cracking each other up with inside jokes and impressions of the other guys while they were supposed to be counting to a hundred. Not only could they make each other laugh, they both felt indescribably separate from everyone else in the group. Dwight had a secret, which he'd shared with no one until he told Bill during a Commando Tag game the summer before eighth grade, about a year into being official best friends.

'I want to be an actor,' he told Bill while they crouched behind a dumpster. 'Don't tell anyone.' The other guys would think he was a fag.

Bill nodded. 'I've been writing jokes,' he said.

From that moment, their relationship took a turn. They were partners as well as friends. 'We talked on the phone every day, saw each other for lunch, between classes and we walked home together as long as we could before we had to go our separate ways,' Dwight said. 'And then we spent every weekend together. Most of it was just sitting around, talking about comedy and writing in our journals about the pretty girls at school who liked the jocks. We called them "depressors".'

Bill was unwelcome at the Slades' after Dwight's mother had caught the boys reading the skin magazine *Dapper* the previous summer (which they had pinched from Dwight's brother's stash and folded into a copy of *Boys' Life*), so Dwight usually arranged an alibi and went to Bill's house. Not that he was ever really comfortable there. Mrs Hicks would offer him an apple and ask what church his family went to and Dwight would squirm as the truth came out that the Slades rarely went.

Bill did his best to spare his partner. 'We would walk in the back kitchen door and there would be a little plan. Bill would go, "My parents are in the den, just walk through, go upstairs, don't stop, don't talk to them. If they ask you a question, don't stop." It was a battle plan, every time.' Bill would lead the way, rushing Dwight through the den, past Mr and Mrs Hicks's reclining chairs, right by the door to the master bedroom and vault up the stairs. 'Bill would just be moving, moving and I would be behind him and then, "Bill ... Bill! Where have you been? Hel-lo, Dwight! How's school? What kind of grades you making?" So I would stop, and Bill would be at the top of the stairs going, "Come on!" Then Mr Hicks would go, "I'm askin' him questions!" And I'm stuck in this fight all of a sudden.'

Once they shut the door to Bill's bedroom, Bill played Dwight stand-up sets he had taped with a little audio recorder off *Merv Griffin* and *The Tonight Show*. The boys' favorites were Richard Lewis, Ed Bluestone and Billy Braver. They played Steve Martin's first ever *Tonight Show* set over and over with Bill acting out the essential visual gags each time. Dwight wasn't exactly sure why Bill had chosen to recruit him to his comedy mission, but he felt he might be kind of like a mirror that said it was okay to be different. The only one, except for Steve, who also said, 'Yes, be funny, yes, write more jokes.'

'I looked at Bill differently from then on,' Dwight said. 'He educated me that humor was not something one just *did*. It was something that was labored over, embraced and cultivated.'

About four months into eighth grade Dwight's older brother Kevin brought home an audio tape of Woody Allen's nightclub act. It was a coup for Dwight: he never had anything cool on Bill when it came to comedy and now he held unheard work of the master. The boys listened to Allen's act until they could say it with him and Dwight started writing jokes with Bill. They decided they would be Mel and Hal (shorted versions of their ridiculous middle names, Melvin and Haldon), misfit twin brothers.

'We have problems, many problems,' they said into the tape recorder, choking with giggles.

'Yes, and this started when we were young ...'

'We were once Siamese twins ...'

'But we were separated at birth ...'

'When the doctor spanked us with the scalpel still in his hand ...'

Coming up with one-liners to volley back and forth was a grind, their comedy homework, but what the guys did effortlessly, for pure joy, was spend hours perfecting drawling impressions of their parents. Their mother characters were nattering phone friends, heartlessly obsessed with the grotesque misfortunes of the neighbors, their swelling purple tumors and pets squashed by speeding cars. The boys saved their most vicious lampoons for their fathers, who became a pair of drawling, racist boobs who compared lawn mowers, admired each other's buttocks and visited Chinese restaurants together.

Now the menu looks fiiine, Chang.

But may we puh-leese have some waffles?

Sometimes the father friends morphed into father and son having a passionate affair and sometimes they became incestuous goody-goody twin brothers, Aaron and Terry. There was also the dorky principal and the stern, yet clearly homosexual, football coach.

The only figure of authority Bill had any use for was Mrs Linder, his eighth-grade English teacher. He thought about her all the time. He told Dwight he had this recurring fantasy/nightmare about leaving English class and dropping his jockstrap from the pile of gym clothes he was taking home to be washed. The thought was mortifying and yet ... compelling. Dwight thought Mrs Linder was perfectly attractive but he thought it was weird that Bill had crushes on a middle-aged woman, and he teased him mercilessly about it.

Bill and Dwight had been compiling material for almost four months when they went on their first professional audition in the spring of 1976. During their weekly scan of the *Houston Chronicle* job section they found a wanted ad for performers for the local Easter Seals Telethon. Auditions were in one week and since there was no way their parents were going to give them a ride to something like that, they carefully mapped out a two-hour bike route which avoided all freeways. So it was, a week later, that they stood, drenched in sweat, in the hallway of a city school for the deaf surrounded by magicians, jugglers and rouged little girls in tutus.

Standing in front of a row of judges seated in the school auditorium, they introduced themselves as Mel and Hal.

'We were sick and tired of being pushed around, so we threatened to run away...'

'...Our parents were very strict and when they heard about our threat they punished us cruelly...'

'...Yes, they took away our legs for a week...'

The judges chuckled politely. A guy with a cigarette nodded whenever he thought something was really good. 'You guys are great writers,' he said.

But they didn't get picked.

When notices for the Eighth Grade Talent Show audition appeared in the hallways at school, Bill and Dwight decided they needed a sure-fire routine. They didn't think stand-up would go over well with the teachers and they had no intention of blowing another shot with an audience. They turned once again to Woody Allen, writing a scene called 'Death', about a guy who gets a knock on the door from Death, which they basically lifted from Allen's 'Death Knocks (A Play)'.

'We thought we were being smart. But you can imagine being a teacher in this very white, Christian, upper-middle-class school,' Dwight said. 'Okay, who's next? It's Bill and Dwight with "Death".'

Bill came up with his own bit for his stage entrance. He gave the stagehand some directions about the spotlight and marched out to center stage in shorts and Sunday shoes with thick-soled seventies platform. 'So he's got these pale bony legs and he's clomping across this wooden stage toward the light. Every time he got near it, it would move to the opposite end. He finally got his foot into the light and the spotlight centered right on the shoe and Bill modeled his feet with these huge dorky shoes.'

'Hi, I'm Quincy Marple,' Bill announced, 'and I had a very interesting experience with Death. I'd like to share it with you now.' The curtain pulled back to reveal a little apartment set with some furniture. Dwight, playing Death in a white sheet with holes cut for the eyes, knocked on the door.

QUINCY: Who are you?

DEATH: I'm Death!

QUINCY: (speaking very slowly and attempting sign language) Oh,
      I'm sorry, do you need a donation?

Bill and Dwight were crushed when they didn't make the cut.
How could Woody Allen fail to get into the talent show? They found
the speech teacher and asked for a meeting. She said they were very
funny, but that the scene needed a little polish. She offered to let
them perform 'Death' in front of the speech class if they shortened
it. Excited to receive some direction, the boys tightened up the script,
rehearsed some more and brought 'Death' to the classroom.

'It just killed,' Dwight recalled. 'People were shaking their heads
and going, "I can't believe you wrote that!" That was a huge boost
for us.' The real payoff was that a few girls were suddenly paying
attention to them. In a few weeks, the boys' yearbook would include
a few acknowledgments of their talents: *Dwight, you and Bill are about
the funniest things in this school. Keep on being funny. Love, Valerie ... Good
luck next year and have a great summer! Stay funny. Love, Debbie.*

'So we're practicing, we're trying to figure out how we can
perform more, if we're getting better. It was hard to judge. There
was no one else. No one knew we were writing jokes, no one knew
we were thinking of becoming stand-ups. That was a secret dream
of ours. We know we have the talent because we blew away the
speech class. And we know we have this driving ambition. So let's
go! What else is there?'

'We need an agent,' Bill told Dwight when school let out that
summer. They called the few talent agencies listed in the phone
book and asked if they needed stand-up comedians. To get an agent,
the two discovered, you needed a tape of your act and an eight by
ten glossy.

What was a glossy? they asked. And where could they get one?
The receptionist at the Universal Talent agency patiently explained
all, and back they went to the Yellow Pages to search for a
photographer. Most wanted $50, but they finally found a guy who
would take one roll for $35. The boys got their map out again and
plotted their route to the guy's house with a black magic marker.
For wardrobe, Bill stuffed a couple of Mr Hicks's wool sweaters into
a backpack.

When the envelope containing their contact sheet arrived at Bill's house a few days later, Mrs Hicks opened it. There was Bill, in Mr Hicks's cardigan, the shoulders dropping to mid-arm, and Dwight swimming in one of his turtlenecks. She wanted to know what this was all about but Bill was hardly willing to explain. He was furious she had opened his mail. You could have two prints for $5 so the boys picked out one to send to Universal Talent, along with a thirty-minute tape of their act, and another to keep for themselves. They stuffed that one into Bill's briefcase with their jokes, practice tapes, 'Career Journal', movie ideas, notes from girls at school, Woody Allen's play and the bicentennial issues of *Penthouse* and *Playboy*.

A week later, all Beverly, the assistant, would say over the phone was that they had received the package and the tape was funny. Obviously, if they wanted to be taken seriously it was going to take a personal appearance at the agency offices downtown. According to their map it was going to be a seventeen-mile bike ride each way, in Houston midday heat and traffic. But the comedy of Mel and Hal was worth it. They packed lunches, told their parents they were going to Tower Records and set off. When they finally arrived two and a half hours later, having stopped once by the side of the highway to eat, Beverly greeted them warmly and said, 'We're working on it. We'll give you a call.' Five minutes later, the boys were back in the elevator, their faces still flushed from the ride down, fumbling for the keys to their bike locks.

A couple of weeks later Bill had to go to Bible camp (where he would make his stand-up debut with Woody Allen's falsies joke) and Dwight had to leave with his parents for a beach trip. Bill promised to keep him updated on their progress by mail. 'Hey Dwight, guess what?' Bill scrawled in his tiny print. 'I have some fantastic news, and some fairly poor news on the next page.'

Fantastic News

I called Carry Fox [the agent]. He said he got the tape, and we had a job. Labor Day at Conroe, a pool party, and get this: $60 bucks for ten minutes!

Just think that's how much you make in thirty-one hours at the paper route!

Bad News

We don't get the job! I don't know why, but don't fret. It will happen a lot. I'm sure after we make a few performances our Fame will spread and we will be very popular, and in much need.

Our main problem is: #1 Conroe is pretty far away, we will have to tell your parents. It is imperative!

#2 Our performances are not on school days because our parents will have a fit. And, I might add, if our grades go down we're doomed. Our parents will blame it on comedy. I feel we should fight all opposition and work only for success.

William Melvin Hicks `

P.S. Get home fast! because ... WE'RE GONNA MAKE IT SOON!

In August, Universal Talent called with an even more exciting offer: did the boys want to be in the local Labor Day Muscular Dystrophy Telethon at the Red Apple nightclub? And could they perform for three hours? They would have to go on around 2 a.m.

No problem, Bill said, swallowing hard. They'd figure out material later. The bigger question was how to deal with their parents. They debated convincing Dwight's brother to drive them down in the middle of the night, and then it dawned on them: this was television! They were now a legitimate act. Their parents had to see how great that was.

The first person the boys went to was Mrs Hicks. They stood there in the den and told her all about it. She actually seemed kind of excited. 'Well, you boys are going to be little stars!' she said, smiling. The boys exhaled. Now all they had to do was get it past the Slades. Bill had been gradually reintroduced to the family months after the *Dapper* incident and the two enthusiastically told Mrs Slade the great news. She seemed impressed at first too, but then the questions started. This was going to be in a nightclub? An adult nightclub? Downtown? In the middle of the night? How would the boys get in?

We're the entertainers, they explained.

Mrs Hicks and Mrs Slade exchanged calls and it quickly became clear that Bill and Dwight's first television appearance was about to be canceled. The official reason given was that it was not a school-sponsored event.

'Our parents said we couldn't,' they muttered to their agent. The boys were expecting a little commiseration but instead got a chipper 'Maybe next time'. Fortunately, since Bill and Dwight had been booked in the middle of the night, most of their schoolmates didn't realize when their big TV debut didn't happen. So at least they got some notoriety out of it as they started freshman year at Stratford High School.

THREE

Beep. *You got to look up when you feelin' down ... you got to look up when you feelin' down.*

Stratford High on Avon Street was a brand new three-story brick monolith without any windows (except a few that looked out on an interior courtyard) and inside it was pretty much what Bill and Dwight expected it would be: a perfectly bland mix of 1,600 well-to-do nerds, jocks, heads and freaks. 'It could easily have been mistaken for a state prison,' Dwight recalled. 'But it was a school of kids of upwardly mobile people who had come from all over the country and they were their darlings. It wasn't just proms and keg parties, it was road trips in beautiful cars and seven kegs. It wasn't just shoplifting at the mall; it was "we stole a whole stereo".' Stratford's pride was its athletic facilities, which included a $3 million basketball court and a regulation size football stadium with AstroTurf. The football players had gone to state finals three years in a row and, predictably, were local media figures. Naturally, they cut in the lunch line, drove jacked-up trucks and had Serious Relationships with the leggy girls with Farrah Fawcett hair. What Bill and Dwight marveled at was the fact that each football player had three Spirit Girls assigned to him. Spirit Girls were way beyond cheerleaders. The sole purpose of being a Spirit Girl was to bake cookies for the team and decorate their lockers with streamers, candy and notes before every game.

Bill and Dwight were just two more gangly freshmen wandering the halls – Bill with his bowl hair-cut and white T-shirt tucked into his jeans – and whatever acclaim they got out of their brush with television wasn't enough to help them when they auditioned for the 1976 Stratford Talent Show a couple of months into the school year.

They performed 'Death' and did twenty minutes as Mel and Hal, including their new 'shock' joke.

'We babysat for abortions . . .' Bill said.

'It was an easy job . . .' Dwight added.

'I mean, the babies didn't make any noise . . .'

'Even if they had we wouldn't have heard 'em in those little glass jars . . .'

Mrs Barni, the Biology teacher in charge of the show, told them they just weren't loud enough.

'Weren't we funnier than the football players who dressed up as girls?' Bill asked.

Mrs Barni said that unfortunately not everyone who tried out could be in the show.

'We just thought, "*Goddamnit*". We've ridden our bikes all over Houston, found an agent, gotten booked on television, and gotten shot down by our parents,' Dwight said. 'And now we're not even good enough to be in the high school talent show.'

Bill tried to remain optimistic. All this rejection was preparing them for Hollywood, where, as Bill had read, only the most dogged performers made it. And hadn't every audition netted them more exposure? Even this talent show debacle had sprouted them a tiny fan base.

The few students who had seen Bill and Dwight perform for Mrs Barni gathered around the guys in the cafeteria at lunch and egged them on as they tested out new jokes, did their parents and pulled stunts like running through the cafeteria, trying to balance raisins on spoons. Most of the student body, however, thought they needed to have their asses kicked. Class clowns were one thing, but these two were just losers. The jocks hurled food off their trays at them and one afternoon Dwight got wedged between a Coke machine and the wall. Dwight's brother Terry, who was a junior, told them that they were about to laugh their way right out of school. 'And you, Mr Bill Hicks, I heard that you said that your father breast-fed you,' Terry added. 'If that's your idea of humor, I feel sorry for you.'

But the only thing that made six hours a day at Stratford bearable – the only point of showing up every morning – was performing. If they couldn't do that, they might as well run away. (In fact they had started mapping out a hitchhiking route to Los Angeles, linked by KOA Kampgrounds.) Bill's most despised class was Typing, run by Ms Hazy. Ms Hazy was big on conduct charts and punishment scales, the kind who practically begged for insubordination. The entire class would chant 'Haz-ee, Haz-ee, Haz-ee' while her back was turned, or yell 'This sucks!' in disguised voices. Bill usually tried to sleep through the whole thing, but one afternoon when Ms Hazy stepped out, he grabbed a roll of masking tape off her desk, lay down on the floor and proceeded to outline his body like a murder victim. For that, for napping through Algebra, for delivering his English class book report like a stand-up routine, and for countless other infractions, Bill ended up in Vice-Principal Buddy Allen's office at least twice a week.

Even Buddy Allen, assigned to guide the class of 1980 from freshman to senior year, had his uses. Mr Allen, a balding man with a W. C. Fields nose who wore three-piece polyester leisure suits, was Bill's perfect new nemesis. After their meetings, in which Bill invariably received another detention, he ran home and spent hours in front of the bathroom mirror perfecting Mr Allen's facial expressions and pragmatic Texas accent. He was a fantastic character, for whom it was almost worth enduring the weekly lectures on school citizenship.

As for baseball, Bill had lost interest. Mrs Hicks cried when he announced he wasn't going to pitch for Stratford, but at least he agreed to join the freshman track team. He and Dwight hid in the pit at practice while the other guys did circuits around them. There was something perfectly symbolic about watching their teammates run themselves ragged in a big circle.

One day Bill sat on a wall near school, reading a book. A carload of boys from across town pulled up. 'Stratford sucks!' they yelled.

'Yeah, I know,' Bill said. 'I go there.'

That summer, Bill and Dwight, both now fifteen, got grill jobs at Wendy's. When management gave Bill his uniform, he printed his home number (497–8817) on his name tag where it should have said HICKS. A courtesy to attractive customers, he told Dwight. Some nights the boys had to close the restaurant, which meant they had to stay until after midnight, mop the whole place and lock up. They were supposed to ride their bikes straight home afterward, since it was after curfew, but one night they stopped off in the Handy Andy parking lot. The lot was perfectly quiet at this hour, and they stood under a streetlight, which swarmed with June bugs. Dwight wanted to talk. He'd had a dream that he died and the experience had put him on to a book called *A World Beyond* by Ruth Montgomery. It was all about reincarnation and destiny.

'We've lived before!' he told Bill. 'It's all pre-planned. You know the life you're going to go into before you live it!'

'What do you mean?' Bill asked.

Dwight explained everything he'd found out: that before you are born you plan your life much like the screenplay of a movie, arranging characters and scenarios that best help your evolution. These scenes and characters are set by your karma. Each life is a gift and you live them one at a time like the beads on a necklace, growing and evolving, experiencing a multitude of lives, genders and cultures in a quest for enlightenment.

Bill got it immediately. He was on earth for a *reason*. And there was a *reason* he was so pissed off at this philosophy of life where you got married, moved to the suburbs, set the thermostat at 68 degrees, expressed your creativity through your yard work and played the same song on the piano for thirty years.

He spun his bike around in a circle. 'Do you realize what this means?' Bill asked. 'We were destined to meet. We were destined to be comics!'

The boys talked for almost two hours about surrendering the small ego for that of the will of God. Meanwhile, Bill's mother had gotten worried when she called Wendy's to check Bill's progress and there was no answer. She'd driven to the restaurant, traced the roads Bill should have taken and finally returned home and alerted Dwight's parents. When Bill walked in the door a few minutes later, she was so upset that she decided to make him get up at dawn the next morning and wash windows. He didn't utter a single word of protest.

The boys had already been meditating since April. Dwight's brother, Kevin, was heavily into the Transcendental Meditation movement and Bill and Dwight thought they had seen him levitate. A few months later, in the fall of tenth grade, they found out about a TM retreat, a 'Residence Course' over Thanksgiving weekend in Galveston, a small island in the Gulf of Mexico about an hour away. They had saved up money from Wendy's and a guy named Paul from the Houston TM center had said he would give them a ride. Bill gave Mrs Hicks a crash course in TM, explaining all he knew about mantras and how they would help him relax. 'Anyone with half their salts could repeat a word over and over again until they pass out,' she replied. Finally, Paul called Mrs Hicks and assured her everything would be fine and even said that TM would turn Bill into a model son. Bill and Dwight heard all about that conversation on the ride down.

They arrived in Galveston on Thanksgiving afternoon and devoured the vegetarian dinner. They were so giddy they couldn't stop laughing. This was a *total* triumph. While their schoolmates were staring at their boring relatives across the dinner table, they were doing something revolutionary. TM was a concrete process, a way to explore all the mercurial concepts they were trying to grasp in *A World Beyond*. They spent the weekend learning yoga positions and meditations, watching hours of inspirational films featuring Maharishi Mahesh Yogi, and having lengthy conversations with the group leaders. They called home once or twice the whole four days.

On the way back to Houston on Sunday night they stopped off at McDonald's for Big Macs. They'd been kind of hungry all weekend. 'This is the best thing I've ever eaten,' Bill said.

Gradually, Bill's spirits were lifting. He and Dwight had even taken on another friend, Kevin Booth, who had seen the guys doing their weirdo schtick in the cafeteria and decided he had to meet them. A year ahead of Bill and Dwight, Kevin was in with the party crowd and so, by mere association, Bill and Dwight were no longer complete social pariahs. Not that either of them wanted to go to keg parties; all Bill really wanted to do was hang out at Kevin's and play music. Kevin, who had a life-size cut-out of Jimi Hendrix in his bedroom window, was the first guy Bill had ever met who was as into music as he was. In fact, sometimes Bill couldn't say for sure what he planned to become: a *Tonight Show* comedian or a rock star. Since seventh grade, he and Dwight had been having rock-out sessions to KISS *Alive*, complete with scarves around their heads and yardsticks for guitars. Recently, he'd received a little guitar for Christmas and Dwight had bought a child's drum set, the Blue Denim, at Kmart for fifteen bucks.

With Kevin, they were getting heavily into Led Zeppelin, Ted Nugent and Bob Seger and Bill started saving up for a Fender Stratocaster and an amp. Kevin already had lots of audio equipment, a bass guitar and a friend named Bruce Salmon who knew how to play it. More importantly, he had parents who went off to their ranch in Fredericksburg, Texas, almost every weekend and who let the boys make as much noise as they wanted in the garage. Before long, the four were set up out there with the Blue Denim having regular practices and taping their favorite numbers, like 'Moment of Ecstasy', on Bill's little recorder. 'They were funny bizarre songs with lots of distortion,' Dwight said. 'We were having a blast. The only thing missing was a name and any musical talent.'

One of their favorite activities before band practice was to pile into Kevin's Winnebago RV and drive around to the homes of various girls they had crushes on. They would sit there, hoping for some activity, before someone noticed the presence of a massive camper idling at their curb. Once in a while, they scored big, such as the night the beautiful Tammy Blue practiced her Spartonaire drill team routine in her parents' living room. They collapsed in hysterics when she spotted the camper and scrambled to close the curtains. Their cruising episodes became known as the 'Nipple Tours'.

If only they could levitate, they could get all the beautiful girls they wanted, and so over Christmas break Bill and Dwight went on another TM retreat. Seven days long with more intense meditations, it was a preparatory course for the TM Sidhis program, which taught the technique for levitation. Listening to the many lectures that week on how effectively TM reduces stress, Dwight came up with the perfect name for their band: Stress.

Kevin and Bill loved it and they started designing a logo immediately. Kevin worked on plans for a fifty-foot papier mâché penis that would shoot steam onstage and they staged elaborate 'concert' photos with smoke bombs, lights and costumes. Bill's 'stage outfit' was his terry-cloth bathrobe. The photos made the rounds at school, and, fueled by their embellishments and lies, Stress grew in stature without their ever having played a note for anybody. One afternoon as Bill sat in the vice-principal's office waiting to see Buddy Allen, he looked down at the table in front of him. Etched into the wood by some other student was the Stress logo. A valuable lesson in hype, Dwight said.

The guys were having so much fun that Bill wasn't entirely surprised when Dwight called him with devastating news just before Christmas: the Slades were moving to Oregon at the end of the school year. It figured that things couldn't go on this smoothly. How the hell was he going to perform without Dwight? Already he began to feel the loneliness creeping in. Dwight promised he would figure out a way to get back to Houston eventually, or maybe they'd meet up in Los Angeles. Whatever, they'd keep up their act. And at least it wasn't happening until the end of the year. They still had five months to perform together.

Wendy's proved an ideal platform for 'impromptu' stand-up sets. The restaurant was right across from Stratford so on weekends, when they weren't scheduled to work, Bill and Dwight dropped by just as a game or a dance was ending and kids were coming in for food. Sometimes they waited for a group to gather, but even one friendly face was enough for them to launch into some wild, improvised routine. Once they had everyone's attention, they performed a mix of their own jokes and borrowed material from the professionals, especially Ed Bluestone and Billy Braver. For the encore, they took requests from the audience, which were almost always for their parent characters. *Tell us about your mother! Do your dads!* The Wendy's shows were such a success that they added Pizza Hut to their weekend rounds.

And then something amazing happened. In February, Bill and Dwight were skimming the newspaper for auditions, as usual, when they saw an ad for the brand new Comedy Workshop. Two months earlier, the Workshop had opened in the hip Montrose section of Houston as an improv theater, but they had recently decided to try out stand-up comedy on Mondays and Tuesdays, their 'off' nights. Bill and Dwight called immediately and Lucien Cullen, the bar manager, told them they could drop in for the next amateur show. Three days later, on Monday night, Bill told his parents he was going to the library and Dwight told his he was going to an organ recital. Kevin waited for them at the end of Bill's street in the 'Stress-mobile', the light blue station wagon that usually hauled around their band equipment.

As soon as they walked into the Workshop, a former topless bar with red vinyl booths and a large stage, they found Cullen and asked if they could go on early so they could get home as soon as possible. The six or seven other comics seemed okay with that. The first guy who went up did a bit on smoking pot. The next guy went on in flippers, a mask and a snorkel, and said, 'Just got back from Bermuda. Boy, my legs are tired.' Bill and Dwight smiled at each other. This guy obviously had not been studying the masters. 'We knew what great comedy was,' Dwight said, 'and we knew what our benchmark was going to be. We were pretty conceited, considering we had barely ever gone onstage.'

Bill was across the room at the bar checking to see their place on the list as the MC introduced him and Dwight. As a result, they approached from opposite sides of the room, met in the middle and walked up the small center-stage staircase. The fluke entrance looked very polished and gave the guys an extra shot of confidence as they tried to adjust their mikes. They'd been working on their set list in Bill's room all week, and had decided to go mostly with one-liners about their inability to get women.

'We were sexually abused when we were younger . . .' Bill said.

'Yeah, we never got any,' Dwight finished.

'At some birthday parties you get a naked girl popping out of a cake . . .'

'We were so poor all we could afford was a naked dwarf hopping out of a cupcake.'

To their delight, they were killing. If people weren't necessarily responding to the jokes themselves, the sight of these two awkward kids talking about sex was infectious.

After they got off, Cullen told them they had lots of potential and another comedian, Steve Epstein, a kinetic twenty-five-year-old originally from New York who'd watched them intently (murmuring 'Woody' when they did one of Allen's bits verbatim), went out of his way to encourage them to come back.

It was official. They were professionals who got laughs in the real world. Fuck Mrs Barni! To celebrate they went to the Zipper Lounge, a strip club around the corner, and watched a XXX movie – now *this* was education on a school night. They even got offered a drink, but neither Dwight nor Bill ever touched the stuff.

It was, as Bill said, enough to try it again and well worth the fury of their parents when they discovered the recital and library had been a ruse. Dwight's father said Dwight would be grounded for the rest of his natural life if he pulled that again. The next week Bill and Dwight just sneaked out, climbing out their bedroom windows to the waiting Stress-mobile. Dwight left a stack of records on his turntable that played automatically and a note, just in case, that said, 'I've gone down to the Comedy Workshop because I have to.'

FOUR

Beep. Dude, I'm gonna vomit at your fuckin' messages. I'm gonna fuckin' heave my goddamn guts up. First of all, you're not at the movie with anybody. 'Cause you have no fuckin' friends. Admit it. A. And B, what the hell's this personalized shit? What, don't I get a personalized fuckin' message? I don't get a personalized message. Ah, forget it.

Bill and Dwight made it down to the Workshop two more times before the Slades were set to move and when they walked offstage for the last time on 5 June 1978, Bill had no intention of returning to the club on his own. He could have adjusted their jokes to a solo act, but he just couldn't imagine standing up there by himself.

And he'd met someone. The last day of tenth grade, he'd finally summoned the courage to ask a girl named Laurie Mango on a date. He was working the Wendy's drive-through when he'd first seen her a few weeks earlier. She was stunning, a tall brunette with pale freckled skin and dark eyes, nothing like the bottle blondes crowding the hallways at school. 'Hey, Laurie Mango, you wanna go on a big high-school date?' he blurted as he walked by her locker. Laurie looked up, surprised. They had exchanged maybe three words before. She wondered if this was one of his pranks.

'I really want to go out,' he told her when he called that night. Laurie was still puzzled. She'd never sensed even a glimmer of interest from him, but then, like Bill, she kept pretty much to herself. Laurie had moved to Houston from northern California three years earlier when her dad, a geologist, came to work for an oil company and she was still in culture shock. This would be her first real date.

Bill took Laurie to dinner and afterward, before their movie started, he pulled her into Toys 'R' Us. They roamed the aisles playing with action figures and water pistols, and Bill bought them a family of bendable plastic Toys 'R' Us giraffes, which, inexplicably, both found hilarious. They could barely stop talking long enough to sit through the movie.

Bill, who had been studying astrology, couldn't get over the fact that Dwight and Laurie's birthdays were six days apart, same year. 'All I know,' he told Dwight over the phone, 'is if you were born with a pussy, we'd be married right now.'

All summer, they went to drive-in movies and to see Bill's favorite music, mostly blues and jazz groups. They sat around in his room (with the door open three inches), talking about the best books, the worst assholes at school. Bill showed her the little comic strip he had been doing called 'The Adventures of Sane Man'. Sane Man was this existential superhero whose one gift was the ability to react to all situations with total logic. He was a sober lone ranger who traveled the world seeking out narrow-minded irrational people, guilty of logic crimes, whom he would defeat with his razor-sharp wit.

Laurie had never met anyone like him. It wasn't just that he was witty or that he wrote her six-page love letters. He seemed much older than sixteen. His goal, he told her, was enlightenment. 'When you're with someone who can look at anything and point out something that twists your whole perception of it, that's kind of what laughter is about,' Laurie said.

Between his all-consuming love affair that relieved him of his virginity and Stress rehearsals, Bill hardly had time for comedy in his junior year. His guitar teacher had told him he was a natural and he was completely taken with his new white Fender Stratocaster. He and Kevin found a new Stress drummer and they practiced constantly, with Bill on lead guitar and vocal and Kevin on bass. Any night they could, Bill and Kevin went to worship local guitar god Eric Johnson. If Johnson was playing the Whiskey River four nights in a row they were there right in front every show, staring at his dancing fingers.

Bill and Dwight planned their reunion over the phone. They had a system worked out for hours of free long-distance calls. Dwight would go to a payphone and call the operator to request a third-party call. 'This is Dr Slade,' he'd say. 'Would you please bill this call to my office?' He would give her the number of the payphone next to him and when the operator called his 'office' to accept the charges, Dwight picked up and approved it. Bill would be waiting on a third pay phone in Houston.

Gradually, Laurie was overwhelmed by Bill's intensity. He was professing his love and devotion all the time, and she loved him too, but it was kind of scary. Everything was 200 per cent with him. He wanted to hold her hand all the time and kiss in front of people, which Laurie thought was embarrassing. Bill and she wrote furious notes back and forth debating it. *I'm only sixteen!* she kept writing. At the end of their junior year, almost a year after they'd met, Laurie gently told him she wanted to be just friends. But he could barely stand to talk to her after that. She'd said she loved him and now she was leaving him.

Everyone he cared about was leaving. Dwight was gone. Kevin was about to graduate and Bill didn't have any friends in his own class. His only consolation was when Stress got to play their first real show, a cacophony of screaming and Hendrix-inspired speed guitar, at the Senior Follies.

'I've been seeing a shrink,' Bill told Dwight one night. He'd grown close to a friend's mother, a woman considered a shade different from the other mothers, a 'free spirit' who worked and didn't care about house beautiful. During their long talks, she'd become concerned about how often Bill mentioned being depressed, and offered to set him up with a friend of hers, a psychiatrist named Dr Saltzman. Despite his relationship with Laurie, his dark moods seemed more frequent and Bill's parents, no doubt confounded over what to do with their maudlin son, agreed it was a good idea.

Bill looked forward to seeing Dr Saltzman. He told his friends that he basically went in there and tried out material. Bill reported that Saltzman, who'd seen Bill and then his parents, had told Bill that it wasn't him, it was them.

As if steeling himself to be alone in the fall, Bill decided to spend the summer of 1979 reading in his bedroom. If you wanted to go visit him, there was one rule: don't bring anyone else. Even David Johndrow, an old junior high school friend of Kevin's who came from California to stay with the Booths for the whole summer, wasn't welcome. But Johndrow was dying to meet this guy who meditated and knew astrology and, after weeks of Kevin's vouching for him, Bill was finally swayed. 'You can come along,' Kevin told David, 'but it's going to be in his bedroom and it's gonna be really cold and dark.'

'It was freezing, just freezing,' Johndrow recalled. 'He had on these little gym shorts and this little white shirt too small for him. He was real pasty and thin. He sat there on the floor playing his electric guitar under this drawing of Jeff Beck near the Woody Allen poster. I started singing a line from *Live in Cook County Jail* and Bill looks up and yells, 'B. B. King! Muddy Waters!'

It turned out David had grown up in a family even more religious than Bill's. The Johndrows were fundamentalists who belonged to Houston's controversial Berachah church led by Colonel R. B. Thieme. Thieme, who later counted Dan Quayle among his fans, preached in full World War II military regalia and exhorted his followers to 'prepare for battle' while 'preparing for rapture'. In the church lobby was a poster of General Patton pissing in the Rhine. When David met Bill he was intensely agnostic, going through a religion-is-an-opiate-for-the-masses period and they immediately started having intense religious discussions. Though Bill shared David's hatred for organized religion, he was floored that David didn't believe in God. 'I had all these sort of philosophical theories that sort of danced around it,' Johndrow recalled. 'He was going, "What do you mean? What are you talking about?" And then he started talking about the Bible, symbolically what it meant, and how these stories were the same as the stories in the *Bhagavadgita* but they're just coming at it from different cultures. And a huge light went off in my head.'

Even when Bill was in one of his loner periods, he somehow managed to connect instantly and intensely with certain people. They almost always became lifelong friends – or, like David, someone Bill called 'his brother'.

In late August the Workshop called. The stand-up nights at the
Workshop had been such a wild success the past year that the club
had opened a ninety-seat room next door called the Comix Annex,
a small, dark club on South Shepard, where they were featuring
stand-up (no sketch troupes, no improv) seven nights a week. They
needed performers badly and they asked Bill to come in as much as
he wanted. It had been over a year since Bill had been down there
and the timing was perfect. David and Kevin had just left for the
University of Texas in Austin and Bill was at a loose end. He began
writing material for himself every afternoon again, newly inspired by
Richard Pryor's tour de force 'Live In Concert', and he got down to
the Workshop as many nights as he could. He was meeting really
cool guys down there, a core group of new stand-ups like Jimmy
Pineapple, an urbane Cajun from Baton Rouge, Louisiana (with
whom Bill had an ongoing debate about who was the greatest
comedian of all time: Chaplin or Buster Keaton); Riley Barber, a
husky six-foot-five character comedian; Steve Epstein, the New
Yorker with a penchant for the Marx Brothers, and his brother,
Louis Epstein.

Riley, Steve and Louis had gone to high school together in
Houston and were the city's first real stand-up comedians. In 1976,
they started performing together at the Rice Hotel downtown before
the Comedy Workshop existed and they'd even gone to New York
together and tried out at an open-mike night at Catch a Rising Star.
Barber's main bit was a five-minute impression of Jimmy Carter,
which ended with him hitting himself in the face with a cream pie.
When the young MC at Catch, Jerry Seinfeld, saw Barber sitting
backstage with the pie on his lap, he said, 'Hey, please don't make a
mess out there because I'll have to clean it up.' Barber started to
protest and Seinfeld said, 'I'm not telling you how to do your act.
I'm just saying, please don't make a mess.'

A few minutes later, as Barber reached the mike, Seinfeld smiled
and whispered one last time, 'Remember, no mess.'

Barber bombed. He lost the Carter voice right away and it took
him so long to get through the torturous set in front of the dead-
silent audience that the shaving cream in his pie liquefied. When he

went to hit himself in the face with it, the liquid cream flew right over his shoulder and sprayed the floor. As Barber got offstage, he looked back and saw Seinfeld on his knees wiping up the stage as he announced, 'This next guy is from Brooklyn . . .'

Between sets at the Annex, the guys hung out in the green room, a tiny backstage den with a small black and white TV and a ratty sofa, trying out material, drinking and smoking – except for Bill who refused to indulge. 'How can you do that to yourselves?' he would ask, shaking his head as they lit up. But he stuck around anyway. 'I felt more alive when I was around other comics,' he recalled. And the guys put up with his straight-edge routine, not only because he was five years younger than the youngest of them, but because he was one of the funniest guys there.

'They talked about him as, "He's a genius",' Ron Shock, another Annex comedian recalled. 'People bandy about the word *genius*: "He's a genius. She's a genius." No they're fucking not. They might be kind of good. But Billy was a genius when he walked in the door. And everybody fucking knew it. Just like they knew it when Rembrandt showed up.'

Bill had barely started school again when his parents announced that General Motors was transferring Mr Hicks to Little Rock. Mr Hicks would need to leave immediately and Mrs Hicks would be spending the greater part of the fall in Little Rock as well, looking for a new house. At first the plan was for Bill to join them at Christmas and finish his senior year in Arkansas, but when their bid on a new house fell through, Mr and Mrs Hicks realized they'd be living in a motel for several more months. It simply made sense to allow Bill to finish at Stratford and they agreed to leave him in Houston with the family car. Finally, Bill joked, his parents were divorcing him.

Bill was now free to perform every single night as long as he kept his grades up – and in Bill's case that meant passing. After all, he was making money at this, as much as $400 a weekend when he headlined. He even booked a 7.30 a.m. Christmas breakfast party at

the Sakowitz department store. He stood next to a breakfast buffet
and told jokes to sleepy store executives holding plates of powdered
eggs.

By the late seventies, comedy was decidedly hip. Members of the
'Me Decade', as Tom Wolfe dubbed it in *New York* magazine, craved
some form of personal address and stand-up had been picking up
momentum for the last few years. *Saturday Night Live* was changing
television, and rock and jazz journalists – captivated by Richard
Pryor unleashing a fierce new voice in his post-Berkeley concert film
and Steve Martin in his white suit filling concert arenas – were taking
comedy seriously while hyping it as the new rock & roll. New York
City's Improv and Catch a Rising Star and LA's Comedy Store were
playgrounds for Andy Kaufman, David Letterman, Elayne Boosler,
Jay Leno, Larry Miller, Paul Reiser, Richard Lewis, Robin Williams,
Roseanne Barr and Jerry Seinfeld.

In 1979, when Bill began hanging out at the Annex, Americans
were especially looking for something to laugh about. The nation
was having, in the words of President Carter, a 'crisis of confidence'.
The year began with the incident at Three Mile Island, the worst
nuclear accident in US history, got worse with the energy crisis and
ended with 500 Iranian students seizing the American embassy in
Tehran in November. Americans were stunned at the television
images of embassy workers blindfolded and handcuffed. At the edge
of the malaise was Ronald Reagan, angling for the Republican
nomination and starting to say things in the press like, 'Liberalism is
no longer the answer. It is the problem.'

At the Annex, people packed into tables and along the bar every
night and what the club needed most was acts to keep customers
laughing and buying rounds. Riley Barber, who had started doing
stand-up in 1976 at Houston's Rice Hotel, said they were 'anything-
goes nights. From the get-go they were packed. They encouraged
you to do as much time as you could because they only had eight or
nine comedians and they had a three-hour show to fill.' Young Los
Angeles and New York comics would have sold their souls for that
kind of stage time, which was out of the question in cities, where

you already had an upper echelon of guys like Leno, Richard Lewis and Andy Kaufman. At the Annex, if you walked in the door in 1979 you *were* a senior guy.

Audiences loved the six-foot baby-faced Bill Hicks, a lanky kid with a lopsided haircut and lousy posture. He looked very much the middle-class son, standing slightly hunched with his shoulders rounded, perpetually vexed by the sacraments of American life: the prom, the family road trip. He paced the stage easily, one hand shoved in his pants pocket, his fluency betraying slightly the geekiness he played to constantly.

'I live in the suburbs,' Bill would say, seated on a stool pushed up against the back wall of the Annex stage. 'Just tell me if you have fathers who sit around like this.' He crossed his leg at the knee, pulled his pants leg up to mid-calf, exposing a few inches of pasty skin and black sock, slouched down and wrapped his arm over his head, his hand dangling near the opposite ear. Lips pursed, eyes dumbly focused, a drawling pretzel in an invisible La-Z-Boy, he was the picture of the fatuous American. *One of the herd.* Bill would hold the pose for fifteen seconds, letting the laughter build a little before he blurted – 'My dad makes $100,000 a year' – then snapped back into position.

'Come downtown to the Comix Annex tonight,' he said when Steve was home from Texas A&M one weekend. 'I went down there and ... he was a star,' Steve said. 'It was unbelievable. The show was sold out, lines waiting to get in and I had no idea that's what he had been doing in his room.'

One of Bill's biggest fans was a comedian new to Houston, a screaming bolt of evangelical fury, a round-faced former preacher from Illinois by way of Oklahoma named Sam Kinison. Kinison came from a family of preachers and he had been spreading the word on street corners since he was a teenager. When Sam got a divorce in 1978, he had to leave the ministry. He wanted to be a comedian and he came to Houston to check out the scene. He figured he had made people in church laugh, he could do it in a club.

Kinison constantly told Bill how talented he was – the 'little prince' he called him – and Bill looked up to twenty-six-year-old

Sam, who wore a three-piece suit onstage and railed against the get-rich-quick televangelists who built amusement parks in the name of the Lord. *And this spring, God willing, God willing, we will have a log ride!* Sam considered himself a believer but he said Jesus wasn't coming back; he was already inside you. 'You can deliver yourself,' Sam told audiences.

Kinison brilliantly expressed for Bill his own lifelong battle with organized religion. Certainly he spoke a language familiar to Bill. They were operating out of the same middle-American evangelical Christian universe, both wildly enraged by its literal interpretation of the Bible and deeply imprinted by it. Discovering larger-than-life Sam was a watershed moment for Bill whose previous heroes – Woody Allen, Richard Pryor, Richard Lewis – hardly resembled the white *goyim* surrounding him.

But it wasn't just what Sam said. It was the way he said it. He was fearless. The first night Bill ever saw Kinison onstage he was in the Annex audience with a date. Kinison was doing his rants against church corruption, talking about baby Jesus being a brat, but it was Sam's signature bit that blew Bill's mind: near the end of the show, Sam stretched a pair of red panties over his head and screamed, 'Call Me Mr Lonely!'. Then he jumped into the audience and started simulating intercourse with a guy in the front row. (Some people said Sam landed on Bill that night, but it was just one of those apocryphal tales that followed the two of them for years.)

'He was the first guy I ever saw go onstage and not ask the audience in any way shape or form to like him,' Bill said. 'I found that highly reassuring. There were nights when he would drive the entire room out the door, and the other comics would be rolling on the floor as the last person out would be screaming, 'This is horrible!'

The more Bill immersed himself in life at the Annex, the higher his star rose at school. The school newspaper ran a profile of him, and on weekends carloads of Stratford students came down to the club to yell hello while he was onstage. He would have preferred they just let him entertain them at school. At the spring talent show, Bill's set killed, but when he used the word 'ass' Buddy Allen came onstage, wrestled the mike out of his hands, and pointed him to the exit. In June, Bill graduated at the very bottom of his class. '417 in a class of 427,' he half joked. 'Ahead of the AC/DC fan club.' That probably lessened the shock when Bill told his college graduate parents he wasn't planning to pursue higher education. He wanted to go to Hollywood with Sam.

Back in April, Sam had gotten into trouble at the Annex. There was this flimsy little stool up on stage and Kinison was at his heaviest weight, around 240 pounds. He was already self-conscious about it so when the stool broke beneath him he went postal. 'What is this cheap piece of shit?' he screamed, throwing the stool to the floor.

'Then he picks up one of the chairs in the audience – heavy wooden and vinyl sixties chairs – and he's going to smash it into a cross beam in the wall,' Riley Barber recalled. 'And he misses the wood and he just hits the plaster with this big heavy chair and he rips this big gash in the wall. And the chair jams in the wall. Sam sees this and he goes, "Well, I can't follow that. Good night." And walks off. The next day the club owner comes in, sees all the damage and says, "Fuck him!"'

Sam was suspended for two weeks. The first night of his leave he came down to the club in a rented limousine and held a mock crucifixion across the street. Stripping naked, with only a towel to cover himself, Sam doused his body with ketchup and tied himself to a convenience store sign. 'Help!' he screamed. 'They're crucifying me! They're crucifying my talent across the street!' Having called the Houston media in advance, he had gathered quite a crowd by the time the police arrived an hour later. Kinison, whom the *Dallas Morning News* had already named Funniest Man in Texas for the second year in a row, got so much publicity out of it that when the two weeks were up and he did his 'comeback' show, the club promoted the hell out of it and packed the house.

Not long after, Kinison had a set-to with Steve Moore, the club's artistic director, with whom he had never gotten along. Moore strongly objected to a Pryor-influenced bit Kinison was doing called 'The Adventures of Baby Jesus' and kicked Kinison out. Sam came back to the club later that night, the two got into a fight in the parking lot and Moore ended up with a broken leg.

Sam's onstage time in Houston was up, but he had been talking about heading to Los Angeles anyway. When Rodney Dangerfield was in Houston doing a concert date, he had stopped by the Workshop and seen Sam onstage doing his 'fucking cops' bit where he played an arresting officer – 'Up against the wall! We're the fucking cops!' – who starts doing the crook from behind.

'That's the funniest thing I've seen in years,' Dangerfield was heard to say. With his encouragement, Sam was ready to get out to Hollywood, with a few Annex guys in tow, and blow them away at the Comedy Store.

'There's no reason to stay in Houston,' Sam advised Bill. 'I don't care if you're just out of high school. You're way beyond what they're doing here.' Bill required little convincing that Los Angeles was his next move – he'd been planning this for years, really – and Kinison began to plan a fundraising show for their move to the coast, with Bill, Riley Barber and another Annex comedian, Carl LaBove. He also invited Argus Hamilton, a hot young Los Angeles comedian who had just made his *Tonight Show* debut. Sam borrowed thousands of dollars from his girlfriend and Epstein (who was already living in LA) and reserved the 1,100-seat Tower Theater in downtown Houston for the evening of 13 September 1980. He called the event 'Outlaw Comics on the Lam' and they nailed up posters all over town. At home in Houston that week, Mrs Hicks brought a stack of posters with her when she went shopping. But Sam sold barely eighty tickets and his efforts only benefited Bill.

'Bill had an incredible set and Argus had trouble following it,' Barber recalled. 'Argus did an hour, they took an intermission and then Carl and Sam went up. It was anti-climactic and plus they were both in bad moods because Sam realized he'd just lost about $8,000.'

Argus, who was dating Comedy Store owner Mitzi Shore, told Bill that Shore would love him. And Argus thought he might be able to get Bill on an HBO Young Comedian's special about to go into production.

Sam had dinner with Mr and Mrs Hicks at their home in Houston to try to convince them to give their blessing to Bill's plans. He assured Bill he could get through to 'church folks' like the Hickses, but Bill's parents immediately disliked Kinison's pompous style, and it was probably the prospect of the HBO special coupled with Bill's molten determination that won their approval. They decided to think of Los Angeles as Bill's 'comedy college' and they offered to pay the rent on a studio apartment. Mr Hicks even bought Bill a white Chevette to pick up in Los Angeles. So as it turned out, Bill reached Los Angeles before Sam, who had to go on the road preaching to try to recoup the money he'd lost on the Lam show.

FIVE

Beep. *WHERE THE* FUCK? *Yer* lyin' *man, theah ain't no whea fuh you to* be. Shiiit. *Go back to youah hole, man. Go back to that hole and dig deep. Let the world go about its crazy ways without youah confusin' glances. Go back to whea you come from,* man.

'Well, I'm here to be a comic!' Bill announced to the wiry young guy answering telephones behind the front desk of the Comedy Store. He'd taken a cab straight from Los Angeles International Airport to 8433 Sunset Boulevard, walked through the Comedy Store's heavy double doors, and climbed the stairs to the main floor, carrying his guitar case and dragging his suitcase by a rope. He had the HBO audition this evening. 'When do I go on?'

Andy Huggins, a young stand-up who'd recently come out from Charlottesville, Virginia, looked up at him. Three-piece corduroy suit. Bowl haircut. 'Eighteen, and he looked younger than that,' Huggins said. 'I would have guessed that this was someone who had never done comedy before.'

Bill thought it was a great gag, the cornball rookie arriving in Hollywood with a suitcase and a dream. He brought his luggage onstage, letting it hit the floor with a thud, playing the rube all the way for the HBO casting executives.

The Comedy Store was a dim cavernous maze of a place with three large show rooms and several narrow hallways connecting a web of lounges, green rooms and dressing rooms. The nearly windowless club had black floors throughout and glossy black walls covered in head shots, dimpled black Naugahyde booths, plastic chandeliers and lots of mirrored surfaces. One lounge had a giant glass coffee table shaped like a piano.

Mitzi Shore and her then husband, the nightclub comedian Sammy Shore, had opened the Comedy Store on the Sunset Strip in 1972 and Mitzi got the club in their divorce settlement a few years later. 8433 Sunset had an intriguing history. In the 1960s it housed a rock club called It's Boss, where the Byrds and Bob Dylan played, but originally it was Ciro's, the studio-era nightclub opened on New Year's Eve 1939 by *Hollywood Reporter* founder Billy Wilkerson. Throughout the forties, everyone from Lana Turner to Albert Einstein spent boozy much-photographed evenings there being entertained by Ella Fitzgerald, Bobby Short and Dean Martin and Jerry Lewis.

Since the Shores had rescued Ciro's from its last stumbling days in the seventies, the club had gradually come alive again, and by the time Bill arrived in the autumn of 1980 Monday night at the Store was the place to be in Hollywood. It was an open-mike experimental night when patrons like Burt Reynolds, Sammy Davis Jr, Beverly D'Angelo and Mick Jagger packed the place out to watch Pryor, David Letterman and Robin Williams, already a huge star on *Mork & Mindy*. The especially funny guys hung out after hours in the private backroom bars partying with the movie and rock stars who were their biggest fans.

Mitzi was mercurial, to put it mildly, but if she liked you she could be a huge help. Just up the hill from the club, she owned an old white Spanish mansion called Cresthill. The after-hours club party house since the Ciro's days, Cresthill had come with the property and Mitzi let lots of struggling comedians stay in its five bedrooms. 'The most elegant exquisite crash pad of all time,' comedian Jackson Perdue, who moved in there in 1978 as a twenty-one-year-old newcomer, said. 'Two inches of dust all over. There were double balconies peering down the hill over the city, a sun room, a couple of fireplaces, maids' quarters and a big long Last Supper table where everyone sat around doing blow.'

The year that Bill came out, Perdue's roommates included Argus Hamilton, Yakov Smirnoff, Andrew Dice Clay, who lived in the maids' quarters, and Ollie Joe Prator, a rotund guy from Michigan who was infamous for stealing everybody's act and often doing it

better than they did. 'Man, you killed in Cleveland!' he would say
when he returned from the road.

Argus had told Bill he could stay in his room at Cresthill until he
found a place, since he usually stayed with Mitzi, and that Bill could
pick up the keys when he arrived. But Argus was doing a *Tonight
Show* appearance the afternoon Bill got to town, so when Bill asked
for him at the desk he got to meet Mitzi instead.

Mitzi sat in the back watching Bill's audition and, though he
didn't get the HBO special, she liked him right away. He was wry
and boyish at once, like Gomer Pyle channeling Woody Allen. The
way it usually worked at the Store was that a new comic started out
on the Monday night open-mikes, vied for a six-minute showcase
with Mitzi and, eventually, if she gave you the thumbs-up, you got
on as a regular. She made Bill a regular from that very first set and
paid him to help out around the Store a few days a week. 'Bill's a
peach,' she told the other comedians.

In a good week, Bill was doing three fifteen-minute sets at the
Store's second location in Westwood. Some weeks there were no
spots, and when that happened he was always devastated, sure he
had fallen out of favor. But nobody, particularly Riley Barber or
Steve Epstein, who had come to LA just before Bill, wanted to hear
him moan when they themselves were struggling to get even one set
out of Mitzi. Whether or not he was booked, Bill hung out at the
Sunset club late at night, intently watching the line-up – Jay Leno,
Billy Crystal, Jimmy Brogan, Garry Shandling, Jerry Seinfeld – many
of whom he had taped off television at home.

'Guess who was there last week?' he wrote to David Johndrow.
'Give up? Richard Pryor. And of course I wasn't there that night.
Boy, I'd sure like to meet him. I'd love to have him call me over
after I get offstage. "Boy I think yo funny. But what the fuck wrong
with yo hair?"'

Bill did entire routines around his kitchen haircuts (provided, of
course, by his father) and, like Pryor, he was becoming highly adroit
at setting up a premise and then illustrating it in a rapid stream of
characters, sound effects and bodily contortions. Like most comedians, he believed Pryor was 'the only and only master of stand-up'

and he and Dwight, now a freshman at the University of Oregon, traded his sets back and forth on audiotape. He wasn't aping him, as he had done with Woody Allen when he was a kid, but he gleaned from Pryor a heightened awareness of technique. Bill was carefully honing his timing, his pacing, even his syntax.

He'd come up with some great new bits since living in Los Angeles. One of them was about how, although he was a fairly nice guy, he just didn't like bums on the streets of Hollywood. The very idea, Bill said, that they wanted him to just *give* them the hard-earned money his parents sent to him every week. A nice solid one-liner, the bum joke was one of Bill's favorites, and even as he turned over his act dozens of times over the next decade, it was one of a few crowd-pleasers that he never junked entirely.

Having established his attitude, he often expanded on the bum theme with the story of a 'mean, ungrateful bum' who had just recently come up to him and asked if he could spare a dime.

'Mister, a dime's not going to help you any,' Bill protests sweetly.

'Well, it can't *hurt* me now either, can it?' the bum growls.

Bill bends over the imaginary bum holding out a dime. 'You don't know *shit*,' he says poking him in the eye with it.

'That guy is great,' Robert Aguayo, who ran the Store's open-mike night, told Riley Barber one night at Westwood while Bill was onstage. 'That guy is better than just about anybody I've seen.' Aguayo shook his head and Barber realized, for the first time, what high expectations the Store had for Bill.

If Bill wanted to go right to the top with this act, it was a done deal. He was sharply observational but generally nonconfrontational – his material the sort that would label him a junior curmudgeon but not seriously controversial.

'I finally have my own place!!!' Bill wrote Dwight in October. 'My own *home*, hooray. I love it. It's the neatest little place.' He had signed a lease on a tiny furnished studio overlooking a courtyard pool at the Olive Tropics, a converted motel in Burbank. He bought a black and white TV for twenty bucks and proceeded to fill the room with stacks of used books from the Burbank Book Castle a few blocks away. He acquired an entire collection of Mark Twain for under a dollar.

'I sure wish I could meet a neat girl here because I've got such an ideal situation with my own apartment and all,' he wrote in another letter to Dwight. 'I've become so paranoid about girls now – I'm so afraid to get hurt again. The Depressors have done their job with me.' Anyway, it was practically impossible to meet a girl his own age at the Comedy Store, and with everyone there from the performers to the line cooks partying into oblivion, teetotaler Bill didn't exactly fit in anyway. 'Bill was always looking so hang-dog and forlorn, just kind of depressed all the time so I told him one day, "You know, Hicks, you need to smoke a joint or something, man. Lighten up,"' Jackson Perdue said. 'And he got really indignant with me. "Fuck you, man! I don't need some Hollywood asshole telling me I need to do drugs."' Bill felt really far away from all his friends having fun together at school in Texas and he was still pining for Laurie Mango. He was actually thinking about going to church just so he could meet some more people – anyone but another comedian.

Steve Epstein got Bill a part-time job telemarketing for a company called the Preview House. You were supposed to call people at home and invite them down to watch allegedly new TV shows or movies (in fact, they were usually test-marketing commercials), but Bill couldn't get one caller to say yes and lasted only two weeks. With his afternoons to himself, he hung out at the Burbank Public Library where he had a crush on one of the librarians. He read Hardy Boys mysteries and checked out film projectors and silent movies, mostly by Charlie Chaplin. Ever since he had seen *City Lights* the summer after graduation, he had become captivated by Chaplin, and now he devised a sort of crash course in him. His favorites so far were *Modern Times*, *Easy Street*, *The Rink*, *The Pawnshop* and *The Floorwalker*. 'Chaplin and Pryor,' Bill said, 'you can't say enough about them and you can't see them enough.'

In the excitement of soaking up all that film history, Bill started thinking about a movie idea he and Dwight had hatched as freshmen at Stratford about life in a concrete brain jail of a high school. It was

called *The Suburbs*. Their hero, 'Kevin', was stuck inside this thoroughly bizarre family with, of course, a buffoon father and a mother
obsessed with morbid thoughts and the gross misfortunes of the
neighbors. In a way it was another incarnation of Sane Man, the
protagonist stuck in an irrational world bent on invading his private
logic island.

He wanted to begin working on the script as soon as possible.
'We must! We've got to!' he exhorted Dwight. 'Didn't those years
make a mark on you?' Stratford was perfect, 'such a contemporary
school *filled* with funny jerks!' Their success was *assured*. 'Because I
think that deep down, under all the facades life presents to people,
almost everyone thinks the way we do,' Bill wrote. 'Sanity and basic
logic is a large facet of *Right* and the absolute. And there is a Right.
There is sanity in this sick world. Hopefully people need it and more
hopefully we can produce it on the screen in the most pure, original
and hilarious form possible. This is Classic Comedy.'

'Some incredible things may be happening in the near future,' Bill
wrote his partner in late October. 'I can't tell you what right now,
for fear they might not come true. (You know that story.) But let
me say this. We've got to be prepared to deliver our A-1 script
within the next three to five years. My main fear is this – Woody
Allen is snapping at our heels and there's no telling who else will hit
up on our point of view within this time . . .'

The development Bill was afraid to talk about was that ABC was
casting a small but visible part in a sitcom pilot called *Bulba*. An
ensemble show of the *Gilligan's Island* variety, it was set in an
American embassy on the fictitious Indian Ocean island of Bulba,
where diplomatic personnel wore short shorts and halter tops. Mitzi
thought Bill would be perfect for the part of the bumbling marine
corporal, Phil Repulski, and got the network to come down to the
Store and see him. They must have loved his father character because
they cast him immediately and Bill later played the idiot rookie as a
junior version of that, with pursed lips and a heavy twang. It was an
abysmal show. Bill had no illusions, but he was thrilled to be cast on
television less than four months after his arrival in Los Angeles. He
made $8,700 for one week of work and, whether or not the show

got picked up, he was now represented by the William Morris Agency. If anything, all the attention made him even more focused on his project with Dwight. He told his new agent about his idea and the guy said if you had a good comedy script you'd always work in Hollywood. Bill was already blocking out scenes.

In late March, as Bill was wrapping work on *Bulba*, he was practically begging Dwight to move to Los Angeles. Dwight wanted to know if he and Bill were still truly partners. Or was he just going to be someone to hang out with while Bill pursued his career? Dwight could see how well Bill was doing without him and he wondered if there was any point in teaming up with him. Bill had a destiny; he was miles beyond everyone they knew.

Bill responded emphatically, circling the words *us* and *we* to make his point. He didn't want to make just one movie with Dwight, he wanted to make movies. This was their career. Happening right now. 'Those are Bill & Dwight, Dwight & Bill movies! It's our *life!*' he wrote. 'We must get together somehow and work! How? How? How? Is there any way you could transfer to UCLA?'

'Heavenly days!' he added, imitating his mother. 'There is no reason to jump down across the country to go to the YWCA. It's out ah da question. My stars! Go clean up your room.'

Bill's immediate success in Los Angeles was doing little for his social situation and no doubt contributed to his desperation for his best friend to move in with him. 'My God, I'm depressed right now,' he wrote to Dwight. 'Have been for the past three weeks.' He couldn't get over the politics at the Comedy Store: even if you were 'refreshing and unique' to start with by the time you made it through the Store system you were 'just a jaded anybody'. And, Bill admitted, 'I've got it good by Comedy Store standards. I mean, my situation is excellent. It's just awful. I have no friends out here. No real friends, you know?'

Bill was looking forward to Sam coming out at last but when Kinison finally drove into town in January 1981, it was hardly the good time Bill expected. Kinison was shocked and furious when Mitzi refused to gave him stage time, and instead offered him a job as a Comedy Store doorman. Not only that, he was totally broke, still recovering from the losses of the Lam show. Sam knew Bill had some money on him from the *Bulba* pilot so he asked if he could borrow a thousand dollars.

'Look,' Bill said, 'it's not like I made $100,000 on this. After taxes, I didn't bring home that much.' Sam was in heavy party mode and Bill knew if he gave him money he wouldn't see him again.

Kinison was beside himself. How dare Hicks turn him down after all he had done for him? A night or two later as Bill walked down the hill toward the Store, Riley and Sam pulled up in Sam's car. Sam slammed on his brakes and rolled down the window.

'Hey, Bill!' he screamed. '*Why are you out here?* You're out here because I put you on that show that I lost *eight thousand bucks* on! And I hooked you up with Argus! That's why you're out here! I went to your parents' house—'

'Sam—'

'And I don't need Mitzi telling me how smooth you are onstage because you're doing me! You do my act! I brought you out here!'

Bill tried to interrupt again and Sam threw a can of soda at him. 'You stuck-up little prick! People helped you and you forget that!' Sam started to get out of the car but then he just drove off. Bill gave Sam the money the next day, but their friendship was pretty much finished for now.

SIX

Beep. This is Willy, and I've officially gone insane at this point. I'm officially insane and I'm writing letters of 'welcome to my insane party'. Anyway. I'm going to go see Thelma and Louise. I don't know why I'm tellin' you. I don't give a fuck. There's nothing to do and I'm out of my mind. So I'll talk to you later.

When the *Bulba* pilot aired once (featuring Bill, in a USMC jacket and boxer shorts trying to twirl his rifle) and got canned Bill barely flinched. 'I'm working on a theory that will prove that every desire guys have to be the best and most successful they can is motivated by an urge to get back at his first love,' he wrote Dwight. 'It's just a theory.' Bill was taking things lightly in part because he was thrilled that Dwight had finally agreed to come live with him in LA as soon as school let out in Oregon. After all, Bill had an agent who would read *The Suburbs* and Mitzi had even offered to lend them money to have their script typed up properly.

As soon as Dwight arrived in July 1981, a particularly muggy summer in Los Angeles, armed with bags of non-perishable groceries Mrs Slade had sent, they got to work. They had just two weeks before Dwight left for an advanced Transcendental Meditation course at the Maharishi International University in Fairfield, Iowa. At eleven each morning they rose and sat opposite one another on unmade twin beds. Heaps of clothes, record albums, books, tarot cards and tiny Buddhas commingled and Bill's old briefcase sat open, so stuffed with reams of jokes he could no longer close it. They wrote furiously on lined yellow notebook paper, trading dialogue straight from their Houston dinner tables, until the air conditioner gave out around four o'clock. They loved coming up with situations for their stable of characters, including of course their parents and a blustering principal 'Buddy Pores' (in reference to the man's skin condition). With the addition of an ape jock called 'Brad Maxi' and a revolting goody-goody brother for 'Kevin' called 'Aaron', *The Suburbs* amounted to a wickedly cathartic bloodletting against their boyhoods. Bill and Dwight could feel the success they'd been planning for seven years just months away. Bill had made it to the small screen and this script was a hundred times funnier than *Bulba*. The country would eat them up. They would change thinking in America to sanity and basic logic. Their father character would be as popular as Archie Bunker.

The reward at the end of the day, when neither of them was scheduled to perform, was going down to the Comedy Store main room to sit in back with Cokes and watch the line-up. They never got over the thrill of seeing the *Tonight Show* guys live. After they came home around midnight, Bill usually went out for a long walk, a five-mile trek up dark winding Mulholland Drive to Laurel Canyon. Sometimes Riley Barber or Dwight went with him, but Bill was perfectly happy to set off on his own. He loved to walk the quiet hills fragrant with night-blooming jasmine, and look down on the sprawling city with its millions of twinkling lights from Hollywood to the edge of the Pacific Ocean.

Bill was thinking about his look. He disliked the gap between his front teeth and he wanted to lose some of his baby fat. He was always joking about the buzz cut he got for *Bulba* making him look like a punk rocker and, though he wasn't really a punk fan, he was into the attitude and the lean mean Sid Vicious look. He started taking over-the-counter Dexatrim and, between the diet pills and all the walking, Bill lost weight rapidly. His major obsession, however, was with his name. He hated *Bill Hicks* and he was forever trying to come up with something new. (It was a lifelong preoccupation. In later years, he called himself Willy and asked his friends to do the same, but it never really caught on.) 'What comedian besides Bob Hope has ever made it with a single syllable name, first and last?' he asked Dwight. He obsessively counted the syllables of the big guys. 'You know, like Jon-Nee-Car-Son, Woo-Dee-Al-Len, Rich-Ard-Pry-Or...' He went on about it for weeks and when he discovered numerology, he decided to pick a new name that would numerically spell success.

While Dwight was away in Iowa, Bill punched up their rough draft and delivered 186 handwritten pages to the typist Mitzi had arranged. A few days later he got a call from the typist who informed Bill that she had done a hundred pages and was only a third of the way through. At this rate, she said, you'll have a 280-page script. 'You better stop typing,' Bill told her.

'Hurry back,' Bill wrote Dwight. 'Stop. Situation hopeless. Stop. Can no longer write. Stop. Had to stop. Stop. Yes, Stop! Stop.' As soon as Dwight got back, they began drastically to cut scenes and tighten dialogue. They worked intensely and, charged by Dwight's TM trip, Bill began to meditate with him again for the first time since high school. Meanwhile, at his parents' behest, Bill enrolled for the fall '81 semester at LA Community College. He signed up for a film course and karate but he only made it to classes a few times. One of the guys in karate gave him a black eye.

The only higher learning that really interested Bill was his spiritual adventures with Dwight. The two went vegetarian and Bill, typically emphatic, not only stopped eating meat, but studied holistic nutrition books, bought organic flour and made batches of wholewheat biscuits from scratch. Bill and Dwight's new diet meant giving up their favorite dish, Brunswick Stew, a concoction made of canned chili and corn niblets.

They made trips to the Bodhi Tree bookstore in West Hollywood and investigated all manner of metaphysical technique, gurus and literature: meditation, TM, Judeo-Christianity, Buddhism, psychic phenomena, astrology and numerology. Copies of the *Rosicrucian Cosmo-Conception*, *A World Beyond*, the Bible and numerous astrology texts joined Twain and the Hardy Boys on the floor of their tiny apartment. Bill sent David Johndrow a copy of the book *The Unity of All Religions* and tucked inside a picture of himself 'levitating' over his bed.

On Friday nights, Bill and Dwight started going to see Charlie Lutes, an early cohort of the Maharishi and one of the first meditators in North America, in a small room over a recording studio on

Santa Monica Boulevard. Nicknamed Captain Kundalini by John Lennon, Lutes was this really straight-looking guy who wore a tie while he led a group meditation and gave lectures on fate, karma, destiny, and the nature of the universe. The first Friday Bill went, Lutes talked about the importance of discipline in your spiritual path. All paths led to enlightenment, he said, but the important thing was to stay on one so you could move forward.

'This is a little uncomfortable,' Bill whispered to Dwight.

The guys talked for hours about the problem: how to attack the outer world while exploring your inner world? Spiritual freedom, they agreed, was the key to creative freedom. But, Bill pointed out, neither Chaplin nor Keaton meditated. How did Dwight account for their success? Dwight replied that it depended on your definition of success.

'Bill was constantly in search of the balance between the two journeys,' Dwight said. 'He'd go too hard in one direction and counter with a dive in the other but his devotion to both never wavered. On top of that was Bill's impatience. Impatience with the plodding pace of humanity, impatience with people's lethargic driving, their inane ideologies, impatience at his own spiritual development. He wanted spiritual evolution but he'd be damned if he was going to sit in a cave or go to Fairfield for three months to achieve it.'

They saw the movie *Altered States* and Bill became fascinated with sensory deprivation. 'He fashioned his own method by tying a king-size foam pillow around his head and fastening it with a belt,' Dwight said. 'The belt buckled at the bridge of his nose allowing him to breathe through the crack. He would lie prone on his bed and do a variety of mental exercises that he picked up from books on sensory deprivation.' Bill thought he might be able to market his invention as a portable deprivation kit.

On the whole Bill seemed more buoyant than usual, though many nights he slept poorly. He thrashed around in his bed so wildly that he woke Dwight, who watched groggily from across the room as Bill jumped up and frantically stripped his bed, searching for snakes in the sheets. Once he sleepwalked into the bathroom, turned on the light, looked in the mirror and yelled *HA!*

Bill's new astrologer told him the package his mother had sent him, whatever it might be, was important. 'It's a little crucifix,' Bill replied. The astrologer told him to wear it because wherever he was going every night made him too heavy. 'You are full of light,' she said, 'and the place you are in is very dark. You attract negative things.'

'She nailed it,' he told Dwight excitedly. 'Every time I go to the Store I'll be really excited about my set and I'll feel all energetic and creative. Then I get there and it's just like – *whoooosshhh* – I'm tired and I want to go home.' Despite the fortune the club had brought Bill, the place depressed the hell out of him and he'd grown to hate being there. Dwight had to agree that the Store was physically about the darkest place he'd ever seen. That was to say nothing of what had gone on in its back rooms over the years.

The only thing that excited Bill about Los Angeles anymore was the prospect of selling *The Suburbs*. He and Dwight finally finished the script at the end of January 1982, split the cost for another typist and dropped it off at William Morris on Friday 12 February. Bill's agent had arranged a brief meeting for them with an agent named John Levine in the motion picture department.

'How old are you guys?' Levine asked. 'I've never had such young people in my office before.'

'That's why it's such a great script!' Dwight said. 'It's written from our point of view and we're just out of high school.' The guys gave him a quick pitch – a loner kid, a clever rebel reacting to the absurdity of life in the cookie-cutter 'burbs. In fact, considering it was just two years before the rash of successful teen angst comedies like *Fast Times at Ridgemont High*, *Risky Business* and *The Breakfast Club*, the concept of the script was on target.

Levine promised to read it over the weekend. Monday the boys waited in the apartment all day. Nothing. They stuck around Tuesday, Wednesday, Thursday. Nothing. Finally, two weeks later they got the call. 'It's good,' Levine said. 'You guys are definitely screen-

writers. But it has no ending. I'll tell you what. I want to see another
one. And after that I want to see another. And after that, we'll start
to talk.'

The guys were elated at first (Levine had called them *screenwriters*),
but profound disappointment set in as they realized *The Suburbs*
wasn't going into production any time soon. They were disabused of
any notions of a direct path to success and it was the end of a dream
that had been very real for both of them. 'It was devastating to us.
We weren't guys who were trying to get long-term screen writing
careers,' Dwight said. 'We wanted to get *The Suburbs* made. We put
every ounce of our heart and soul into that thing.' On the other
hand, they had been kicking around a script called *Sane Man*, and
Dwight was into it if Bill was. But Bill took the rejection hard and,
though he didn't say it overtly, he sort of lost interest in the whole
writing thing. It was driving him crazy, both he and Dwight down
in the dumps living together in one room. Bill was desperate to get
out of LA and fortunately, he was starting to get booked out of
town – an opening spot in San Francisco, a week of work in
Sacramento. He figured the way to recharge himself was to begin
focusing again on his first love, stand-up.

At the beginning of the summer of 1982, Bill got a call from the
Annex to do a few dates in Houston. They were willing to bring him
home as a paid road act and Bill was really excited about getting
back to Texas, mostly because he'd been thinking about Laurie
Mango. He'd never really stopped missing her, and he'd heard
through friends that she was now a pre-med student at Rice
University in Houston. As soon as Bill got to town he got her
number at the dorm and, if Laurie was surprised to hear from him
after months of silence, she still said yes when he asked if she
wanted to go see *ET*.

Laurie was amazed at the change in him in the year and a half
since graduation. He was eating nothing but rice and beans and
talking about having a mantra. His latest incarnation was hard for
Laurie to relate to but their old connection was there. 'It wasn't just
fond memories,' Laurie said. 'We always had this bond. I think it
was a bond of relating to each other's philosophies, of being the first

one. And not just first love, but where you feel like you are soul mates, where you speak to each other without pretense. We had that, too.'

That one encounter was all it took for Bill to start thinking about moving back to Texas. When he returned to Burbank in July he was beset by frustration. Laurie had her college life and Dwight was off to Iowa again, having these great spiritual breakthroughs. Everyone had a passion but him. What did he have? No girl, no partner, no project. He was stuck at the stupid Comedy Store doing his routine by rote. He was simply outgrowing his own act and it almost embarrassed him now, getting laughs for being so 'cute'. He didn't care about being the boy wonder. He didn't even have head shots. 'Even cab drivers in LA have head shots,' he said. But Bill didn't have the energy for that stuff. He couldn't even say why he was doing this anymore. 'I never thought it was funny, what I was doing, and I was always frustrated by it,' he later recalled. 'Maybe it came too easy.'

He was beginning to fumble around for a way to shake things up. It occurred to him that most of his heroes – Richard Pryor, Keith Richards, Jimi Hendrix, Kinison, for that matter – had stimulated themselves through psychedelics and he was getting sort of curious. Dwight would never approve – it was against everything they subscribed to – but then he was in Iowa. One afternoon in August, Bill got some acid from a guy down at the Store. He took it home, locked the door, sat down on his bed, carefully dropped a tab and began to write furiously in his journal. Once he was fully on, he took off his shirt and went into the bathroom to look at his body in the mirror. He flung his arms out to the side, as though crucified, and hallucinated his nipples and navel becoming the face of Christ.

On 17 August, Bill called Dwight at Maharishi University to tell him he had decided to start spending more time in Austin, where the Comedy Workshop had just opened a club. He could hear the confusion and hurt in Dwight's voice and he tried to explain how he just had to get out of LA and how much he missed jamming with Stress. He'd be back and forth because of work but Kevin Booth, David Johndrow and another old friend, Brent Ballard, all students at the University of Texas, had a house together in Austin and he wanted to be based there for awhile. He didn't mention his acid trip just yet.

As soon as Bill settled into the Austin house, he found a new cause. He, Kevin and David began setting up a production company called Absolute Creative Entertainment. Nobody was using the term *indie* yet, but running an operation where the three would have total control over producing original, uncompromising music and comedy had been their dream since high school. It was kind of an offshoot of their teenage ambition to be a band and, just as they had taken promo pictures before they could play instruments, now they ran around buying office supplies and having stationery and business cards printed. 'Because our house on 42nd Street was going to be the production center and we were going to somehow need stationery right away,' David said. 'Before we even had any ideas. But it was all kind of pumped up by Bill's thing, by his renown or whatever you call it.'

For their first project, they started working on a video spoof called *Ninja Bachelor Party*. They'd all grown up with *Kung Fu*, starring David Carradine and they sat around in the morning giggling at old kung fu movies. Kevin bought a video camera, a rarity in 1982, and they started fooling around, shooting little scenes here and there. They planned to make the stupidest karate movie ever.

Bill loved being in Austin, the ultimate college town, with some 48,000 students, and an intellectual oasis in a state whose Board of Education had yet to approve the teaching of evolution as fact, not theory. The hippie enclave was a tolerant home to all things experimental and the ideal playground for Bill's metaphysical wanderings. He and David spent hours in Grok Books, a big occult bookstore on 6th Street that reeked of incense and overflowed with esoteric texts of ancient philosophy. Bill always said he was 'going to have a baby' when he came upon an incredibly great idea and as they roamed around David heard him a few aisles away going 'Psshht! *Waah!*' every few minutes.

David, Bill and Kevin joined Float to Relax, a new club with flotation tanks that promised 'weightlessness' and, only half jokingly, they started testing their telepathic powers by trying to send each other cake ingredients from different rooms of the house. They'd spread out their religious, occult and mystical books across the floor of the den, comparing notes, underlining passages and cross-referencing ideas. Bill was particularly excited about Alan Watts and John Lilly, whose book *Center of the Cyclone* he couldn't stop talking about. Mostly, though, Bill and David studied astrology texts, trying to test the compatibility of their charts with their girlfriends'. Laurie was an Aries to Bill's Sagittarius, both fire signs with fire rising. 'Bill had this duffel bag full of books that he would carry when he was going to go talk to his parents or have a discussion about religion with somebody,' David said. 'Then it became a joke: The Duffel Bag of Knowledge.' One day, much later, Bill threw away the entire bag. He'd devoured those ideas and he was moving on.

'He was the first guy I knew who would go to serious astrologers. The next day it would be, "Oh, it means nothing" just as easily. He could just change from day to day and it wouldn't be a problem. It would be like, "Well, Bill, I thought you said *this*." And he would say, "I was hot yesterday and today I'm cold. That just the way it is. One doesn't invalidate the other."'

By the end of September, Bill was back in Burbank for a visit. He and Dwight planned a massive prayer session in their apartment that they envisioned as a cosmic Woodstock, a jam session of every God, Deva and Angel. 'We had been dabbling with prayer and decided simply to go for broke,' Dwight said. 'Open ourselves up to the universe; to every conceivable idea of God, invite every being into our presence and then surrender ourselves to their will.' They got up early the morning of Sunday 26 September, lit candles and incense and observed silence until noon. They continued with a half-hour of TM and then Bill put on a tape of Kathumi, a New Age guru he had found. Dwight asked for protection around the apartment and invited the presence of 'the Master Jesus, Sri Sathya Sai Baba and those angels and beings that would hear our prayers'. Bill asked to be purified and for the Lord to take his will and make his life a tool for the Divine. He asked for creative inspiration and, especially, that his stand-up grow. They listened to some Sama Veda chanting and at the end of the day they felt completely spent, like they had pushed as far as they possibly could. 'This prayer session had a profound effect on us both,' said Dwight. 'Although at that time, I thought it cemented our relationship together as two guys who would really tear up Hollywood, I now realize it was really a fundamental turning point for Bill. It was as if all of his purpose in life was waiting to drop on top of him and this prayer session was the opening of the floodgate.'

SEVEN

Beep. *Hey, man, it's Willy. I just realized I learned a very, very important lesson tonight. Anyway. Ummmmm . . .*

One night in Houston that fall, Bill and Steve Epstein, who had moved back from Los Angeles, sat on the makeshift porch behind the Annex. 'What's this going to be like?' Bill asked. He had just swallowed three of the mushrooms he had asked Eppy to procure. All of the studies with Dwight and David, the prayer session and the acid trip had opened him up but he was still stymied for a way to integrate his spiritual advances into his comedy. Kinison was an enthusiastic proponent of mushrooms. He told Bill they helped with the writing like nothing else.

Bill kept questioning Eppy. 'How will I know I'm high?'

'You'll know,' Eppy replied.

Bill chattered nervously and then suddenly stopped mid-sentence, with a massive grin on his face. 'Wait a second,' Bill said about forty-five seconds later. 'I know. *Yes.*'

The MC appeared at the back door. 'Bill, you're on.'

Bill started in with his Jim Bowie museum joke, a constant about the kind of Southern landmarks his parents liked to tour during the summer. 'What could they have in this museum?' he blurted, beginning to shake with laughter. 'A knife,' he croaked and collapsed in hysterics. He held his hand up to illustrate the size of the knife and the audience began laughing with him. The more overcome he became the louder they roared. He was killing and he had only done about two minutes of material. He felt as if his very infectiousness had been enough to get them.

Mushrooms were a miracle. 'I'm a comedy god on those things!' he cried.

He'd just been talking to Eppy about how the ultimate comedy perfection would be the ability to transfer ideas without actually saying a word, communicate by osmosis like Keaton and Chaplin with just the imperceptible arching of an eyebrow. 'He would just be able to be so in the moment that people would laugh at his pure joy in being connected to them,' Johndrow said. Truly connecting with the audience, that's what he hadn't been able to do yet.

Bill had yet to experience the paranoia-inducing aspects of mushrooms but the next time he gobbled a few and went onstage, they slapped him hard. No eye candy and bonding that night. The audience wasn't buying him at all and with each second of awkward silence he freaked a little more. Midway through the set he had worked himself into a fetal huddle on the corner of the stage. The audience pelted him with coasters.

'What's a good drink?' Bill asked.

It was a few weeks after the Houston mushroom adventures and Bill was hanging out at the Workshop bar in Austin before a show with Eppy and another Houston comedian, Dan Merryman. Bill wanted to try everything available. He was now off on a substance quest, a complete departure from the purification tear he'd started a year ago. Sure you could sit cross-legged and pray for ten hours, but drugs, Bill now realized, were an express lane to transcendence.

Merryman suggested Cuervo Gold.

'Will it really get me off?' Bill wanted to know.

Bill was the closing act and he had a good two hours to get acquainted with the powers of top-shelf tequila. Seven or eight shots later, he was standing at the edge of the stage, glaring at his audience, seeing them for Reagan-loving middle-class fucks. (Forget that he was in one of the most progressive towns in America.) He'd never before been so filled with pure contempt. They were the reason everything was so mediocre. Who was he, their little monkey boy?

'You people,' he spat. 'You're responsible for Gary Coleman's career. You are the reason *Diff'rent Strokes* is the NUMBER ONE SHOW ON TELEVISION.'

Bill dragged his sleeve across his forehead and lay down onstage.

He cupped the mike with his mouth and began to chant. 'GARY COLEMAN GARY COLEMAN GARY COLEMAN GARY COLEMAN.' All you could see was his feet.

David watched agape from a table about three rows back. He was with a date, a girl he had just met. He'd never seen Bill like this. 'I had been talking about this friend of mine she had to see. Oh, God. It was horrible, she hated him. And she had every right to hate him. "Every fucking one of you ... blah blah blah." Just incoherent, and then he started doing something about how stupid war is and how the first two people that put on uniforms were the first two original morons.' The $180 million military package that Reagan was pushing for, at a time when joblessness was at 10.8 per cent, had been a subject of fierce debate for the last several months.

Bill sat up again. 'You stupid fuckin' old people,' he slurred, crawling around the stage. 'You just send your kids off to war. What the fuck do you care? You got all the money. Let them die. Just stay home and watch on your TV sets. You don't give a shit.'

An older woman in front stood up. 'I'll have you know my son died in the war for your freedom!' she yelled, pointing a finger at him.

'He didn't die for my fucking freedom!' Bill screamed.

As she and her husband left their table and made their way to the nearest exit, Bill said, 'All right, all right, maybe I was a little out of line ...'

The audience stared.

'Fuck you all,' he groaned.

'Every time I party too hard I remember Keith Richards is still alive.' That was one of Bill's favorite new lines. Barely taking a day to recover from the horror show in Austin, he'd started drinking every night, Jack Daniels, no chaser. That first night notwithstanding, everyone talked about how alcohol had brought out a sharpness in his wit. It disinhibited his critical voice and his comedy went to a deeper level. He was experimenting, improvising material onstage though not always coherently. 'He came alive,' Laurie said. 'He knew that and other people knew that. I think that's what propelled him to continue at first.' Offstage, of course, drinking also made it a lot easier for Bill to deal with the streams of new faces he came into contact with almost every night.

Kevin said it was like putting gasoline on a fire, the way alcohol and Bill mixed. His grimacing Sane Man was giving way to a new persona, the Prince of Darkness, an anti-hero for all. Bill was tapping into his outrage at a system much larger than his family. It was slow at first; as he scaled back on needling his parents, he moved on to the Christian Far Right, personified by the Reverend Jerry Falwell, the plump bombastic host of *The Old Gospel House*. Falwell's political group, the Moral Majority, supported a strong defense and 'family values'. 'Get in step with conservative values or prepare to be unemployed,' Reverend Falwell said in the papers.

If not politically sophisticated at the start, Bill was a natural social critic starting with his outrage at society's soldiers of banality and hypocrisy. His ire was great fun to watch simply because he was a natural showman. He hilariously punctuated his rants, skipping around the stage, wrapping the microphone cord around his neck like a noose or dipping into a quivering arabesque to underline his fury.

'He was pretty much a traveling circus,' David Johndrow recalled. 'I mean, he made it to shows and some of them were so funny it would just kill you. He was absolutely amazing when he was doing this thing about Falwell. He would get the audience chanting, "Jerry Falwell, first to go!". And he's marching around the stage and just doing those kinds of outrageous over-the-top things – that's what the alcohol sort of lubricated. But they would always degenerate because he'd be saying, "Someone bring me a drink" and people would make him drinks and bring them onstage. And he would turn into the bitter guy lying on his back and screaming, "WHAT DO YOU WANT? WHAT ARE YOU HERE FOR?"'

Drifting between Houston and Austin, Bill was very much back together with Laurie, who took his sea change in stride. 'He was smoking cigarettes, Marlboro Reds, he was drinking straight Scotch, he was talking about acid trips, it was literally 180 degrees,' Laurie said. 'Forget vegetarianism, forget meditation! It was the decadent screw-the-world-everything-sucks-the-end-is-coming-so-we-might-as-well-go-down-in-fun kind of totally opposite thing. And the timing was great for me because I was just ending a relationship with someone who was Mr Mountain Climber. I was ready to rebel against all that, too.'

Bill celebrated his twenty-first birthday at the Annex in Houston. It was an especially momentous occasion, as he and Dwight had always talked about how the numbers twenty and twenty-one kept popping up in both their lives. Their joint address at the Olive Tropics, for example, was 2021 West Olive. They firmly believed that when they reached twenty and twenty-one years old, respectively (Dwight being four months younger), it would be a groundbreaking period. But when Dwight called Bill at the club to wish him a happy birthday, Bill was partying with Laurie and the guys. He was completely wasted. Dwight hung up the phone, disgusted.

Bill's new train-wreck style was nothing if not rock & roll and the city of Austin, led by those in the music scene, fully embraced him. Long a tightly knit blues town and home to Willie Nelson, Austin in 1983 was a hotbed of funk, rock, punk, bluegrass and new wave, supporting over sixty live-music clubs and opening about ten new ones by 1984. On any given night, you could go see Joe Ely at the Opera House, the Skunks at the Ritz, the Fabulous Thunderbirds at the Coliseum, Stevie Ray Vaughan and Double Trouble at Antone's, Stephen Doster and the Scissors, Little Charlie Sexton and Bill's teenage idol, Eric Johnson. When musicians had a night off, going to see Hicks perform was the thing to do, and it was a mutual admiration society. Bill became friends with revered guitarist Stephen Doster through Doster's roommate, comedian Johnny Torres. Bill loved to hang out with Doster's cover band, the Austin All-Stars, and belt out 'Satisfaction'.

'The first words I ever heard out of his mouth were, "Good evening, ladies and gentlemen. My name is William Melvin Hicks. Thanks, Dad",' Doster said. 'Then he proceeded just to tear apart his whole upbringing. It was the funniest thing I'd ever seen. And he looked like he was about fifteen years old. Back then, he was really baby-faced for a twenty-one-year-old.'

Bill had been in Austin barely six months when he got a call from the Workshop to open for Jay Leno there the second week in February 1983. Thirty-three-year-old Leno, who packed clubs 300 days of the year and was becoming well known through his appearances on the new show *Late Night with David Letterman*, was considered the sharpest, best road act in the country. Leno was a hero to Bill. Beside himself, Bill asked Laurie to come to Austin for the engagement. 'This is really important,' he told her, 'really significant.' The *Austin Chronicle* was promoting the shows well in advance, noting Jay's Carson and Letterman credits and calling Bill 'the most promising up-and-comer of the stable', ensuring the two would play to full houses all six nights.

Leno brought his wife Mavis and the four hung out all week, having dinner at Steak & Ale together before the shows. Bill and Laurie couldn't get over how warm and genuine Jay and Mavis were. 'Bill was thrilled to be with him,' Laurie said, 'and kept telling me what a great guy he was. There were very few people Bill would say were funny: Seinfeld, Jay and maybe one or two more but that was it.' Leno seemed to have an affection for Bill, and he had lots of advice for him: if you want to get on television, he suggested, you should clean up your material and make it more palatable for general audiences. Leno said Bill didn't need to swear or get graphic about sex; he was powerful enough without that stuff.

Bill took it all in, but he was even more interested in hearing what Mavis, a professional astrologer, had to say. Despite the buzz of opening for Leno, Bill was still feeling restless and confused about his life path. Austin had a lot going for it, but Laurie was in Houston and Bill hated being apart, writing her long lovesick letters from Austin, sometimes twice a day. 'The rest is so meaningless,' he wrote. 'It only takes on meaning when I'm with you – my love. And when we're apart – motions. Without love, life is meaningless motion.' He could see what 'an irresponsible infant' he was, he told her, and 'how much other people take care of me', and now he realized that this was the year of growing up and doing his part, 'just like Mavis said'.

'And it's sort of scary but now I think I have the incentive to do it. Us, you, we ... I love you and I love us and I want it to work.

You go around a thousand times in the world of experience and this time I want to go around with you.'

'I gotta go,' he announced one day to Kevin and David. Bill had all but moved in with them and just as quickly he was leaving. He was driving out to California to pick up his stuff and move back to Houston where he was going to live with Laurie's parents. He left Houston on 21 March in his Chevette with his new pet, a ferret called Neil. Two days later, around 10 p.m., he reached the California border and agricultural inspection informed him he could not bring a ferret into California. He turned back to Arizona, parked at a rest stop and wrote Laurie a letter while he waited for the border guard to get off duty so he could stash Neil in a suitcase and try again.

'A lot of things are changing,' Dwight wrote in his journal a couple of days after Bill's arrival at the Olive Tropics. 'And they all seem to be stemming from the return of a gentleman named Bill Hicks. A man who I can't figure out if he is near enlightenment or a black beast. I don't know. He's a genius and a putz and a child and a Master all in one. And with the return of him on Wednesday, my life has been shaken like thunder. I have experienced every emotion and every shade of feeling since he's been back. Elation, joy, bliss, anger, depression, awe, love, hate, wonder, laughter, disappointment, fear, pain, have all passed through me. And generally all at the same time.'

Dwight had no idea what to make of the new character before him. Bill was dressed head to toe in black, wearing a Members Only jacket and shades. He was chain smoking and talking some deep shit about sex and relationships – no surprise there, given his reunion with Laurie. But they both *loathed* smoking. The illogicality of it irritated them so much they even had a code when someone lit up. 'WDPS?' they would ask one another, meaning 'Why Do People Smoke?'

Bill kept talking about his left side. Sometimes he felt something there, he said. A presence more than a pain. One night when he'd been tripping on mushrooms in Laurie's dorm room, he'd gone through a birthing experience with Laurie in the role of the mother.

He said that, as he relived his birth, he remembered something about his own pain being born. He felt it had been a difficult passage, that he'd been hurt somehow. The result, Bill believed, was an imbalance.

'He started to think of everything in those terms,' Dwight said. 'If there was some abnormality on his body it was in his left side. He felt his left side and right side were uneven and he had to balance them.'

If Dwight was shaken by Bill's latest incarnation, they still managed to have a pretty good month together. They came up with a new character for *The Suburbs* and went down to the Comedy Store every night to watch, awestruck, as Richard Pryor worked out material for his concert movie *Live on Sunset Strip*. They hung out a little with Kinison, who was still working as a doorman – and before Pryor came on they watched twenty-one-year-old Jim Carrey blow audiences away, set after set.

When Bill got up early on the morning of Wednesday 18 May to drive home to Houston, he left a farewell note for his roommate before he closed the door. On the top he had scrawled, 'The dream doesn't end . . . the rainbow changes directions', and at the bottom he'd drawn a little Lennon, with guitar in hand and a long cigarette hanging out of his mouth. It said, 'I'm in a band now, ya know.'

EIGHT

Beep. *Hey, man, it's Willy. You've never gone this long without checking your messages or calling me. Okay. Be that way. Be any way you want to be.*

For all of Bill's bravado with his friends, he didn't know what the hell he was doing back in Houston. He was performing at the Annex almost every night, but something was wrong – even the flow of whiskey couldn't entirely ease his malaise. In fact, it was probably the worst thing for his depression. After almost every set, Bill imploded. He and Laurie would be in the car on the way home and he would start: 'I'm not funny. The other guy got just as many laughs and his material is stupid. I'm not as funny as him.'

'I would say, "You're just not seeing it right. They loved you. They adored you,"' Laurie recalled. 'It was true that sometimes people wouldn't get what he was trying to do or it was too harsh or sometimes it was that he was drinking too much and he would just go on these rampages and he wouldn't get offstage. Those were just horribly embarrassing. But even when he killed we would go through this.'

Really, Bill knew his talent wasn't the issue, but he had this ongoing love-hate relationship with performing and he seemed continually to search for reasons to get away from it, in favor of a more consistent existence, only to be pulled back in almost immediately. 'I was so miserable,' he said later, 'that I said to myself that I was going to college ... even if I had to be a frickin' accountant – anything but getting onstage again.'

It really bothered Bill that he had never gone to college, especially now that he was with Laurie, who was dedicated to her studies and heading for med school. His college-educated parents had always put a strong emphasis on education and made it clear they thought he should get one. 'He was always feeling less than others, less educated,' said Laurie. 'In reality, meanwhile, he was reading books that were beyond me in complexity and was more intelligent than 99 per cent of the population anyway.' Even Frank Mango, Laurie's father, privately couldn't imagine what Bill Hicks was going to learn in a classroom.

Bill enrolled at the University of Houston for the 1983 summer session, signing up for philosophy and a couple of drama classes, and in late May he and Laurie drove to Austin for his big farewell show at the Workshop. Word got around that Hicks was quitting comedy for good and the last night, Sunday, the room sold out to students, faculty and his musician buddies. He began drinking well before the show and once he was onstage, friends started sending him shots. It looked like it was going to be one of his marathon shows and after about two hours people slowly started to leave. Unmoved, Bill waxed sentimental about what made a truly great skin flick. None of this just showing the guy's 'hairy ass' pumping. 'It's not an adult feature unless at the end someone is gooey,' he said. 'Arcing ropes of jism hitting chins, that's an adult feature.' The crowd groaned. 'Women licking up semen like kittens under a cow udder, *that* is an adult feature.' 'Ya'll are staring at me like a dog that's just been shown a card trick,' Bill sighed.

About thirty serious fans remained, drinking with him, and finally the club turned off the lights. When Bill didn't miss a beat, they turned the microphone off, too. By now, everyone was just laughing at the absurdity of it all. 'He's drunk as shit and he sits down at the edge of the stage with his legs hanging off and just starts yelling and doing his bit,' said his friend David Cotton. 'Well, it's going pretty well. He's getting funnier! Because he's having to work. He doesn't have lights or a microphone and he gets everybody back. Instead of just being the sloshed drunk, there's a challenge before him. And he starts concentrating and being funny again and comes back around, does a couple of bits, winds up the show, tags a nice ending and – boom! – gets applause. Ends the show despite them!'

Bill loved living at the Mangos' while he went to school. He

adored Joyce and Frank, Laurie's parents, and being in their home
had a calming effect on him. They all sat around the kitchen table
playing poker and Bill and Joyce spent hours in the study, drinking
red wine and talking about life. Despite the thirty-year age difference,
Joyce considered him a good friend. 'He loved to talk,' she said, 'and
he just loved exploring any kind of idea. It was incredible to watch
his mind work.' If Bill was adrift, he didn't appear to her to be
agonizing over what direction his life was going to take. He
sometimes talked about wanting to be a preacher. 'That was a high
goal in the back of his mind ... He used to tell me he wanted to try
every single thing before he died. That was his motto: "I want to try
everything once." '

The Mangos took Bill to see the blues folk singer Odetta, a
favorite of Elvis, when she came to Houston. Frank Mango had
known Odetta years before in San Francisco and after the show they
went backstage to say hello. When Odetta heard Bill was a comedian
she said that was about the hardest, loneliest thing a performer could
do. 'You're taking the long road,' she told him.

Meanwhile, Bill was barely making it to classes at the University
of Houston: six weeks later, when the Annex called to ask him to
sub for another comic at the last minute, his retirement promptly
ended. So much for 'earning a degree, getting a nice safe job and
earning a stupid living,' he said.

1983 must have seemed like a bad time to leave the business.
With the death of the disco era, the country was littered with
graveyard nightclubs, which only needed a mike and a brick wall to
be turned into comedy clubs. Modeled on those in New York and
LA, clubs were springing up in heartland cities like Cleveland and
Pittsburgh, and there was a windfall of road work. Customers were
drinking so much, a cover charge wasn't necessary. As Bill put it, 'It
literally went like this: "Bill, we have a gig for you in Victoria, Texas.
Oh, and while you're there, a club just opened in El Paso." It
happened in every state.' The immediate potential to make thousands
of dollars a week was there. 'It felt right all of a sudden,' Bill said.
'Suddenly I am making great money as a twenty-year-old kid. I'm
thinking, 'Wow, let's not be foolish.'

Mostly he missed the life. He loved being around guys who lived and breathed comedy the way he did and several of the original Annex comedians – Pineapple, Barber and Epstein – had returned to Houston from Los Angeles. Between them and the arrival of an offbeat mix of characters new to the Annex, comedy in Houston was getting ever more intriguing. There was John Farneti, a thirty-three-year-old lawyer and former high school Latin teacher, with a wife and a two-year-old daughter, who performed after work and whose droll act was considered 'intellectual' (a notion he scoffed at by quoting Dick Cavett, 'Well, maybe compared to Totie Fields.'). Ron Shock, a forty-year-old from Amarillo, Texas, who had turned twenty-one in prison and run several businesses before becoming a full-time stand-up comedian, had a small-town drawl and a gift for hyperbole that made him an unrivalled storyteller. Andy Huggins, (whom Bill had met his first day at the Comedy Store in 1980) had just moved to Houston; he was soft-spoken but had a razor-sharp wit.

At the Annex, all the guys were stars. As Bill's friend, the Annex comedian Tracy Wright put it, they were all college age and living a rock-star life. 'Everybody was excited about comedy,' Bill said. 'It was new, it was the most happening thing, people were getting laid in the bathrooms, cocaine on the bar, crowds were waiting an *hour* to get in.' One night the pretty girlfriend of a guy who had been heckling Jimmy Pineapple throughout his set followed him into the bathroom after he got offstage. While Pineapple was having her, he asked, 'How's that for a comeback?' Or so the story went . . .

Bill was now making enough money to get an apartment of his own and in the fall he and Laurie found a grim one-room flat on Richmond Avenue in a seedy part of Houston. But it was a place for just the two of them and they adopted another ferret, a friend for Neil. They'd always had a passionate, highly charged relationship, but this time they were more deeply committed and they talked about getting married. 'We were extremely close, we had a real affectionate bond that time,' Laurie said. 'We took care of each other. Also, I love the dramatic, too. I vicariously got a lot out of his being on the stage and sought-after and in a cult-like way. I thought that was fascinating and wonderful to share . . . It was like I had the serious, conservative track of life and his was this wild adventurous, extreme, exciting one . . .'

Laurie was with Bill most nights at the Annex. Bill loved to be with her, but he didn't really like her watching him every night. 'It's my work,' he said, 'and I don't want to worry that you've heard it all before.' Laurie reassured him that it was funny no matter how many times she heard it.

All of them — fifteen or so including Huggins, Pineapple, Wright, Farneti, Barber, Shock, and an aspiring comedian named Mark Wilkes — hung out between sets in the green room, a small dark space with fake-wood paneling and a beer-stained floor, talking and drinking, all of them wired from stage time. It was a tough bunch. No hacks allowed. As stand-up became more of a business, the unwritten Houston credo was comedy for comedy's sake. The point was to write the most original material possible. And if one guy wrote a line perfect for another guy, he handed it over.

'It was just a crapshoot that came together,' Huggins said. 'The guys were all very creative. Everybody there loved stand-up. Nobody was using stand-up because they thought one day they'd get their own TV show. Everybody was doing stand-up because they loved doing it, because it was fun. We were very insistent on originality — to steal or be derivative was a sin — and this may have been a bit snobbish on our parts but we had a distaste for prop comics or any-one who went up there with something other than original thoughts and original words. And to be around that kind of creativity just spurred everybody on. You kind of fed off it. You found yourself growing in spite of any laziness you might normally have.'

'It's fascinating how different areas brought out different kinds of comedy,' Bill said years later. 'Like Boston, the guys were real political, and in Houston, all the guys were kind of social, or humanist, but they were also kind of philosophical and spiritual in a way. I don't know why it came out that way, I just know that we all kind of had a similar philosophy about God. It could be that we tripped so much.'

If Hicks was the youngest, he was the undisputed leader in a group of alpha males. As Farneti liked to say, 'There's Hicks and then there's everybody else.' There might have been more grudging feelings if Hicks weren't so goddamn funny.

Laurie was often the only girl back there, smoking cigarettes and listening to them. She thought they were hilarious but she wasn't sure they liked having her hang out all the time. 'You did have to show, if you were going to be a woman back there, that you weren't going to get offended by anything,' she said. 'They wouldn't put up with that. They sort of hazed me a little.' The guys warmed up pretty quickly though. It was hard not to appreciate a woman who gave Bill the line, 'I smoke because I need the tar to fill the potholes in my soul.'

NINE

Beep. *Hey, where's my buddy when I need him? Where's my buddy when I need him? Where's my buddy when I need him? I'll just call one of my other hundreds of buddies. Really, give me a call, dude, we gotta go to New York.*

Jay Leno had promised to help Bill get on *Letterman* and he was true to his word. He'd told *Late Night* segment producer Robert Morton what a great act Hicks had, and on a Friday morning in early February 1984 Bill got the call. Actually, the Workshop got the call because Bill didn't have a phone just then, it was forever being cut off due to $1,000 long-distance bills. 'Letterman's looking for you!' Workshop co-owner Sharon Menzel yelled when she pounded on Bill's door around noon. The show producers wanted Bill to call in that afternoon to discuss a booking. The thing was, he planned to spend the afternoon doing some mushrooms he had gotten from the friend of a guy who worked in an Unclaimed Mail room in Colorado. Also, John Farneti was coming over any minute to go on an urban hike.

'I have to call Robert Morton at three,' Bill said when John arrived.

'Maybe we should hold off until after then,' Farneti suggested.

'No, no,' Bill scoffed. 'Let's take them now, go for a walk.'

As Bill headed out the door, he picked up a globe from a nearby table and tucked it under his arm. 'In case we get lost,' he said.

The two meandered down to Rice University, toward the football stadium. John glanced at his watch. It was time.

'You want to call him?'

'Ohhhhhhh, *man*,' Bill groaned. 'Call him? Where from?'

'There's a payphone. I got a quarter.'

'I don't even know the area code.'

'Gee,' John said, 'I wonder how we could find out the area code for *New York City* here at the *university*?'

Bill's friends marveled at how work came his way without his ever picking up a phone. None of them could remember him ever once calling a club to ask for a set. Bill wrote new material regularly but he seemed to have little energy for pursuing his career.

After several miles and two hours of musing, Bill and John sauntered to a phone. Mr Morton, the secretary informed Bill, had already left for Connecticut for the weekend. He couldn't be reached.

'Did I just fuck up?' Bill asked as he hung up.

Farneti did not want a psychedelically depressed Bill on his hands. John said when Bill got bummed it was as if a houseful of Barrymores were bummed.

'And I said, "Not at all! Not at all!" I'm thinking *total total total fuck up. How can you possibly be this self-destructive?* So we go out for another walk and every eight steps he asks, "Did I fuck up?"'

This time they walked a few miles west to Greenway Plaza, a futuristic civic complex that looked like something out of *Metropolis*. They sat in a sunken concrete structure amid the skyscrapers and eventually they started talking about Ethel Merman, whose recent death had been in the news. Suddenly Bill started doing Ethel Merman. 'And he's never seen her in her prime but they were showing clips of her singing on television. And he's just shrieking *There's no business like show business* ... cutting loose, doing this tremendous Ethel Merman and we're roaring, laughing, and we look up in the sky and there's this plane way overhead towing a banner. But it's much too high for us to read it.'

'Bill looks up at it, craning his neck for several seconds as if he can make out the words, and reads very slowly, "You ... fucked ... up ... pal. You ... know ... who ... I'm ... talking ... to."'

Ten months later, on 5 December 1984, Bill was standing in NBC Studio 2-E inside 30 Rock, puffing hard on a Kool Menthol as he watched Letterman chat with sports announcer Marv Albert and Chris Elliot do his sixth appearance as 'The Guy Under the Seats'.

This was actually Bill's second visit to *Late Night*. A week before he'd been booked and bumped when, fifteen minutes before air, NBC wanted to excise the last bit in his set.

The three cardinal broadcast rules at NBC were: no making fun of religion, schizophrenia or the handicapped on the air. The bit Bill wanted to do was known as the pencil-in-the-eye routine.

'It was one of the ones he did most often and was known for in the early days,' Farneti said. 'Many people could do it for you verbatim. It's "Teacher leaves the room in the first grade and you're throwing the pencils back and forth – *hey! hey!* – and I'm the one that throws it right in the kid's eye. Blinds him.

'"Everybody pulls a chair out from somebody. When I pull the chair out, the guy who falls down? Paralyzed. For the rest of his school career he's being pushed around in a wheelchair.

'"By a kid with one eye."'

The joke was a classic example of Bill's deftness in setting up a surprise ending, something he delighted in. He would cleverly drop in a detail in the set-up, lead the audience away from it and suddenly wrap back to it for an even bigger laugh.

'The audience would just explode at that. He was the king of tags. What he really liked about this joke was in the end he portrayed himself as the *victim* of it all. And then it ended with, "And what do you say to this guy?"

'"Well, you can park closer to the school now." That was a big big laugh. The guy wouldn't let Bill do that one.'

A few minutes past six, Bill heard Letterman introduce him for the first time. 'My next guest is a stand-up comedian who is making his network debut on this program tonight...' Bill mashed out his cigarette, ran a sweaty palm through his hair – '... Please give a warm welcome to Bill Hicks!' – and walked on to the small stage to face the studio audience. His confidence kicked in as he faced the cameras and, almost turning a shoulder to the audience, launched into stock favorites, mostly amusing stuff about his 'goober' parents. The highlight of the set was a routine about taking a summer school class in philosophy, one of his earliest bits to weave in a spiritual message. He'd taken the class with a bunch of jocks, Bill said, guys who were in there trying to make up credits. First day of class the professor explains the core of life: God is consciousness. And we are all God trying to realize our full potential.

'Guy in the back goes, "Yeah, are we gonna need to know that?"'

Bill raised his hand, a blank look on his face.

'Is that gonna be on the quiz?'

Five minutes later he was done, not a beat missed, and Bill heard Letterman murmur, 'Very fluid, very funny' as he came off. Bill's friends were all watching from Houston House and reported later that the best part was when he raised his hand and you could see the stain under his arm. They said it made him look like a real person, to be nervous.

At twenty-two, Bill was the first of the Houston guys to do *Letterman*; not even Kinison had made it yet. But what Bill was thinking about was that he'd been on his personal favorite show, the one that had pushed Leno to the next level. It was confirmation, he said, that he hadn't been wasting his time. He appeared, however, plainly surprised at the red tape involved in getting approved to perform on television.

'The first time I went up there was harrowing,' he told the *Houston Chronicle* when they profiled him a week later under the heading 'Bill Hicks: A hostile Bob Newhart'. 'The second time wasn't so bad. I imagine the third time will even be fun. I really dug the set. If I could have done what I wanted, it would have been memorable. As it was, it was sufficient . . .

'I was basically just tying one-liners together smoothly, but they almost literally picked them for me.'

Brandishing an all-important TV credit, Bill's club price went up to $1,000 a week. But after an initial wave of offers, Bill was having trouble getting booked. With every road gig his reputation for outrageous behavior grew. Drinking brought out his physical side – he'd end up outside in the parking lot destroying things, kicking apart two-by-fours, punching his car so hard he dented it, hurling shot glasses on to the roof ('Drinks are on the house!'). Word travels fast on the comedy circuit and Hicks stories grew with each retelling.

Before Sandy DiPerna, a club manager in Richmond, Virginia,

met him she'd heard the wild Bill stories too, but the first time she saw him onstage in Virginia Beach, 'it was like nothing I'd ever seen in my life'.

Typically, jobs came Bill's way through word of mouth, but DiPerna knew comedy club owners all over the country and thought she could get him booked more regularly – even with his reputation. When Bill got offstage, Sandy asked him if he was working with anyone. After they exchanged numbers, she noticed him at the bar drinking pretty hard but she didn't think much about it. It was the eighties after all and there were clubs that paid talent in eight balls.

Bill assured Sandy that he was serious about putting his career on track. He followed up with her as soon as he got back to Houston, sending a bunch of press cuttings and some head shots. 'I hope we can work together,' he wrote. 'I will not let you down!'

The first couple of months of DiPerna acting as his agent, Bill lay low and Sandy got people to book him, some very reluctantly. The trouble was that Bill could rarely keep a job.

More than his bad behavior, the problem was his act. As the decade progressed, comedy clubs began to demand 'clean' material for a changing audience. 'Because there were so many of them, clubs started to get more competitive,' said Jimmy Miller, who booked clubs on the West Coast. 'Club owners began papering the rooms, giving away two-for-one coupons or sending out Tuesday night freebies to mailing lists. If you didn't paper Tuesday night you got maybe ten people. This way the club owner got 150 people who didn't pay but who were drinking and eating food. It might sound like a small thing but it was a big thing for a thinking man's act. You don't want to throw Bill Hicks or my brother [Dennis Miller] into Little Rock, Arkansas, on a Wednesday night, particularly when they're giving the audience away for free. Who do you think those people are?'

Not a few of them were Reaganites. It was 1984, 'morning in America', and Reagan, who campaigned on the feel-good phrase, had just won re-election in a landslide. The economy was turning around and high school Young Republican clubs had record memberships. Bill's routine about how we live in a world where 'good

men are murdered and mediocre hacks thrive' didn't always go over.
How was it, Bill asked onstage, that Gandhi, Kennedy and King
were murdered and Reagan was wounded?

Plenty of comedians did Reagan-the-ancient-B-actor jokes, of
course, but the sheer ferocity of Bill's Reagan material wasn't exactly
daiquiri-compatible. He liked to tell a long graphic fantasy about
bursting into the White House to murder the Reagans, not to get
Jodie Foster's attention – Hinckley was *clearly* insane – but Phoebe
Cates's.

'He kicks in the door and he's shooting the President,' said
Farneti, who wondered how many 'bullets' Bill had gone through in
his career. 'And he says, "Where's Nancy? Come here, you assless
bitch!" *Boom boom boom.* "Where's the dog?" *Boom boom boom.* Next
he's sitting on the electric chair. But he got Phoebe Cates's attention.
"Any final words, Mr Hicks?" And Bill's sniffing his middle finger
and looks up and says, "Whaaaa? What'd ya say?"'

'The craziest thing about Bill Hicks was he just didn't care
whether people laughed or not,' said Brad Greenberg, who booked
comedy clubs in the south-east. 'We had lots of guys using foul
language and stuff. I could never really use Bill Maher because he
was too sarcastic. Dennis Miller was just out there. But Bill, Bill was
a Southerner. He could do what was necessary to entertain the
crowd, but then he'd start drinking or get on a soapbox about
something and then it would be back to talking about shit that
people just had no idea about. He'd think nothing of talking about
religion and Christ. To the average person out there just trying to
get away from their troubles, it wasn't their cup of tea.'

At a Michigan club Bill got into such a conflagration that it was
written up in the newspaper. The club owner, John Yoder, phoned
Sandy and said, 'Well, I just want you to know I had the worst
review ever from his show and I'm going to send you this article.'
Sandy apologized profusely, as she always did, and then called her
client. 'I was saying to Bill, every time you get thrown out, it's not
so much what you're doing to *your* reputation because your reputation is shot. But *I* have a fairly good one!'

Now and then Bill was contrite – as when he got fired in Fort

Meyers, Florida, for getting into a scuffle with some bouncers at a disco after a show and breaking a $500 vase, but when it came to toning down his act, there was no discussion. 'He'd go ballistic. "Don't you *ever* tell me how to do my act. Don't you *ever* tell me what to say onstage."'

Darkening Bill's mood considerably was the fact that he and Laurie were drifting apart, which Bill thought had mostly to do with his being on the road all the time. But their distance had at least as much to do with his drinking. Laurie was usually the one to get him home in one piece and she listened to endless self-loathing diatribes. 'He would be inconsolable. Be ranting about how he was no good, life was no good.' He even turned on her sometimes. When Bill was drunk he easily became insulting and jealous, overly demanding. There was no reasoning with him. He was inconsolable: he was no good and life was no good. Laurie realized she thought of Bill as, first and foremost, an angry person.

'We didn't have anything in common anymore. I was going off to med school, he was going on the road and drinking. It was kind of like, there's nothing left here to fight for anymore.'

There was no big dramatic break-up, just a series of fights and trial separations that pushed them a little farther apart each time until Laurie finally moved back into the dorms. 'It was a mutual decision,' Bill started saying from the stage. 'She said she didn't want to see me anymore and I said, "Okay."'

Sandy could never stay mad at him. A few clubs requested that she chaperone her unruly client to his gigs and when she did they always had a great time. With her, he was always sweet, a perfect gentleman. They'd play tarot cards at the hotel all day and if Bill didn't like what they said he'd just reshuffle them. One weekend in Charlotte, when they got restless Bill found a palm reader in the Yellow Pages and called a cab to take them to her home.

When they got to her door, the palm reader's place was a mess and she had all these wild kids running around. 'You'd think she would have known we were coming,' he whispered to Sandy.

Back at the hotel, Bill presented Sandy with a beautiful crystal necklace she'd seen in the hotel gift shop. He was always buying nice things for her and her daughters, but this was too much; a few hundred dollars and no occasion. Maybe he was just in a happy mood. The palm reader had told them both that Bill was going to be a big star.

And he could be, Sandy gently insisted, if only he would back off just a little. Grudgingly, Bill came up with a few lines to soften the blow. One of his favorites, after a long bit on cunnilingus, was 'My mother wrote that one.' His other favorite was 'I am available for children's birthday parties.' He was discovering he could go pretty far out there if he had one good line to reel them back in.

TEN

Beep. Where are you, man? I signed up for Prime Time. *I went and got CDs. I'm in hell. I'm in CD hell. Or CD heaven, actually . . . Um, this looks like it's gonna be a Dylan fest, but I would like to branch out. I got all three Lyle Lovetts and I got* Kind of Blue. *So. Life is happening on many levels. Ohmygod* 'Visions of Johanna' *singing!! AWWWWWWWWWHHHHH. AWWWWWWWWWWWWWWWHHHHHHHHHH.*

By the time *Houston City Magazine* began profiling Bill in June 1985 the electric company had cut off service at his Richmond Avenue apartment, and he was sleeping on Mark Wilkes's floor. The night that writer Bob Daily met him before a show at the Annex for their first interview, Bill admitted he had just $15 to his name. 'It's all right, you know?' he told Daily. 'I mean, I'm a young guy. I'm not going to quit.'

'Like punk rockers, who he admires,' Daily wrote, 'he is cynical, contemptuous, full of what one critic called "youthful indignation". Onstage he is openly critical of nearly everything and everybody that falls in his field of vision. (Including, it should be noted, himself – the source of most of his frustration.)

'"Sometimes I feel like an alien in this world," he admits. "I don't get along with it at all. Like, I don't want to work – I think it's an inhuman aspect of life. I think we should get paid for being ourselves . . ."'

Bill's state of mind reflected the irony of the moment: he was noticed and respected and becoming more unemployable by the day. 'It seems absurd that this young man – funny, successful with an exciting, high profile career – should talk so frequently of pain and depression,' the reporter noted.

'I'm changing though,' he assured Daily in the piece. 'That's an illusion, to be a suffering artist.'

Daily followed Bill for a week or so more, and on Friday 21 June found him in a much better frame of mind at Houston's Tower Theater hanging out backstage with Jay Leno who, Daily wrote, was about to entertain 900 screaming fans. Bill told Daily he had just gotten two weeks of work in Austin and St Louis, Leno had offered to help him get on *The Merv Griffin Show* and, best of all, Bill was about to move into Houston House, a luxury high-rise downtown. He and Mark Wilkes were moving in on Monday.

Wilkes, somewhere between an acolyte and a friend of Bill's, had started coming around to the back of the Annex when he was a waiter at a nearby seafood place. Eventually he'd put a set together, heavily influenced by Hicks. Wilkes would do absolutely anything for him – get him girls, party aids – and Bill, meanwhile, looked the other way when Wilkes did his material verbatim on the road.

Incredibly, Wilkes had managed to talk the manager of Houston House into letting him and Hicks live there in a one-bedroom apartment on the twenty-second floor with a balcony and an unparalleled view of downtown, rent-free. He exploited Bill's local renown and his recent Letterman appearance to its full potential. It would be great publicity to house Houston's King of Comedy; the *Houston City Magazine* piece, due to hit the stands in December, would be the first example of free notice for the building. (Indeed, Bill mentioned the building by name to Daily.) Wilkes had also promised that he and Hicks would do shows for tenants in the building's party room.

The day Bill and Mark moved in they discovered a book on the floor of the empty apartment called *Making Your Dreams Come True*. Bill chucked it. 'I guess we don't need this,' he said. Wilkes let Bill have the bedroom, and Bill covered all the windows with aluminum foil to block out the sun.

Bill and Wilkes had their first big party at Houston House a couple of nights after they moved in, an all-night coke and booze fest. It was an after-party for a sixty-minute stand-up special several of the guys, including Bill, Farneti, Shock, Huggins and Epstein, had just taped for Channel 2, Houston's NBC affiliate. Epstein and Ron Shock, who organized the whole thing, called the show 'Texas Outlaw Comics'. Epstein had recently trademarked the Outlaw name; he felt he had some claim to it, he said, since Kinison still owed him money from the Lam show five years earlier.

When the show aired in July it got solid ratings and ran twice more that summer. The moniker caught on quickly, due in part to Kinison's notoriety, and *Houston City Magazine* ran a story on the 'Outlaws' and their plans for a second special. 'We want total originality,' Epstein told the reporter. 'We're looking for people who speak their minds, whose comedy comes from themselves – the people who aren't interested in selling out.'

Spurred on by the success of their collective voice, the guys poured their energy into a vision of Houston as the entertainment nexus of the future. They imagined not ever having to leave their city to find success, their sensibility capturing the attention of the nation, Houston becoming to comedy what San Francisco had been to the Beats. 'It's kind of like 1910 in Hollywood when it was just getting started,' Bill said in an interview with the *Houston Chronicle*.

Bill's look now, which went nicely with the Outlaw thing, was an all-black ensemble, usually jeans and a leather jacket. He had black 'Sane Man' T-shirts made up in North Carolina during a week when his shows were going particularly well, and wore one when he opened for Ray Charles at Rockefeller's in downtown Houston. Bill loved being paired with a band. The most resonant stand-up comedy requires a sense of rhythm and pacing, and comedians are often serious music lovers. Bill was a most enthusiastic one; his friends said he'd much rather talk about music than comedy. When Bill turned on to something, he steeped himself in it and, for a period, Dylan was all he listened to. Johndrow never forgot the huge grin on Bill's face as he kicked back in his La-Z-Boy at Houston House and howled at 'It's Alright Ma (I'm Only Bleeding)', a song he began quoting from onstage. His other loves included Miles Davis, The Clash, Arlo Guthrie ('Hobo's Lullaby' was the ultimate comedian's song, he said) and Tom Waits (particularly 'The Piano Has Been Drinking' and 'Pasties And A G-String').

During intermission at the Ray Charles show at Rockefeller's Bill
hung out backstage with the band and watched as a fan tried to get
Charles's autograph. 'Mr Charles doesn't sign autographs,' a security
guy told her.

'Oh, but I came from so far away,' the woman begged. She
persisted and finally one of Charles's entourage said, 'I sign autographs for Mr Charles.'

'You *do*?' she cried, rushing over to him, paper and pen in hand.
'Oh, thank you!'

'Hey, I can give you John Lennon's,' Bill offered.

From that first night, Houston House (where Pineapple and
Huggins had also gotten a one-bedroom apartment), with its sprawling view of the city, was the official hangout. The guys pretty much
had the run of the building and Bill, Kevin and David were shooting
more scenes for *Ninja Bachelor Party* up on the roof. It quickly
became the last stop for a revolving cast of comedians, musicians
and hangers-on, plus the core group – Pineapple, Barker, Huggins,
Wright, Eppy, Wilkes, and a younger comedian, Bill's good friend T.
Sean Shannon. Johndrow was there too most nights; now a photographer, he'd moved back to Houston after graduating from UT
and had been doing head shots for all the guys. The parties, big,
informal and raucous, with Tom Waits, Dylan or Sinatra on the
stereo, often went on all night with lots of drinking, snorting,
Ecstasy, card playing and a career's worth of lines floating out with
the soundwaves.

They wholly rejected the notion, suggested by reporters over the
years, that they were some kind of roaming fraternity and Pineapple
mocked the Outlaw moniker, refusing, with rare exception, to take
part in group shows. The guys were an intriguing entity nonetheless,
a brotherhood of staunch individualists with a million inside jokes.
Within the group, alliances shifted and pairs of guys buddied up for
a time.

One guy got into Jerry Lewis or the Three Stooges and pretty
soon they were all into it, watching, reading, quoting. The big phase
was Sinatra, spurred on by Pineapple, onstage a cocktail-swilling

romantic whose act referenced Sinatra constantly. *I won't dance, don't ask me.*

Pineapple and Bill, suddenly closer since Houston House, especially loved Sinatra's Columbia years, ring-a-ding-ding meet-me-at-the-Copa Frank, and they got deep into *My Way*, Kitty Kelley's biography of Sinatra, particularly his tortured affair with Ava Gardner. Bill loved to play dumped lovesick Sinatra. Hanging out with the guys in a hotel room before an out-of-town show, he would jump out of the shower, race into the room dripping wet with a towel wrapped around his waist and cry, 'Did Ava call? Was that Ava?'

As the Annex audience crowded the bar for a last round, the guys had a few drinks too and picked up some smiling girls. 'We'd often as not segue over to a place called Birraporetti's,' Huggins said. 'It was owned by a guy who just loved the comics. A nice place but it was a real yuppie place. We would come in there: loud, obnoxious, if we weren't drunk, we very quickly got drunk. We would insult all his regular customers, who spent more money than we ever had. By all rights, we should have been barred but he thought we were great. He was always buying us drinks.' The owner even gave Jimmy and Bill a special Birraporetti's credit card. They ran up quite a tab, by some accounts as much as $3,500, and later ended up doing a show at the restaurant to pay it off.

From there, they might head for Farneti's large home, and, as his wife and daughter slept upstairs, Bill perched on the living room couch for hours and channeled Elvis, back from the dead and taking questions about the afterlife. At times he morphed into his parents, sitting in their Little Rock den entertaining Bill's friends in their son's absence.

Bill had a great bit about how when his parents came to visit him at Houston House, he was going to pull the same rise-and-shine routine on them that they did on him. Around three in the morning it would be, 'Hey, we got lines of coke! Mary! Jim! What you doing sleeping? Get up! Come on, let's go! We're going to eat sushi at four!'

'Until the day he died that's what the audience wanted more than anything,' Farneti said. 'Don't tell us how to think, don't explain the government, *do your parents.*'

Girls were barely tolerated at late-night gatherings (the phrase was 'fun sponge'), but Bill, now officially single, was seeing a few girls, intense liaisons that never lasted. There was, briefly, Lisa the law student who lived at Houston House. She left him a farewell note that said, 'You may be a star someday but you'll always be an asshole.' Then there was a steady stream of sexy questionable types, whom Farneti called the debauchees. 'Wilkes would pick 'em up on the airplane or something. They'd be from River Oaks, a wealthy part of town, and after they left, a couple days later you could still smell their perfume on that goddamn doorknob.' Bill had a weakness for the especially unstable types. One of his paramours famously tried to stab him in the throat with a fork. 'I love you!' she shrieked. 'If you really loved me, you would have used a spoon,' Bill replied.

When the guys got the bad news that on 1 July 1985 Ecstasy would be declared illegal, Eppy went out and bought a hundred pills for seven hundred bucks three days before the deadline. 'He bought wholesale,' Barber said. 'That first night there is a big party. All these guys are sitting around Bill's place. Saturday night, coming up to Sunday morning, they're tripping. Eppy drops a bunch of Ecstasy and acid together, locks himself in the bathroom, starts hallucinating about this girl he's dating whose dad is a Persian mob guy or something, and this guy is going to flip out ... He's going to kill the girl and they're going to come looking for Eppy. And they're going to come to Bill's and find Eppy and arrest all his friends for having drugs. He's got this in his mind, this is actually happening. So to save his friends he flushes about eighty hits of Ecstasy down the toilet. And then walks out and tells everyone what he just did. "Hey guys, guess what I just did? I did it for you!"'

The counterpoint to the debauchery was mushroom trips, which Bill considered a serious experiment with consciousness. 'Do you think psilocybin mushrooms growing on top of cowshit was an accident?' he said. 'Where do you think the phrase "That's good shit" comes from?' He'd long ago stopped taking them before performances; now he'd go with Kevin and David to the sprawling

Booth family ranch in Fredericksburg, Texas, for major ritual tripping. The idea was to assimilate the LSD experience back into daily
life. The guys always fasted for a day or so, practiced yoga and
meditated the day before. 'We were having lots of breakthroughs in
those days,' Johndrow said. 'It was a constant thing. That was our
whole thing. Taking everything as far as possible.'

From practically the first time, every trip Bill was preoccupied
with his left side. There was something there. He clutched himself
just beneath his ribcage, his face a grimace. He described it as more
a weird presence than a pain. 'This time I'm going to get it out!' he
would declare. 'I'm going to get this demon out of my side.' The
guys joked about staging an exorcism: wrapping Bill in foil like a
baked potato and putting him in the field until he sweated it out,
this upside-down cross.

Bill would go along with the fun and then, without warning, he
would become genuinely agitated. 'It was always something that was
really *bugging* him,' Johndrow said. 'And we couldn't stop laughing.
Because the more unhappy he gets the funnier he is. And he's going,
"What's so funny? It's not funny." Something was bothering him
and it would always connect to "I've got to get it out – there's
something there. What is it? What is it?"'

ELEVEN

Beep. *Hey, man, what's the deal? Such a weird night.* Very strange night. *And you aren't around. Very, very strange night. Ohhhh. Man. It's 4.35 here, and the sun's going to be coming up any minute.*

Bill asked Wilkes and Farneti to come to New York with him for his second appearance on *Letterman* in late August 1985. Farneti figured he was invited in part because he was the only one with any money. ('Considering the first thing Mark asked me when I got to the apartment was, "Hey, can I borrow money?"')

Late Thursday afternoon, 22 August 1985, Bill stood in a dressing room at *Late Night* with Robert Morton and an executive from NBC's Standards and Practices department. The S&P guy was there to approve Bill's set. 'The guy literally had gray hair, gray mustache, gray clothes,' Farneti said. 'And the guy is standing there with his back against the wall and says in a gray monotone, "Go through the routine, I'll tell you what you can't say. I don't laugh." So Bill goes through the first minute of it, and the guy hasn't laughed at all. He's just listening. And Bill just trails off like any primate would. The guy says, "I *don't* laugh."'

Bill tried again to get his pencil-in-the-eye joke past NBC and, for the second time, they rejected it. What aired was Bill, more confident this time, motoring through six minutes of almost entirely innocuous fare – 'I like my job. It's a good job. I like the hour' – and signing off with a line Farneti gave him: 'Have a spiffy eternity.' Bill, Farneti and Wilkes went on to the Hard Rock Café for a night of feckless drinking, the three of them in a booth, Wilkes telling Bill over and over again that he had 'X factor' and Bill, inexplicably, yelling at Farneti, *Don't ever patronize me, John!*

Bill was bemused by his two *Letterman* experiences but he felt as if both had been worth it in terms of exposure. Unfortunately, though, Bill was not really coming across on television. What the audience saw was a smooth, intelligent act by anyone's standards, but with only about six minutes Bill lacked time to build momentum or really work an idea and it robbed him of the fiery crescendo so critical to his act. The demand from network television for a quick witty spray of set-up punchline fare seemed designed, however insidiously, to abbreviate anything approaching actual social commentary. Just as Bill started to build, one sensed him halting as he shifted down, changed gears, moved to the next bit.

The following week, Bill landed in a place where he could let loose – Austin, where he was performing at the Workshop. Whenever Bill came to town now, it was a major social event and all the musicians came out on Sunday evening (their night off) to catch Hicks and party well into Monday. Bill's friend David Cotton started promoting after-parties at Steamboat Springs, a bar on Sixth Street, for Bill's sold-out Workshop shows. 'We would print these little cards,' Cotton said. 'Friends, mainly musicians and comedians and nightclub owners, would come down late. The first after-party we threw, we passed out buttons that just said "Hicks" on them.'

If Kinison happened to roll into town, as he did from time to time, all bets were off. One time when Bill was headlining a seven-night sell-out run at the Workshop, he called Kinison onstage with him and Sam started screaming about getting divorced. 'I WAS MARRIED FOR TWO FUCKING YEARS! HELL WOULD BE LIKE CLUB MED!' It got more outrageous by the second and the crowd, full of University of Texas fraternity boys, started getting rowdy, yelling and disrupting the show. Security began to hustle out the troublemakers and Sam told the audience to go fuck themselves. The club manager, Arthur Jahazik, quickly called a cab and when it pulled up in front of the club, he grabbed Cotton. 'Get these guys out of here now,' he said.

'Jahazik grabs Hicks and shoves him in the cab, and then takes Kinison and throws him next to Hicks,' Cotton said. 'Doster and I get in and tell the guy to Go! The pissed-off fraternity kids are pouring out of the club and literally running down the street following the taxi.' As they pulled away Bill looked over at Kinison next to him. He had passed out.

Sam came to by the time they got downtown and they drank kamikazes at Steamboat Springs until they got kicked out. 'Man, I'm finished,' Doster announced as they stumbled out the front door. Bill and Sam, just starting to warm up, followed Cotton back to his apartment where they plopped down on his couch. 'I threw down a gram of coke and we sat there and these boys talked religion. The conversation was way over my head. Both of them had read about every religion and about how this scripture really meant this or it could mean this or this or this. Five different things. And not just Christianity, but Buddhism and all these offshoots of stuff. If it hadn't been my own house I would have left.'

They did several more grams of coke, half Bill's and half Cotton's, snorting their seventh as the sun rose. Cotton had been mixing drinks for them for hours ('which was a full-time job') and finally, at eleven o'clock in the morning, he cut them off. 'Bill, we've got to be back at the club in eight hours,' Cotton said. But now Bill and Sam were too paranoid to leave. 'So they're sitting there and I've cut them off and Sam Kinison reaches down into his sock and pulls out a quarter ounce of the most beautiful pink and purple flake cocaine I've ever seen to this day. The sorry scumbag had not shared one bump all night long. I couldn't get them out of my apartment.' Finally, around noon, a good friend of David's, a law student who was a Hicks fan, agreed to pick up Bill and Sam and drive them to their hotel. 'Hicks and Kinison had a liquor store bring stuff over to the Villa Capri,' Cotton said. 'They showed up at the Workshop to do the Saturday night show in the same clothes, both of them. I slept all day, ate, took a long hot shower and sweated it out. And there they were in the same clothes still on a roll. Not only did they each do two shows, nobody knew nothing. They didn't drop a beat. And then they partied all night again.'

Two months later, on Halloween, Bill was out having fun with Tracy Wright, Wright's girlfriend Lori and comedians Cindy Olivarez and Brett Butler at a Houston bar called Blythe Spirits. Bill had a few drinks and started getting nasty with Olivarez for no good reason. He was insulting her, needling her over nothing, which was especially stupid since the bartender serving them happened to be her boyfriend. The bartender wore a kilt, a detail that Bill did not fail to note. Before long, again for no apparent reason, Bill was pissed off at everyone and stood up. 'I'm leaving,' he snapped, throwing a handful of coins at the bartender. He turned and headed for the door. The bartender turned red, came out from behind the bar, caught up with Bill and grabbed him from behind. 'You fucking asshole,' the guy snarled as he shook Bill. The two scuffled, a few chairs got moved around and the bartender threw Bill to the ground. Bill's foot and ankle wedged under the jukebox near the door and when he hit the floor he twisted and something in his shin snapped.

Wright was coming down the stairs from the second floor of the bar when he heard the yelling. 'The guy in the kilt is on top of him, he's got his fist cocked back to hit him – and you know quite frankly the way Bill behaved sometimes it was amazing somebody hadn't clocked him before,' Wright said. 'Brett's kicking the bartender in the ribs and everybody's hollering. The first thing I said when I came down the stairs was, "*Bill*, what did you do?"'

By the time he was released from the Emergency Room of a private hospital in the Heights, Bill was openly admitting he had had it coming. If two serious fractures and a metal plate in his lower leg had him thinking, there were no immediate signs. When Bill visited Austin a week later, he was using his crutches as a prop to make crucifixes. 'Is Bill Hicks the Funniest Man in Town?' *Houston City Magazine* asked on its December 1985 front cover.

The second week of February 1986, Bill flew to New York for his third *Letterman* spot. It looked like he was becoming a regular. He had worked up a great set, much of it having to do with televangelists. Despite NBC's dislike of anything religious, he had gotten away with a light bit on his second appearance in August which went, 'I like Southern evangelists. Real powerful dudes. You see stuff in the *TV Guide* on Sunday like "Brother Dave heals the deaf. Show Closed Captioned".

'How powerful *is* Brother Dave?'

In Bill's club act, the joke was about Oral Roberts, but NBC most likely made him drop in a made-up name. The Brother Dave reference was a nod to the Southern satirist Brother Dave Gardner, whose records Bill devoured.

Bill and his friends, Doster, Johndrow, T. Sean Shannon and Dwight, had been faithfully watching Jim Bakker and Jimmy Swaggart for years. They watched *The PTL [Praise the Lord] Club* like some people watch *The Simpsons*. If Bill was on the road he'd get on the phone with one of the guys when it came on. The best was when his wife Tammy Faye, looking like a $3 Reno hooker, sang to the Lord. The guys screamed with laughter and made bets on how many minutes it was going to take Bakker to meander from Jesus to dollars.

And Bill was in near-genuine awe of the 'Swagmonster'.

'As many times as I've watched Swaggart, obviously he's a formidable adversary,' he told Dwight. 'That's what makes me watch him. I'm going, "Look at that guy perform!" It's phenomenal! It's like, "For those of you who never got to see Elvis, you're gettin' it right now."'

'Ahm all shook up!' were the first words out of Bill's mouth on the night of 13 February as he hit his mark on the *Late Night* stage. Bill did a couple of standards before starting in, after two previous rejections, with the pencil-in-the-eye routine. He did the whole thing, all the way out to the classmate breaking his back and ending up in a wheelchair pushed by a kid with one eye. Next he performed a couple of light jokes, using one about watching cable television as a segue to assailing a dirty televangelist. 'Found out one of these TV evangelists has been audited by the IRS,' Bill said without using any names. 'Very interesting fact: the $25,000 donation meant for a hunger fund went to buy him a brand new Corvette.' Bill laughed his bitter machete laugh. 'He said it would help him spread the word quicker. But—'

How the joke ended or who that televangelist might be remained a mystery to TV viewers watching Bill hours later that evening. In post-production, *Late Night* cut into the joke, interrupting Bill mid-sentence with canned applause. Meanwhile, the camera awkwardly cut to the studio audience (too brightly lit and from what appeared to be a different part of the show) smiling blankly. The edit was so crude that not only was the punchline buried but Bill was not even shown saying thank you or goodnight to the crowd. The next bizarre shot was of Bill walking over to Letterman's couch for some stiff patter.

The same kind of edit was used to excise the pencil-in-the-eye routine. The pencil thing itself appeared to be approved; it was when Bill got to the part about the kid being in a wheelchair – the essential tag, the meat of the bit – that NBC bristled. In fact, the program's editors cut off the bit as Bill uttered 'break his back' so that the word *wheelchair* wasn't even mentioned. The joke no longer made sense. It was all set-up, no punchline. Bill's friends in Texas – Doster, Huggins, Wright and Johndrow – watched in shock as the end-of-show credits rolled and Robert Morton made a beeline for Hicks. Bill rose from his chair next to Letterman's desk, and said, 'Man, I'm sorry about that.' You could actually see him mouth those exact words while Morton (his back to the camera) gestured agitatedly. Bill appeared to be protesting as he threw his hands up in the air.

What viewers didn't see was that Morton had already darted over to Bill at the last commercial break. 'What the hell are you trying to do?' he asked. The producer was livid. Bill had been expressly forbidden to do the televangelist bit. As Morton chewed him out, Bill protested his innocence. (It remains unclear as to whether Bill openly defied *Late Night* or genuinely misunderstood the guidelines given him before broadcast.) He swore to Morton he wasn't trying to ruin his own career on national television but he just couldn't see what the problem was. It was just a joke.

Everybody knew these guys were con artists and crooks, didn't they? Club audiences ate up that material. There was one that went, 'Never trust a man that starts a sentence with "What God *meant* to say was ..."' He also had a Falwell face, bunched up and ignorant. 'Is that the perfect face for a crosshairs?' he would ask.

Morton told him the joke wasn't approved, period. For a comedian to do unapproved material for telecast was akin to mooning the producers. Bill said he hadn't had time to change his set before he went on but Morton wasn't buying. Bill knew as he walked away from 30 Rockefeller Center that he wasn't going to be invited back anytime soon.

TWELVE

Beep. *Hey, man, it's Willy. It's Willy. I don't know where you're at. Why don't you help me? Why have you abandoned me? It's Willy. Time of trouble. Time of need.*

In 1986 Pat Robertson was gearing up for a presidential run and Oral Roberts, who had audiences of over two million and daily donations of almost $500,000, announced that if he didn't raise $8 million for missionary medical scholarships by 31 March 1987 God would strike him dead. But Bill wasn't allowed to joke about televangelists on the air.

His Houston friends were feeling similarly frustrated and underused. The road demanded light fare and now business was falling off considerably at the Annex, exacerbated by the opening of a second Houston club, the Laff Stop, which differentiated itself by bringing headliners in from out of town while overlooking Houston's own, even as middle acts.

Epstein had an idea. Encouraged by the success of the Outlaw show for Channel 2, he thought if he and the guys packaged themselves as a group and produced their own live shows they could perform at a higher price, with a higher profile and greater creative control. Each show would be themed topically: politics, drugs, sin, religion. Bill, Farneti, Shock, Huggins and Barber were up for it. They planned eventually to take their show out of comedy clubs and into theater venues, in and out of town.

'We're giving Houston one more shot before we hit the road,' Epstein told *Houston City Magazine* reporter Pat Dougherty, explaining that the Outlaws could make upwards of $1,500 a gig on the road but only about $300 in Houston.

As Huggins put it, 'It was real catchy marketing. There was a bunch of us, we wanted to do some shows together. Just finance it ourselves – it was a way to get more money than we normally got when we played a club. So we wanted to produce our own show and to call it Outlaws was something that caught people's attention.'

'What makes us Outlaws?' Farneti asked onstage. 'Whenever we go driving, we all ride shotgun.'

In February they booked their first road show, 'Outlaw Comics Get Religion', in Baton Rouge, home of Jimmy Swaggart Ministries. But just a few days before the gig, the Baton Rouge club canceled on them for fear of offending patrons and, possibly, the Outlaws suggested in the papers, because of direct pressure from Swaggart's church. If the guys were genuinely pissed off at the cancellation, they made the most of the incident to every reporter they talked to. 'What the guy in Baton Rouge didn't understand is that we went to Swaggart's hometown to promote the idea of freedom of speech,' Bill told the *Daily Texan*, the student paper at the University of Texas. 'When he shut us down, he was acting against precisely what we were fighting for.'

They rescheduled 'Get Religion' at the Workshop on 2 March and a local radio station, KPFT-FM, taped it for broadcast. The show focused almost exclusively on televangelism, though curiously Swaggart escaped skewering while his Oklahoma counterpoint, Oral Roberts, was mercilessly mocked by Ron Shock, who did a hilarious rant about Roberts' claim to have seen a 900-foot floating Jesus.

Bill worked up the perfect character for the show. 'We have a special guest this evening for you, ladies and gentlemen,' Farneti declared. The lights went out. 'Also Sprach Zarathustra' thundered through the speakers.

'The essence of religion,' he yelled, 'is the afterlife and not only is there life after death, there is life after spin-out! He was taken away ten years ago and ten years from the day he arrives, he arrives, he is with us tonight. We don't know who put the *bop* in the bop-shoe-bop, we don't know who put the *ram* in the ram-a-lam-a-ding-dong, or the *Jew* in 'Hey Jude'. But we do know who put the *car* into reincarnation. He is with us tonight, coming back for his Cadillacs & Condoms tour 1987, help me welcome on this stage . . .'

'THE . . . KING! The King! The King! The King!'

'Also Sprach' was quickly drowned out by the swell of 'C. C. Rider', the lights came up and there he was: Bill as Elvis in a plastic garbage-bag cape, paper sideburns and reams of toilet-paper 'scarves' wrapped around his neck. The audience went nuts at their resurrected ragtag King and Bill began tossing his scarves to the audience and landing karate poses. As he turned away for a second, the audience caught a glimpse of the big Elvis photo – as though there could be any confusion – pasted on to the back of his cape.

Bill had spent the afternoon getting his costume together on the living-room floor of his apartment. He and Farneti cut the sideburns out of grocery bags and, as they bent over filling them in with black markers, Bill bellowed, 'Lisa Marie said to stay in the lines!'

Bill had been talking like Elvis for the last three days. At parties he was known to sit on the couch and channel people who knew Elvis. 'Elvis gave me this ring,' he would say, holding out his hand with a large stainless-steel potato-chip bowl balanced on his ring finger.

Another night Bill might wear an Elvis towel for his cape or for an occasion like the Bar Tab show at Birraporetti's he might put on his fancy store-bought Elvis costume, a clingy white jumpsuit with a sparkling cummerbund. And like any really good Elvis, Bill fixated on a particular crumb of the Presley myth and amplified it gloriously. Unlike Andy Kaufman's Elvis, who actually belted out a few songs, Bill's Elvis was a failing Elvis, the gargantuan grunting underbelly of the American dream, reduced to passing out sweaty scarves and brand new Cadillacs. It was the inexorable thirst for acolytes and fans that fascinated Bill – an interesting fixation for a performer who had no compunction about offending his own audiences.

'I don't know, Elvis just cracks me up,' Bill told a reporter. 'He's a hilarious American story. He had everything he could possibly want and he was still completely miserable. It's just mind boggling. One thing I don't like is the idea of the media and corporations pushing "The American Way". The American way is no way at all. Are people happier? You judge a culture by how happy the people are, not by how much money they have.'

As much as Bill was amused by the kitsch of Elvis, there was no question he felt genuinely connected to him. One night Bill and John drove to Bill's old neighborhood, Bill hoping it might spark some good childhood material. They ended up driving around a cemetery, John drinking champagne, Bill snorting coke and listening to an Elvis tape. Bill said that he identified most with the last shot of Elvis in an old documentary where he was fat, high and pathetic, crying onstage and talking to 'Cilla'.

Bill began giving away his paper sideburns and talking to the Workshop crowd, encouraging them to ask him questions about the great hereafter. He said he'd been in purgatory. 'You know why they call it purgatory? No cheeseburgers. And Janis Joplin was there.

'*HUUUH!*' he barked, lunging.

He tossed McDonald's cheeseburgers from a big brown bag to the crowd ('Take that home with ya, darlin'!') and a waitress finally passed up the water glass of whiskey he'd been asking for.

Jack Daniels, 'Elvis' explained to the audience, had helped him through his break-up with Priscilla.

'Ah said, "She left me, Jack. Priscilla left me." And he says, "She's a bitch, Elvis."'

Bill took a swig from his glass.

'I said, "No, Jack, I love her."'

'She's a whore, E.'

'You might be right, Jack.'

Bill chugged as he sank into an Elvis crouch and, as he started to do the bark, he froze for a second from the insult of whiskey. The audience came to his rescue: *HUH!*

'I drink for a reason, folks,' Bill explained a few minutes later when he reappeared as himself in his Sane Man T-shirt holding a fresh drink. 'John Lennon was murdered, Oral Roberts wasn't and Pat Robertson is running for President. I'm fuckin drinkin' through this one ya'll!'

Robertson, Bill explained incredulously, had said that God told him to run. Pretty scary, Bill said, until he realized God hadn't told him to vote for the guy.

'Go back to Virginia, marry your daughter, stay out of my life, you Nazi hillbilly FUCK! That's just my opinion, for what it's worth.'

On 19 March 1987 Jim Bakker resigned as co-chairman of the PTL ministry when he was caught in a Florida hotel room with PTL secretary Jessica Hahn. The Outlaws couldn't help but marvel at their own prescience and while Jim and Tammy Faye made the cover of almost every magazine from *Newsweek* to *People*, the Outlaws planned their biggest, most elaborate show yet. They booked the State Theater in Austin for a Saturday night in April and Barber put up the money. Meanwhile, Wilkes talked the Driskill, Austin's most elegant old hotel, into giving all the Outlaws free rooms. Johndrow designed sepia Outlaw posters with the faces of Bill, Farneti, Shock, Epstein, Huggins and Barber's faces clumsily pasted on to bodies riding in on horseback under the giant title 'Outlaw Comics Get Religion'. They walked around downtown Austin the week before the show sticking them on community bulletin boards, sides of buildings and telephone poles. 'We had so much fun just seeing Bill with a big armload of posters and a huge grin on his face, tacking them up everywhere and giving them to people,' Johndrow said. 'It felt like a religious revival meeting was going to happen.'

With the 800-seat house almost full that Saturday night, they opened the show by projecting on to a wall in pitch darkness a series of giant garish images of Swaggart, the Bakker and Oral Roberts that David had shot off television. The Talking Heads' 'Burning Down The House' boomed along to the slides and screams of appreciation rose through the theater.

Austin American-Statesman reporter Kevin Phinney wrote that, although the show was uneven, 'it also bristles with comedic brilliance'.

Last and best was comic Bill Hicks. After making a not-too flattering appearance as The King of Rock and Roll, who had returned to let everyone know death really wasn't so bad, Hicks launched into a blistering indictment of what he sees as the campaign against individuality masquerading as Christianity. 'I was moved by Oral

Roberts, though,' Hicks confessed. 'I was. And when he said 31 March was his deadline, I sent him a check. Dated it the first of April.'

Yes, folks, stand-up comedy has a future. Unfortunately, it's name is William Melvin Hicks, a moniker Hicks constantly laments.

A week later the Outlaws lost their shirts on a 'Get Religion' show at Snikkers comedy club in Chicago but in July they did their most successful one ever: four weekend shows called 'Outlaw Comics Live for Your Sins' at Rockefeller's, the club where Bill had opened for Ray Charles. Huggins hosted, Pineapple made a special, hilarious appearance in his smoking jacket and Bill closed the show as Elvis. He promised everyone in the house a brand new Cadillac and then pronounced them all doomed to hell: 'But ya'll can keep the Cadillacs.'

The *Houston Chronicle* gushed that the 'Outlaw comics are here and now. They grew out of everything Houston ever was or is, and they point to its future.'

The Outlaw tag started to catch on way beyond Houston, which to some extent helped sell Bill's more provocative material when he went out alone on the road. When Bill played a Norfolk, Virginia, comedy club the local paper called Bill 'one of a growing handful of Outlaw comics who manages to evoke bust-a-gut laughter and make trenchant political commentary' and his performance 'an astonishing night of entertainment'. In early August when he, Huggins and Pineapple played Charlie Goodnight's, a favorite club with three bars in Raleigh, North Carolina, frequented by NC State students, the *News and Observer* called Bill 'an Outlaw comic who packs a .38-caliber wit'.

During his philosophical trip, Hicks launches insightful and often scathing arrows at the world, with crack shots often aimed at sacred cows. No subject is too controversial, no religious or political figure too lofty, for his off-the-wall musings.

'The material is never offensive,' he says. 'It can be perceived by narrow-minded people as such. A lot of people are preaching fear these days and I don't believe in that at all. So I target these people and they soon stand up and walk out, as they watch their extremely fragile world view crumble to the laughter of people around them . . . They call me Kid Compassion.'

Even Bill's offstage hi-jinks, always the bane of his road life, were becoming palatable under the Outlaw umbrella, but Bill himself was growing tired of his own behavior and, if anything, he seemed embarrassed by his reputation.

Houston newspapers have reported that offstage he also lives on the edge, particularly in an incident involving broken bones and a barroom brawl. Wild Bill Hicks? Billy The Kidder?

'Yes, I was thrown into a jukebox,' he says. 'Since I barely remember it, I don't think people should harp on it. There was a time when I was a radical youngster, and that was fine then, but now I save it for the stage.'

Bill's voice was a weary monotone when he called Dwight a couple of days later to wish him a happy twenty-fifth birthday. He said he'd been on the road constantly, that's why he hadn't been in touch, that and his phone getting cut off again. Now he was hanging out at home on the couch waiting to watch his old friend Fred Greenlee on *The Tonight Show* and Sam Kinison in his first HBO special.

Bill and Dwight had kind of distanced themselves from each other the last couple of years. Though Dwight was also touring as a professional comedian, he was married now and living in Oregon. He still wasn't into drinking or drugs. In fact, Dwight was one of Bill's only sober friends and tonight Bill seemed anxious to vent.

'I've been trying to clean my life up a tad here and there,' Bill said. 'You know, I don't know what it is. I don't know how to do it either. You know? I mean, I'll just be honest with myself. I don't know what I've ever done really to get where I'm at and I don't know what I've ever done to prevent myself getting where I want to be. Ahm sure the alcohol helps!' he drawled. 'Go git a whiskey!'

'Uh oh,' Dwight murmured.

'I'm running out of time,' Bill sighed. 'Time is runnin'. *So*. There's no time to feel sorry anymore.'

THIRTEEN

Beep. *Hey, dude, it's Willy. I'm about to go to sleep. I got some great stories to tell you. Some neat lessons learned today. And it all boils down to one thing. How do you perceive?*

Bill was about to be yanked out of his rut. He, Kevin, David, Epstein and Barber – were making plans for an important trip to mark the Harmonic Convergence. All over the world people were preparing for the 1987 Convergence, a major astrological event, a New Age Earth Day of sorts, when they would gather at sacred spots and embrace metaconsciousness. The guys had been gearing up for the big day with Harmonic Convergence seminars, yoga and meditation sessions. 'It was just one of those things where, again, Bill would go into an idea completely and then we would laugh about it,' Johndrow said. 'Everything was tongue-in-cheek which allowed us to do kind of anything that we wanted. The irony was always nearby.'

On Sunday afternoon, 16 August, they drove out to their own sacred spot, the Booth family ranch, and after fasting, took five grams – what psilocybin pioneer Terrence McKenna, author of *Food of the Gods*, called 'heroic doses' – of psychotropic mushrooms.

As always, they tried to time their trip so that they'd peak as the sun was going down. Bill, Kevin and David sat silently meditating toward the sunset by the pond and waited for the mushrooms to kick in.

Once it was dark, David got up and wandered off down the dirt road to take photographs. Bill and Kevin remained at the pond tripping in total silence and they weren't sure how much time had passed when they became fully aware of their physical surroundings again. But as they began to talk, they realized they shared the same feeling of having come out of some kind of craft. Both recalled the same experience: together, they'd entered an alien ship. 'It was almost like being inside of a giant conch shell or something,' Kevin Booth said. 'It was a big spirally thing. We were together, talking to each other throughout the whole thing.'

It wasn't easy to describe what they had witnessed (neither reported physical contact) but Bill described it to David as having seen insect beings inside balls of light. But even that didn't really explain it.

'It was on a higher level than seeing alien life,' Booth said. 'It was as if our brains were plugged in like modems. We were just tapped in to some upper level of consciousness – a free-flowing communication highway. We met a zillion beings all interconnected.' Insect consciousness, that connection with the 'Transgalactic Other', as one of Bill's favorite writers, Tom Robbins, called it, was, of course, a common outcome of a powerful psilocybin experience.

'There was always an expectation of UFOs,' Johndrow said. 'It was also part of a symbology that we had for that transcendence where we were going to break through to some level where we could telepathically send the cake ingredients.'

Bill was so positive of what he had experienced that he found it hugely frustrating when people assumed his encounter was a joke. 'Every time I tell the story, the first thing people ask is, were you tripping?' Bill said. 'And I go, yeah. And they go, oh yeah, right. But it was really profound and I want to experience it again. Totally straight. So I can tell people I was straight.'

For someone who had long bouts of loneliness, who talked constantly of feelings of alienation, whose concerns were largely eschatological, it was a wonderfully uplifting experience. If the story stretched the imagination, so what? That was the point. To Bill, the encounter was absolute confirmation that we are not alone.

As Bill and Kevin slowly sat up in the grass they saw Epstein come walking up the road.

'You guys getting off on these things?' he yelled. ''Cause I don't feel anything yet!'

*

'You've got to read this,' Bill said. He handed his new girlfriend, Pamela Johnson, a copy of *Stranger in a Strange Land*, Robert Heinlein's science fiction cult classic about a man raised by Martians who arrives on earth never having seen a woman and without any knowledge of our planet's cultures and religions. Bill was always passing on important books, 'required reading', to Pamela, a fine-boned brunette with fair skin, a pile of curly hair and wide-set brown eyes. Pamela was a hair stylist whom he had met when Pineapple sent a bunch of the guys to her at a downtown salon. At first Pamela didn't think much of Bill, who never had much to say during his appointment (he was usually just hung over), but one night at Houston House, while she was giving haircuts at Andy and Jimmy's place, she wandered upstairs to check on him and found him sitting there smoking a cigarette.

'I said "Are you alone?" and he said, "Of course. I'm always alone."' Pamela fell in love with him instantly. She told Bill she had barely cracked a smile since her father died a year earlier and Bill made her laugh.

Bill was wildly attracted to Pamela. It didn't bother him that she was seven years older than him, divorced with two sons, aged twelve and thirteen. She was his feminine ideal, a Southern belle of the Blanche DuBois variety, intense and dramatic, though in a soft way. In private, Bill called her Bird and she called him Daddy. He liked to be alone with Pamela, kept his relationship with her separate from his life with the guys. His friends didn't care for her much anyway. 'In front of people, I never spoke other than "hello", she said. 'I listened for him. That's what I did. Because a lot of people stroked Bill.'

After Pamela got off work and saw to her children, she met up with Bill wherever he happened to be working. If he had the night off, they holed up in his bedroom, made love and ordered Chinese food. He could always think of something good to do – 'sweet precious things' – like sitting in bed and painting with oil paint while they listened to music. If audiences might not have believed it of their 'Dark Prince', Bill's quixotic side didn't surprise anyone who knew him well; it was the sunny side of his Errol Flynn.

'I think the best one-word description of Bill Hicks is *romantic*,' said Stephen Doster. 'Not reactionary. Not radical. He was a romantic of unparalleled proportions.'

Sandy DiPerna knew Bill had a market somewhere. 'We'll just have to keep trying until we find it,' she told him. She knew one person who might be able to help Bill, get him out of the clubs and on television again: Rick Messina. Messina booked clubs in the New York area and handled Rodney Dangerfield's club, so he had Dangerfield's ear when it came to finding new talent for his HBO specials.

Sandy knew Rick liked Bill a lot. In fact, Messina thought Bill was brilliant, but Bill had also been fired on a Messina gig in New Jersey. Sandy finally called Rick anyway and he mentioned that Dangerfield was preparing a new HBO special called *Nothin' Goes Right*. So far they had Andrew Dice Clay, Robert Schimmel and Dom Irrera. 'Rick! Bill would be perfect for it!' Sandy cried. 'Please please let him come and showcase. I know Rodney would really like him.'

It would be an incredible opportunity for Bill. Kinison had shot to fame in six minutes the previous year on Dangerfield's special when he did the Scream. And it would mean national exposure for the first time since being kicked off *Late Night* a year and a half before.

Rick agreed to give Bill a shot, but there were two conditions: Bill had to come up to New York a couple of days early to work out his set, and he had to promise to stay sober until after the showcase.

Sandy gave her word.

'Sandy, it was terrible,' Bill said into her answering machine minutes after he got offstage at Dangerfield's in New York. 'I had a really bad set. And I'm really sorry. I know you wanted this for me.' He hung up and, utterly despondent, went straight to La Guardia to catch the next flight back to Houston.

A couple of hours later, Sandy's phone rang again, and this time she was there to pick up. 'I already know,' she said when she heard Rick's voice. 'He told me he had a bad set.'

'Yeah, he did,' Messina replied. 'But Rodney loved him.'

Bill was in, provided he passed muster at the HBO showcase in Los Angeles. It was strongly suggested to Sandy that she accompany him to the coast. 'It wasn't to handle him, because I really couldn't handle him. It was that if Bill didn't know you, he didn't feel comfortable with you. And he got really bored when he was by himself. So they just felt that if he wasn't by himself too much – he and I could hang out together and I wouldn't bug him.' Bill, who was barely making rent (Houston House had begun to charge him), hardly had the means to fly his manager out, but Sandy wanted this so badly for Bill she was willing to pay her own way.

The night before the showcase, Bill picked Sandy up at Houston Hobby airport. They'd fly out to LA together the next day. He showed her all over town, took her to all the places he and the guys hung out. They stopped in at Birraporetti's (Sandy couldn't believe they really had given him an open tab) and went to comedian Steve Moore's house where everybody was gathered reading excerpts from a true-crime book called *Cold Kill*. The book was about Cindy Ray, an Annex open-mike comic who had had her parents murdered. 'Then we went back to Houston House and Bill and Tracy Wright got really drunk and they went out on the balcony and they were playing guitars,' DiPerna recalled. 'I was so afraid. I thought, this is it. I've got this HBO audition tomorrow and he's going to fall off the balcony.'

Bill made it to LA in one piece at six o'clock the next evening. His showcase at the Comedy Store wasn't until eleven o'clock so he and Sandy had a few hours to kill. Sandy's goal was to keep Bill from drinking so when they arrived at the Store she asked him to show her his name. Everyone who worked at the Store had their name on the building. 'There were hundreds of names and he couldn't even remember which side of the building he had signed,' DiPerna said. 'I kind of think he knew I was distracting him, but he just played along. We hunted and finally found it. After he did his set, he just stood in the hallway and I went up and gave him a big hug and he just looked at me and said, "Now can I have a drink?"

'I said, "*Now* you can have a drink!"

HBO gave Bill the okay. He had to be in New York two weeks later for two nights of taping at Dangerfield's and each comedian was told to bring a funny intro for Rodney to read. Bill asked Farneti to write his. John was flattered but when he arrived at Rockefeller's for a writing session, he found Bill slumped over the bar, his head in his arms. 'It's an endless hell,' he groaned.

'Very depressed. Being funny about it. But very down – on a scale of one to ten, negative three, the standard when you went to lunch with him – just totally down. Rather than get into that stuff, I said, "We're going to write this and here's how: you do Rodney's intro voice, stop, and I'll do the joke. Just ad-lib." So he has a fairly good Rodney voice and he's going, "But hey, this next guy, ladies and gentlemen—" And then I would say something. It was like working dry toothpaste out of an old tube, but I finally came up with one he liked . . . And then he just slumped over again.'

Farneti, who had been through counseling, talked to Bill for hours about depression, but Bill seemed uninterested in seeking out help. 'It was the opposite of, "Boy, it must be so fun to write with Hicks for Dangerfield!" But his misery wasn't ignored. There was just no changing that, no being talked out of it.'

Bill was the only one who arrived in New York with a finished intro in time for a week of rehearsals. He'd agreed not to drink all week and Messina had encouraged him, as he did all the comedians, to time his set precisely to minimize the possibility of being edited. 'It meant repeating the same act every night and planning it out specifically,' Messina said. 'No riffing. He was sober, and he was doing that same spot like a parrot every night for a week before the taping and he was dying.'

The line he and Farneti had settled on was, 'I'd like to say this next guy is ahead of his time but his parents haven't met yet.' Not John's favorite, but Bill liked it. The first night of taping, he tried it out on Dangerfield.

'Not funny enough,' Dangerfield said.

'No, that's funny,' Bill replied. 'Try it.'

If Rodney was startled at a no-name twenty-six-year-old challenging him, he went ahead and tried out Bill's line on the first audience. Surprisingly, it got a good laugh. The next day before the second taping Bill walked by Rodney's dressing room. 'Hey Bill,' Dangerfield called. 'That line, it's real funny. What the fuck do I know?'

Saturday night, after his final taping, Bill drank all night with Messina, who nursed a Heineken while Bill downed double whiskeys and regaled him with funny road stories. They were celebrating Bill's perfect set, which made up for his rather lukewarm first one on Friday. Bill was just relieved it was over and that he'd delivered HBO something they could work with. About four in the morning Bill meandered down 38th Street to the Doral Hotel; once in his room, he picked up the phone and called Oregon.

'Hello?' Dwight whispered groggily.

'How do you sleep?' Bill asked.

Bill's friends were used to these calls. When he was on the road, all alone and drowning in whiskey, he might call you in the middle of the night and scream into the phone something like, 'All women are WHOOOOOORRRES! I can't stand it!' It was just hard to sleep sometimes. Bill told David that once he'd tossed and turned in bed for hours and when he finally found a comfortable position, he realized he was twisted in the shape of a swastika.

One day, out of the blue, Bill's father called Sandy with a suggestion. 'Sandy,' he said, 'it's really nice that you're helping Bill get all those club dates, but I think he needs to be a game show host. When are you going to get him a game show?'

'I've got to get out of Houston,' Bill told Pamela around Christmas. 'This is ridiculous.' The Outlaw shows were fun but he was going nowhere. The UFO experience, the HBO special, hanging out on the comedy scene in New York all week, had woken him up to the possibilities. And recently, Bill had seen a Houston comedian named Richard become nearly destitute because of his severe alcoholism.

Bill and Wilkes began keeping bowls of fruit around the apartment and together they had a new mantra: *live.*

It was the beginning of a shift, a realization that he had to make some decisions. And while Bill was still struggling with drinking and experiencing blackouts more frequently, he had a coherent ambition within him.

'What do you ultimately want to do?' Farneti asked once when they were taking a walk. 'Do you want to make it big like David Brenner?'

'No!' Bill said, scowling. I want to make a contribution to comedy. Like Charlie Chaplin.'

New Year's Day 1988, Bill woke up in a panic. Pamela wasn't on her side of the bed. The night before they'd gone out to dinner with another couple, friends of hers, and then returned to Houston House for a nightcap. Bill had drunk steadily throughout the night and by the time their guests left, he had gone into one of his rages. It wasn't a fight really, just Bill stomping around the apartment ranting incoherently, screaming ugly words until they'd found themselves out on the terrace. He couldn't remember much after that but he had a hazy awful memory of holding Pamela against the railing, threatening to throw her off the balcony.

So she was either on the sidewalk, twenty-two floors below, or she'd gotten away from him.

'Thank God,' he sobbed when she answered her phone. 'That's it,' he promised. He was disgusted with himself. He would never drink again.

'That's great,' Pamela answered. But they were finished. She had no intention of seeing him again.

A little more than a month later, Bill stood onstage at Charlie Goodnight's in Raleigh, dressed in a black leather jacket and sipping Jack Daniels from a shot glass. He was only about fifteen minutes in.

'How many of you think I'm the Antichrist?' he asked.

Listening to the smattering of applause, Bill narrowed his eyes and stared hard at the audience. 'That's not enough,' he said.

'He then went to work to convert the remainder of the Tuesday night audience,' wrote *News and Observer* reporter Michael Hetzer in the next morning's review titled, 'Wild Bill Lives up to Nickname'. 'He screamed into the microphone. His vision of a machine-gun-toting Jesus was positively malevolent. He acted out violent, bloody fantasies toward his former girlfriend, an assortment of politicians – even the Reagans' dog. He unearthed new, unimagined lows in bad taste . . . This is not a warm person. But is he funny? Oh yes.'

At about the same time Hetzer was working up that piece, Bill sat backstage in the tiny green room at Goodnight's about to pull an all-night binge before a morning radio interview. But he had a nagging feeling even as he started on his third whiskey. Every person who came by the green room was either a dealer or a friend offering him drugs. 'I was up all night with the most satanic thoughts,' he said in a 1992 interview with *Texas Monthly*. 'Somehow I did the radio show and was really funny. But my heart was pounding, and I thought I was gonna die.'

The next afternoon Bill dragged himself out of bed and staggered over to opening act James Vernon's hotel room. Vernon was long up, having gone to his AA meeting in the morning. Bill asked if he was going again tomorrow. 'I go every day', Vernon replied.

'Can I come?'

Sandy DiPerna, who was always trying to pair Bill on week-long gigs with comedians who were sober, had been praying this would happen. And not only was Vernon five years into AA, but he and Bill were good friends from Houston. Vernon's first real gig, when he was just a year into comedy, had been opening for Bill at the Workshop in Austin. Bill had taken him under his wing, advising him to quit his day job, and introducing him around when Vernon followed Hicks's advice and moved to Houston a couple of weeks after the Workshop show. Vernon even credited Bill with helping him find his voice. Bill didn't like the stock racial stuff Vernon was doing at first.

'He said, "Why are you doing the dumb nigger shit? We've got a bunch of those,"' Vernon recalled. '"I've heard you talk in the green room, the shit you say back there is what you feel. That's funny. Go up and do *your* stuff with your attitude the way *you* do it and you're going to be okay." And I looked at him for a minute, got up and walked away. I had just gotten in a fight a few nights before when this kid in the audience used the "N" word with me. But after Bill said that, I didn't go onstage for a month. I would go and look, but I wouldn't go up. And then I went up and I started doing political material, observational humor, stuff that was *real* to me. I didn't do "black" humor anymore. I didn't close myself off.'

When James took Bill to his first AA meeting Bill sat quietly, not participating in any way, but listening. He declined a desire chip, the first token of commitment to sobriety, when they came around.

That night at Goodnight's from the side of the darkened room James watched Bill, standing onstage a few minutes into his first set, down a Jack Daniels and ask for another. Bill raised his glass to him, grinning. 'We'll start over tomorrow.'

James nodded. And somehow he wasn't surprised when the sound of Bill knocking woke him up the next morning.

FOURTEEN

Beep. *Errol? Pal. Roy Gene got his diploma. Second one. Tryin'
to make us look bad in front of Papa. In front of Pa and Ma.
We gots to get on that fertilizer job and make some money, show
'em we can make money, too, Errol. Let 'em know Errol and
Pal ain't no Roy Gene. We work for our livin'.*

'I'll sell you this car for $50. Right now. It's yours.'

It was April 1988 and Bill was getting rid of his little white
Chevette. He wasn't going to need it in New York City.

The new owner, a tenant at Houston House, handed over the
cash and asked if he could have the title.

'No,' answered Bill. 'The deal is you take it right now and don't
ask me any other questions. That's why it's $50.' Typical Bill. Any
kind of hassle and it wasn't worth it.

James Vernon had agreed to be his sponsor and Bill had been
going to AA meetings every day since February. It couldn't have
been easy with most of his buddies still going at it (although Huggins,
'hugely affected' by Bill's recovery, had also stopped drinking) but
once Bill made up his mind he had an iron will. He'd lost no time in
reuniting with Pamela, swearing to her that things were going to be
very different. Now that he was sober, he realized that his life was
meant to be spent performing. That meant leaving Houston.

Los Angeles was out. According to Pamela, he told her that the
last time he'd left California he had seen the Grim Reaper in his
rear-view mirror as he drove into the Arizona desert. 'Anyway,' Bill
said, 'when I think of comedy I think of New York.' More than
anything, Bill wanted to get on the *Letterman* show again. Living in
Manhattan might put him back in the loop.

Pamela was coming with him. She had gotten a job offer in

Manhattan and was leaving her teenage boys with their grandmother in Houston. Bill went up at the start of the summer and Pamela followed a few weeks later, arriving by cab in Houston and Avenue B one night around half past ten, stepping over the junkies in her pumps. They stayed with Bill's cousin, Joan Moosy, an actress Bill had become close to as an adult, in her East Village apartment, for a few weeks until they found a one-room studio apartment on Avenue B and 3rd Street that looked out on a brick wall.

That summer was a happy time for Bill. He got stage time around Manhattan right away at Caroline's at the Seaport and the Original Improv and he was writing constantly. He was shocked by the homeless situation in New York and had tons of material about it. 'I'm no bleeding heart, okay? *But.* When you're walking down the streets of New York City and you're stepping over a guy on the sidewalk who – I don't know – might be *dead*, does it ever occur to you to think, "Wow, maybe our system doesn't work."?' He found Manhattan audiences a little cold, though New York comedians he knew from the road such as Dave Attell, Jon Stewart and Ray Romano often stuck around after their own sets to watch him. But Bill didn't hang out much. He was absorbed in AA with his usual doggedness and getting sober had immediately lifted his spirits. He called colleagues and old friends (including Laurie Mango) and even a few club owners to apologize for old trespasses. He and Huggins supported each other, and when Bill's old friend David Cotton got sober, Bill called him every single day to help him through it.

Meanwhile, he and Pamela were enjoying an intense affair in the privacy of their own little place. He said that getting sober had sent his sex drive through the roof and, ever nocturnal, Bill was right at home in a twenty-four-hour city. He and Pamela played chess for hours and, around midnight, they liked to stroll to Umberto's in Little Italy to eat pasta and watch the black stretch limos that lined the curb. Bill never left the house without stuffing his pockets with change to hand out to the homeless. 'I could have been a bum,' he would say. 'All it takes is the right girl, the right bar, and the right friends, man.'

They were both pretty much broke living in Manhattan but

Pamela called her mother and she sent them a television, a bed and a credit card to help them through. The credit card was for Bill to establish some credit so he could travel more easily. He had never even had a checking account. In fact, when Sandy DiPerna started booking Bill she was shocked when she received her commissions by mail, hundreds of dollars of cash tucked into a greeting card.

Just a few weeks after getting settled, Rick Messina called with a nice offer: was Bill interested in appearing in a movie? The idea was to assemble twelve of the raunchiest comics in the business, including Jackie 'The Joke Man' Martling, Steven Pearl, Stephanie Hodge, Tim Allen and twenty-one-year-old Chris Rock, and shoot a live late-night 'blue' show. They were calling it *Comedy's Dirtiest Dozen* and Andrew Dice Clay was going to host. They taped at the Hudson Theater and though the movie (which enjoyed a small midnight-movie theater run with a replacement host, Ben Creed), ended up a fairly underwhelming parade of dick jokes and shit jokes, it was twenty-seven-year-old Bill's first unexpurgated performance on film. And, with a minimum of bad-boy posturing, he easily shifted the show to a new level.

Why, he asked, are all news stories about drugs negative? Why the same LSD story every time? 'Young man on acid thought he could fly. Jumped out of a building. What a tragedy.' Just once, Bill lamented, he'd like to see a positive drug story. Just once.

'Wouldn't that be newsworthy? Just once? "Today a young man on acid realized that all matter is merely energy condensed to a slow vibration and that we are all one consciousness experiencing itself subjectively. There's no such thing as death, life is only a dream and you are the imagination of yourself. Here's Tom with the weather."'

On a trip to Los Angeles in the winter of 1988, Bill was introduced by his old Houston friend Ron Robertson to a talent manager named Jack Mondrus. Bill had Sandy DiPerna, of course, but she was really a booking agent. Mondrus, a tall blustering silver-haired man, managed a few comedians and variety acts; his main client was a ventriloquist act, Willie Tyler and Lester. Robertson suggested that

Mondrus check out Bill at the Laff Stop in Newport Beach. When Bill found out Mondrus would be in the audience that night he treated the manager to Hicks classics such as the bit about Dick Clark – Satan in disguise – giving birth to John Davidson and George Michael being 'a demon set loose on the earth to lower the standards for the perfect and holy children of God'.

After fifteen minutes of watching Bill not bother to tone it down, Jack knew.

'He was stream-of-consciousness,' Mondrus recalled. 'I believed that he'd thought of every word he was saying right there on the spot. It was like that every time I saw him. I never thought he was doing material.'

The next day the two got together at Jack's home office in West Los Angeles. Bill told Jack he wanted to be on *Letterman* again. Mondrus said he should do more television in general. There were tons of new cable comedy shows: *MTV Comedy Hour*, *Evening at the Improv*, *The A-List*. Most importantly, Bill could work the road more consistently and at a much better price. Mondrus felt you should make the money while you could.

Not everyone advised Bill to sign with Jack. 'Now he'll represent two dummies,' Farneti said. A few weeks later, though, Bill and Jack signed a one-year contract with a three-year option. Bill's idea was for Sandy DiPerna to continue booking his road dates, but after about six weeks she bowed out. Jack wanted her to get Bill huge money – around $3,500 a week – when she was having trouble getting him booked at all.

As Mondrus himself tried to get Bill road dates, he realized he hadn't been very aware of Bill's reputation. He was finding he had to answer for the drinking days. He had to give club owners his solemn word that Bill was okay now. There would be no busted toilets, no trashed bars, no freaking out.

But because of Bill's unassailable talent, a few key bookers were happy to give him a clean slate. In San Francisco, Geof Wills, who booked the Punch Line, even lied to his boss so that he could bring Hicks to town. 'Jack Mondrus talked me into hiring Bill,' Wills said. 'At the time, we didn't really hire people without TV credits and though Bill had done *Letterman*, it was a long time ago. So I fibbed to my boss that Bill was going on *Letterman* again and would plug the Punch Line. I did that because I had seen Bill once, about ten years before on his first San Francisco gig, when he was young and stoned. It was crazy, I was laughing so hard I was dying. It was like nothing I had ever seen before.'

Wills's risk paid off. Bill 'set the club on fire' on his return to the Punch Line, and during his late shows that week, local comedians crowded along the back wall and called out requests at the end of his set. The club was so happy with Hicks, Wills got hired away by its silent owner, Bill Graham Productions, to book major touring acts.

Thanks to Jack's dogged working of the phones, 1989 was to be Bill's biggest year on the road yet. It began with a six-week booking in Las Vegas for the opening of Dangerfield's new club, Rodney's Room. Kinison was coming in for a night and so was Dangerfield himself. Bill got top billing on the Tropicana Hotel marquee, a new tux and a suite by the pool for him and Pamela. After the show every night they'd play the slot machines and Caribbean Studs, then head off to swim around 3 a.m.

After the Dangerfield engagement finished in mid February, Bill and Pamela found themselves on a plane almost every Monday. Pamela hadn't taken that haircutting job because Bill wanted her to be free to travel with him. They hit every town in America that had a comedy club: San Francisco, Hartford, Denver, Atlanta among them. Sometimes Bill called Sandy DiPerna just to check in and say hi. 'Wow, Sandy, isn't this something?' he'd say. 'The first thing I used to do when I got to a gig was to look for hookers,' he joked. 'Now I'm looking for massage therapists and AA meetings.'

One week Bill had a gig in Atlantic City where Jay Leno happened to be headlining at another club. Leno invited him and Pamela backstage to hang out before his show. 'He had one of those big deli trays in his dressing room and we hadn't eaten all day and Jay is telling us the story of his first *Letterman* appearance,' Pamela said. 'And he says to us, "Would you like something to eat?" So I'm eating off the tray and listening and laughing and Leno gave us great seats to see his show before Bill had to be back at his own show. So we left there and Bill goes, "I can't *believe* you ate his food." I said, "Well, he offered!" And he goes, "Well, he didn't mean it." I said, "Of course he meant it! Bill, the tray was *this* big!" He said, "No, he didn't, Pamela! Don't ever eat other people's food again when we're invited backstage!"

FIFTEEN

Beep. *Hey, man. It's Willy. Back home after the most, most unpleasant evening. Ah, anyway, I don't know where you are, man. No one's home. Everyone's got a life. Everyone's got a life but me. Actually, I have a great life. I just wish I could appreciate it.*

In West Palm Beach, Florida, there was a club called the Comedy Corner. The Corner had an excellent reputation for top-shelf bookings. Damon Wayans, Chris Rock and Ellen DeGeneres regularly worked there. Jim Carrey and Jerry Seinfeld, whose mother lived in a nearby town, frequently dropped in to do a set.

The one guy missing from the line-up was Bill Hicks. Lots of Corner comics, especially Tom Ryan, a new comedian from Philadelphia who'd left the insurance business, pestered the club manager, Colleen McGarr, to book him. Whenever she asked around about Bill, though, the response from other club owners was almost always the same: 'The guy's a genius, but he's got a major problem with alcohol.'

But then Chris DiPetta, a booking agent in Atlanta, called Colleen singing Bill's praises. He had just had him at the Punch Line in Atlanta and Bill had had great shows and was all cleaned up. No more booze, no more drugs, DiPetta assured her.

Bill arrived in West Palm Beach on a stormy Tuesday morning in May. As Colleen waited at the gate looking for him, she was slightly nervous. 'I didn't know what to expect. I'd heard all the stories. But by the time he got in the car, I just thought, "Oh my God, this guy is so sweet and cool and smart." Just these really bright intelligent eyes and very kind of shy.' It was unusual for Bill to feel comfortable with anyone new, and certainly not a woman, but Colleen, who was also twenty-eight, had a warm earthy quality. She had a quick throaty laugh and she focused her bright blue eyes intently on you when you spoke. Bill could tell she was really listening.

Colleen dropped Bill at the comedian's condo around the corner from the club and said she'd see him at the club that night, but he showed up at her office just a couple of hours later. 'Can I talk to you for a second?' he asked, pulling her into the hall. 'Do you know where there's an AA meeting?' Oddly enough, in her five years of booking comedians, no one had ever asked her that. Colleen grabbed the Yellow Pages, found one nearby and gave him a lift.

The excitement around the club that night was palpable – particularly for Tom Ryan, who was getting to open for Bill. 'Here was this guy I've been hearing about forever,' Ryan recalled. 'He was younger than you might think and almost disarmingly normal. But as soon as he hit the stage you could see he had this polish. This kind of world-weariness like, "This is no big deal. I've got the goods." He opened by saying, "Drunk driving isn't what it used to be."'

'Debbie Gibson had the *number one* album, ya'll,' Bill continued. 'Now if this doesn't make your blood fucking *curdle*. Who buys that shit?'

He had a better idea for what Gibson could do after school: 'Go babysit Tiffany. Spank her little bottom till it's bright red, then lick it all over. There's a video I'll fucking watch of yours.'

'Now, none of us had ever heard any of this before,' Colleen said. 'We were just dying, going insane. The way he moved onstage, the way he used his *hands* was the funniest thing ever. He just blew my mind. He was mobbed immediately when he came offstage. They just went ape over him. It was so powerful and so pure and exactly what I had fantasized comedy could be about.'

'Is it me?' Bill asked. 'I mean, *goddamnit*, I remember – and maybe I'm just romanticizing the past – when music had a conscience and music had *soul* and music had *balls*, man. Does anybody remember that at all? Anybody?'

All the excesses, all the performance extremes that had been unleashed during the drinking days were now bridled with a discipline. He knew all about train-wreck performance. It was as though having gone all the way out to the edge and survived, he was fearless up there. You could stay onstage way past the light, until the audience crawled out. You could lie on your back onstage and chant *cunt* into a mike for five minutes. You could even wrap the mike cord around your neck and pull it up, as though hanging yourself. But now Bill was moving on. Inspired by his recovery, he was honing that ire into something fantastically vital and screamingly funny. He had always been able to access outrage, but now he was able to articulate it in a way that made him not just exciting but exhilarating.

Over the next six nights Bill did eight shows and the Comedy Corner crew watched every single one. 'It was a crash course in Bill,' Colleen said. 'They didn't sell out, but comedy was swinging so it was pretty packed. There would be the occasional person who said, "I thought he was dirty", and we'd be like, "Fuck off."'

Every afternoon, Colleen drove Bill to an AA meeting. The rain refused to let up so she just waited for him in the car with a newspaper. 'I didn't mind at all. It didn't strike me as weird at all. I was actually kind of touched that this guy would bring me into his confidence so quickly.'

'So what goes on at those meetings?' Colleen asked over lunch one day. At some point, Bill explained, alcoholics are bereft of self-esteem because they have left so much damage in their wake. He was mortified to think of the violent episodes fueled by his drinking. So one of the bonuses in going to the meetings was that no matter how bad you thought you were there was always someone worse than you. You could always take some solace from the fact that, 'Okay, at least I didn't go to jail or beat my wife.'

He told Colleen all about his childhood, but it struck her that generally Bill was not a person who looked back much. He seemed much more interested in what was coming. By the time he left, Colleen felt like she had made a real friend – in a business of a thousand acquaintances.

In Chicago, Bill started working at a new club called the Funny Firm, opened by a hilarious, gregarious guy named Len Austrevich.

Len had been a fervent Hicks fan since the Comedy Store days in LA, when Len himself was starting out as a nineteen-year-old comedian. To Len, Hicks was one of the great technicians, like a Leno or Seinfeld, a guy consistently sharp who nailed the set every time. Hicks kept a spare 'A' act in his pocket. But it had been five years since Len had seen Bill onstage and when Bill arrived for his first engagement, Len was stunned by his metamorphosis. Hicks was *saying* something up there.

'For the record,' Bill said as he greeted the audience, 'and let's not mince words because our very lives depend only upon truth, *George Michael is . . . a . . . big . . . girl.*'

Bill's real issue with Michael (other than his music) was that he was now doing Diet Coke commercials. It made him sick. What kind of real rock star would do such a thing? 'Even Madonna fucking hawked real Coke. You little *puss.*'

'What kind of fucking Reagan wet dream is this world, man?' he sighed.

Bill's next booking at the Funny Firm went somewhat differently. The first night, a Tuesday, a rowdy crowd packed the house. Many in the audience, it seemed, had met their two-drink minimum by the time Bill got onstage. A few vocal types kept yelling out to him, helping him out with punchlines, even making requests. One woman in particular, a puffy blonde, to Bill's right, would not shut up. 'My little echo,' Bill called her. He was trying to talk about the Zapruder tape.

'You suck!' the woman yelled.

Wooooo went the crowd.

'You suck,' Bill repeated thoughtfully.

He got off his stool and walked to the side of the stage. 'You fucking cunt!' he screamed, pointing at her. 'Get the fuck out of here right now! Get out! Fuck you! Fuck you, you idiot. You're everything in America that should be flushed down the toilet, you fuckin' turd. Fuck you! Get out! Get out, you fucking drunk bitch! Take her out! Take her fucking *out*! Take her somewhere that's good. Go see fuckin' Madonna, you fucking idiot piece of shit!'

Woooooooo!

'You suck, buddy! You suck! I can yell at the comedian because I'm a drunk cunt! That gives me carte blanche!'

Bill began to skip around the stage. 'I got a cunt and I'm drunk! I can do anything I wa-aant! I don't have a cock! I can yell at performers! I'm a fucking idiot 'cause I got a cunt!'

He knelt. *'I want you to go find a fucking SOUL!!!!'*

Some of the crowd booed. A lot of them cheered.

He sat down on his stool again and rubbed his eyes. 'Sorry you had to see that. I dug a real hole on this one, didn't I?' He started to giggle. 'Gee, Bill, that isn't material you're working out for your next Arsenio spot?'

At this point the audience was pouring out of the club, but the forty or so who stayed pulled their chairs closer. Unbelievably, the heckler was still sitting there with her date.

'I don't care if you stay,' Bill said wearily as he lit a cigarette. 'Just don't yell at me. I don't like to be yelled "You suck" at me. I have feelings, too. So fuck off.'

Bill went along merrily for a little while, ignoring most of the little call-outs and interruptions.

Hard night!

Want to go out?

He tried to do some actual material.

He talked about why his girlfriend left him ('Gee, Bill, what did you do, call her a cunt?' 'No! Not at first!')

Free Bird!

Free Bird!

'Oh please,' Bill groaned. 'God in heaven. I'm gonna leave. I'm gonna go eat a Polish.' He was talking about Jim's Polish, a sausage stand on Maxwell Street on the gritty outskirts of Chicago. 'You guys will have more fun without me. You will.'

The crowd cheered.

'Give it up!' some guy yelled.

'Fuck it, I'm staying 'cause of that, you fucking dick. You will be the first to go, Mr Shirt and Tie Man. Mr Work for the Man. Mr See Traffic Every Day of the Rest of Your Fucking Pathetic Life.'

'I will take off my mask and display my true self to you, you cum-sucking piece of shit. Goddamn it. You want me to take my mask off and display my life to you, you fucking worms? Or do you want me to pretend I'm the comic monkey boy and you are the upstanding citizens?'

He bleated like a goat. 'Yes, Comic Monkey Boy, be our little plaything while we go about our pathetic fucking lives! Fuck you! Fuck "Free Bird"!'

Bill sat on the little wooden stool as though on strike. He put his face in his hands. 'I apologize for this whole show. Generally there's material, I swear to God there is. A point of view and everything. Tonight? Sorry! The airline lost my sense of humor. It didn't work out.'

Free Bird!

Finally, club security started kicking out the drunks.

You suuuck!

One guy in the front row loudly grumbled about having paid for the show. Meanwhile, a bunch of comics from the Improv had rushed over when they got word that Hicks was on fire at the Firm and they were lining the back wall of the club.

'I'll pay you the money,' Bill said. 'Just get the fuck out. The problem with you, dude, is this. The fact that you don't get it or like it is fine. The fact that you want to ruin it for everyone else, that's why you're a cocksucker. That's why. Do you go to, like, Eric Clapton concerts with your own fucking guitar?'

Bill announced that now he really was going home and someone asked for an encore. He chuckled and did his old bit about how great it felt not to have a boss: 'They're like *gnats* on a camping trip.'

'Okay, there's that one,' Bill sighed.

Free Bird!

'Please quit yelling that. It's not funny, it's not clever, it's stupid, it's repetitive. Why the fuck would you continue to yell that?'

Kevin Matthews!

Matthews was Chicago's big morning DJ.

Kevin Matthews!

'Okay. Now what does it mean? I understand where it comes

from. So do you. Now what does it mean? What is the culmination of yelling that?'

Jimmy Shorts!

'Jimmy Shorts. He's not here. He's not gonna be here. Now what? Now where are we? We are here at you interrupting me again, you fucking idiot.'

Bill got up, literally hopping mad. 'We're here at the same point again, *where you, the fucking peon masses, can once again ruin ANYONE who tries to do anything because you don't know how to do it on your own!*' he yelled, jumping up and down. '*That's where we're fucking at! Once again the useless waste of fucking flesh that has ruined everything good in this goddamn world! That's where we're at!*'

He lunged in the direction of the woman. '*HITLER HAD THE RIGHT IDEA! HE WAS JUST AN UNDER-ACHIEVER!*

'*KILL 'EM ALL, ADOLF, ALL OF 'EM. JEWS, MEXICANS, AMERICANS, WHITES, KILL 'EM ALL. START OVER! THE EXPERIMENT DIDN'T WORK!*'

Free Bird!

'Free Bird.'

Bill dropped to the stage in a heap.

Len Austrevich awoke way too early to the sound of his pager frantically beeping. The club's switchboard was jammed and his investors, three straight business guys, were calling a 9 a.m. emergency meeting. Bill's soliloquy was the talk of talk radio. Len got to the club as quick as he could to greet his fuming partners. Dubbing that woman 'drunk cunt' seemed to be the main bone of contention. They wanted Hicks fired immediately.

'I run the stage,' Len told them. 'We're not getting rid of him. I didn't get into this to censor comics.' This was the first time twenty-seven-year-old Len had faced off with his partners.

'This is insane,' the investors argued. 'We lost 200 people last night. We can't have this. It's all over the radio. You don't call anyone a cunt!'

'Yeah, well it's comedy,' Len said calmly. True, most of the room had walked, but the people who stayed were just dying with laughter. 'Just trust me,' Len added. 'I guarantee you if we stick with Hicks, word of mouth is going to spread.'

Meanwhile, the influential Kevin Matthews was standing by Hicks on the radio, telling those who called in to complain about Bill that he thought the show sounded great.

By Thursday, both the evening's shows were sold out, and all the weekend shows too. Len exhaled.

The *Chicago Tribune* wrote him up excitedly, as well as the *Chicago Sun-Times*, which called him a 'firebrand who seems on the verge of self-immolation as he uses his incendiary wit to torch America's hypocrisy'. In a 'bloated comedy business, which is propped up by cupidity, stupidity and timidity' Hicks, *Sun-Times* reporter Ernest Tucker noted, 'kicked the slats out of that triangle in a hurry Tuesday during his opening night here at the Funny Firm, leaving the packed house silent and gasping'. Bill started going on Matthews's radio show every time he was in town and his small fan base became a wide following.

Even better than the appreciation, more fun than baiting uptight Catholics ('Fuck your cult!' was a favorite line), was Bill's ritual with Len.

All Bill wanted to do after a show these days was eat, which suited Len just fine since he didn't drink either. Every time Bill came to town they planned their time around which restaurants they were going to hit. Len said Bill could eat like a motherfucker. Thursday it was ribs, Friday steak, Saturday ribs again. Every night, no matter what, Bill had to have a big greasy sausage from Jim's Polish. Len took all the comics to Jim's but no one loved the place like Bill. 'He became addicted to these things,' Austrevich said. 'It got to the point where I would pick him up at the airport in a limo and we would have to go straight for a hot dog. One time I picked him up, he made me take him to get a Polish, he did the show, after the show he wanted a Polish, then he called me from the hotel at three in the morning going, "Gotta get another Polish." I heard later on that he'd connected through Chicago on a flight so he could go to Jim's. They're very addictive. You get them with fries and this huge bucket of peppers that were just fire hot. He used to say, "Those are my little green friends, Len. Time to take me to my little green friends."'

One night as Len and Bill made their way to Jim's Polish, side-stepping the huge rats running across Maxwell Street, a guy selling stolen porn videos approached the two. 'Porno for your lady?' he enquired.

Bill turned over the cassette.

'No, thank you,' Bill said. 'I believe my lady already has that one.'

SIXTEEN

Beep. *Okay, that's real cute but today's Monday and change your fuckin' message. This is Willy, where are you? Where's my friend when I need him? Okay. All right. All right. All right.*

'Drugs is so bad! Drugs is *so* bad!' Bill whined one night a few months later, pacing the stage of the Bottom Line in Manhattan's West Village with a burning half-cigarette dangling from the fingers of his left hand. He was closing Mike's Talent Show, a hip variety showcase that booked performers like Eric Bogosian and Ann Magnuson.

'Yeah, yeah. Well, how come Keith Richards still walks? Explain *that* Mr Surgeon General. You never hear the Surgeon General mention Keith, do you? Little hole in the theory there.' The club gave him the light, the warning to wrap things up, and Bill ignored it. Keith, he said, defied that stupid commercial with the egg in the skillet. 'Here's Keith's brain. *SSSSSSSSSsssssss.* Here's Keith's brain on drugs.' Bill tore into his air guitar, belting out the opening riff to 'Satisfaction'.

'It's not a war on drugs. It's a war on personal freedom. Keep that in mind at all times.'

Peter Casperson and Steven Saporta, two music industry vets who together headed a management company and an indie label, Invasion Records, turned to look at each other. 'He was that striking,' Casperson said. 'I mean, Mike's Talent Show was this very regimented deal where everyone got ten minutes, but Bill just came out and disregarded all the rules. He was on for thirty, forty minutes, dressed all in black, and he's doing the smoking bit and the Keith Richards bit and some of the bits that are now on his first record. But the thing that stood out was his Keith Richards-on-drugs bit –

Bill was really more like an alternative rock act than a comic, and his rock references were so much more meaningful to him than to most people in comedy. They sort of reflected his passion for music. We saw him as this rock guy and that nailed it.'

The minute the show finished, Casperson and Saporta headed backstage and found Allan Pepper, owner of the Bottom Line. Upon finding out that Hicks not only had representation but a decade of stand-up under his belt, Casperson and Saporta took another tack. 'Hey, you were great,' they said, introducing themselves to Bill. What would he think of making a comedy record with them?

In short order, Casperson and Saporta got in touch with Jack and struck a multi-album deal with Bill. He would receive a $2,000 advance for each record, with each new record renegotiated according to past sales.

It wasn't that Casperson or Saporta thought comedy CDs were going to break out Bill Hicks. Comedy just didn't sell that big anymore, but Bill Hicks was going to break and when he did they would be there with the goods.

Casperson and Saporta talked to Bill and Jack about a plan to separate Bill from the pack and exploit his edge. The two loved Bill's all-black rock & roll look – a far cry from the polka dots jamming the Comedy Channel – and suggested hipper glasses. They could see how ambitious Bill was and Casperson, who had produced Martin Mull's records in the seventies and once managed Madonna, thought Bill could be the new Pryor. They encouraged Bill to play musical venues like the Village Gate and the Bottom Line, places with a rich history, places Lenny Bruce would have played. 'We were staying as close as we could with him because the way Peter and I looked at it, this guy was going to be legendary,' Saporta said. 'The thing was just to do right by him and keep close to him and if we couldn't manage him, we would make records with him and eventually maybe something would happen. So we're trying to get him to focus on jazz rooms, rock rooms, anything but comedy rooms. "Don't work comedy clubs!" That was the main thing.' Of course that presented a bit of a problem since comedy clubs were Bill and Jack's main source of income.

When Bill was at the Village Gate recording material for his first record, *Dangerous*, Casperson called his old friends Bill and Rose McGathy, two influential record promoters, and asked them to come down. Bill McGathy begged off, explaining that he had a bad flu. Come anyway, Casperson pleaded. 'He said, "You gotta trust me on this,"' McGathy recalled. '"This is probably the most special thing I've ever come across." So we went. And Bill came out dressed in black. I think he started the show at that time with the Dylan song "Subterranean Homesick Blues" and he proceeded over the next hour and twenty minutes to verbalize so many things that Rose and I had thought and never really said, I think because we were afraid people would think we were totally paranoid by saying some of these things. He was twenty-seven years old! His whole perception was just so ageless. It was like he just *knew* stuff. This intuition about the reality of things.'

As devoted rock lovers, the McGathys especially loved the way he railed against anti-drug pro-endorsement rock stars and the bit about John Lennon's murder. '*Goddamnit*. If you're going to kill somebody have some fuckin' taste. I'll drive you to Kenny Rogers's house, all right? Get in the car – I know where Wham! lives!' Bill ended the set in his favorite way, by dropping to the stage, 'assassinated'. The next day, the McGathys called Casperson and offered to do special radio edits to promote *Dangerous* when it came out. You can still hear Bill McGathy, sick as a dog, laughing above the rest of the audience on the record.

Bill, who deep down wanted to be Jimi Hendrix, was delighted with this turn of events.

'Dear David Johndrow Esq.,' Bill typed one gray June afternoon from New York on his Smith Corona SL 500. 'I hope this letter finds you well and exalting in the realization of your dreams.' Bill had decided to stay inside and write his friends in an effort to squelch the wrath of the phone companies ('AT&T, MCI and any other random letters that delight in sending me bills').

As for him, everything was going great. While it was in his nature to think really big and expect lightning to flash every time he came to bat ('*à la* Roy Hobbs in *The Natural*'), progression by step seemed to be the order of the day. 'I truly believe God has a better plan than I, only his at times seems a lot slower,' he wrote.

Still, there was no word on a return to *Letterman*. That was okay, he said. He would just keep working, 'traveling the country like some prophetic Johnny Appleseed spreading my seeds of ascension, i.e. dick jokes'.

The real occasion for the letter, he explained, was that he was coming to Austin in less than four weeks, the week of 11 July to shoot his own comedy special at the Laff Stop. He wasn't going to wait for a television executive to give him one. He had some money saved up from the road and Kevin Booth, who had been urging him to do this for months, was a producer at Austin's public access station, ACTV. ACTV had a solid student following, so they knew they could count on plenty of air time there.

David shot the show (called *Sane Man*) using three cameras while Kevin did the sound, and for the first time Bill got to tape a glorious six minutes on his favourite subject: smoking.

'How many non-smokers do we have here tonight?' he asked, pulling a cigarette out of his pocket. 'Non-smokers?'

Cheers and applause.

'What a bunch of whinin' maggots. Obnoxious self-righteous slugs. I'd quit smoking if I didn't think I'd become one of you, I swear to God.'

He had no time for non-smokers who blathered on and on about the lethal dangers of secondary smoke: 'I'll smoke, I'll cough, I'll get the tumors, I'll die. *Deal?*

'Thank you, *America.*'

He was on a roll, and the rest of the set was, much like *Dangerous*, a rant on the culture war between good and evil as personified by pop idols: Jimi Hendrix, John Lennon and Keith Richards versus Debbie Gibson, Rick Astley, Tiffany ('to think someone could use a good liver') and George Michael. 'These aren't even really people!' he cried. 'It's a CIA plot to make you think malls are good. Don't you *see?*'

For all Bill's passion for the classics, be it Dylan, Hendrix or

Twain, he never insulated himself from 'the cultural dungheap' as he called it and got a perverse thrill from watching *COPS* on TV and kidnapping his friends to see *Action Jackson* or *Cobra*. 'He *loved* bad Steven Seagal and Van Damme,' Huggins recalled. 'I think it just amused him as show business at its worst.'

And that night, Bill was at his physical peak, dancing across the stage, fucking a stool for a bit on AIDS, throwing a mike stand into the audience as Elvis and using any number of ear-crunching sound effects (gunshots, Hendrix guitar feedback) to convey the sheer glee he took in hating mediocrity. 'I was just howling,' Johndrow said. 'I had never seen him that focused. Since New York, he'd come back really really sharp.'

He marched around like a robot. 'But. Bill. Malls. Are. Good. Malls allow us to shop 365 days of the year at 72 degrees. That must be good. We are happy consumers.

'I'm a happy consumer! And you know – *hee hee hee* – I'm concerned about what my children consume! *Hee hee hee*. I would like to consume the barrel of a twelve-gage shotgun right now if I could!' Bill shoved two fingers in his mouth.

'*Poownw!*'

'Our next guest,' David Letterman said on the evening of 12 September, 'is a very funny gentleman who has a fairly bleak but utterly consistent view of human nature. He is appearing this very week at the Funny Firm in Chicago. Ladies and gentlemen, please welcome back to this program, Bill Hicks.'

Three and a half years after his last appearance, Bill was back on *Late Night with David Letterman*.

Frank Gannon, the man responsible for booking him, had been a segment producer on *Letterman* for just two years. Gannon had an unusual résumé for the comedy business. He had a Ph.D in Political Science from Oxford and began his career as a speechwriter in Richard Nixon's White House. When Nixon resigned in 1974, Gannon flew out to California with him on *Air Force One* and spent the next four years helping the ex-President write his memoirs. 'I've

worked for the two great laugh-getters of the twentieth century,'
Gannon liked to say. When he joined the *Letterman* staff from a job
as editor-in-chief of the *Saturday Review*, Gannon familiarized himself
by going out to comedy clubs several nights a week and going
through stacks of comedians' reels found in the show archives. One
night Gannon happened to see Bill at the Improv. He couldn't
imagine why he hadn't heard of this kid. As soon as he got to the
office the next day, he pulled his tapes. They were terrific.

'Why wasn't he in the mix at booking meetings?' Gannon asked
Robert Morton, now the executive producer.

Morton said he knew Hicks and loved his work, but they had
had some problems with him years earlier.

Gannon said he wanted to give him another shot and Morton
agreed, provided Gannon could guarantee Bill wasn't going to get
into trouble on air again.

Over the phone, Bill was straightforward with Gannon about his
earlier difficulties. He wasn't contrite about it, just matter of fact.
Point was, he wanted another chance and he was prepared to do
what was necessary. Gannon went around to the clubs with Bill to
work out a solid five-minute set and they had their first tug of war
over what Bill could and could not say on television. Mondrus told
Gannon not to worry, his client would do it however the show
wanted, and then he told Bill to stop fighting it and just get on the
air. 'He would get exasperated,' said Gannon, 'and he would argue
vehemently but ... he didn't actually rail against it that much. I think
he understood that I was a necessary evil.' Actually, Bill liked
Gannon a lot. He loved hearing Nixon stories, and the two enjoyed
lively political debates over dinner. 'He was a libertarian and I was
a traditional intellectual as opposed to a social conservative. I think
we agreed on one thing: That Man [as Bill often said] is a virus in
shoes.'

In the end, Letterman succeeded in delivering to his audience an
easy-to-digest diluted Hicks. Dressed in a black leather jacket, a black
shirt and black jeans, Bill came out to 'Jumpin' Jack Flash' and
dutifully ran through heavily edited bits on smoking and Keith

Richards. But in the absence of the full strength of his words he seemed to posture too heavily, as though struggling to convey an edgy persona as compensation for the antiseptic material.

Milestone though it was, nothing much changed for Bill in the ensuing months except for raising his price a little when he went back on the road to do the usual round of comedy rooms. One night he found himself in a nice suburb of Kansas City playing at a little club called Stanford's and Sons.

'Good evening, ladies and gentlemen,' Bill began. 'I am very tired and I have been on the road for months, so please bear with me while I plaster on a fake smile and plow through this shit one more time.'

A woman in the front gasped and Bill leaned over to her table and winked. 'I'm just kidding,' he told her. 'It's magic every time.'

As Bill plowed, he probably didn't notice tucked away in the back of the room a comedian and kindred spirit in the form of one hefty six-foot-four Fallon Woodland. Fallon's barber had recommended he see Hicks and Fallon already had a fuzzy memory of a bright skinny kid he'd seen on *Letterman* a long time ago. Now he sat alone in the back, mesmerized. Fallon already knew he'd be back for the next show.

The second night the two were introduced and after the show went back to the club condo to hang out and drink sodas. Fallon reminded Bill of Ignatius J. Reilly, the gargantuan hero of John Kennedy Toole's bleak comic novel *A Confederacy of Dunces* who lives with his mother in New Orleans and writes his opus on Big Chief pads he hides under his bed.

'I think my girlfriend is leaving me,' Bill confided to Fallon. Oddly, he kind of wanted her to. He knew it was ending, he even said it was doomed, and yet he really wanted to force it right. She got on his nerves, but sexually he'd met his match. And those rare times when things were peaceful, it was great. 'Johnny Carson's been married four times and he's got an in-town gig,' Bill sighed.

'I was tired of the road,' Pamela recalled. 'We had made a pact that every four months we would take a break. To go breathe oxygen, to eat real food.' The promised breaks never seemed to materialize, though, and Bill didn't seem to mind when she stopped going on the road with him. Pamela thought it was because he was so caught up with his AA friends, a scene she found 'cliquish'. She had a job for a while cutting hair again but Bill didn't really like her working – 'He wanted me at home so he could reach me at any hour of the day' – and she was lonely.

One night when they had split up for the hundredth time, Bill did an entire set at Caroline's about her. He told the eight o'clock audience that she was a crazy Southern woman. All he could think about was that some other guy was going to get to enjoy the crotchless panties he bought for her on Valentine's Day. Then Pamela arrived and found Bill in his dressing room between shows. They shut the door, and the late-show audience got a more standard Hicks set.

The day before Bill left Kansas City, he bought Fallon a copy of *A Confederacy of Dunces* with a picture of Ignatius J. Reilly 'with his fleshy balloon of a head' in his famous earflaps on the cover. The guys exchanged numbers but Fallon wasn't so sure they'd stay in touch. Comedians pass around numbers all the time.

A week later, Fallon's wife left him and he desperately needed to talk to someone. He called Bill and poured out his story. Happily, there seemed to be no limit on how long Bill wanted to talk. They went on for three or four hours at a time. When they weren't talking about women, they talked video games: Super Mario Bros, Zelda, John Madden Football. They played together over the phone, competing, trying out the tricks together. Bill started to call Fallon from wherever he was on the road, from little hotel rooms all over the country, just to check on him and make sure he was okay.

'Fallon, think about it!' Bill counseled. 'A window has opened. Jump out of it. You're free! My God! You can stay up and watch videos. You can play Nintendo any time you want! You can do whatever you want any time!'

Bill's phone habit had something to do with being sober and on the road. He didn't want to be anywhere near a bar, so after a show he headed straight for his hotel room, fixed himself some ice cream with Magic Shell Topping, played Nintendo and talked all night to friends all over the country. 'Stories,' he'd say, 'I want stories.' He'd call Shock, Huggins, Pineapple, Bob Fiorella (a comedian he had met at a gig in Buffalo, New York), Colleen. But especially Fallon. If Bill couldn't get him on the phone, he just left a message . . . or six.

They took delight in comparing phone bills. Fallon's longest call to Bill was 251 minutes – four hours and eleven minutes. But Bill won with a 258-minute call to Fallon. The sick part was that the calls were made on the same day.

They started thinking about the fact that maybe they should get paid for their conversations. They were funnier to one another than anything they had seen on TV. Fallon suggested a staged show but Bill thought they should go right for television.

Occasionally Fallon ran into comics who had worked with Bill on the road during the drinking days. He loved to call Bill with their stories.

'Bill, do you remember that guy Bob from Indianapolis?'

'Yeah! We hit it off.'

'Well, no, you didn't, Bill. You smoked in his car the whole way back after he asked you not to, and you also kept hitting him in the chest with your finger and saying, "*They* may think you're funny. You're not."'

'*Ggggod.* I feel so bad.'

Late Night were so happy with Bill's first performance that they had him back just two months later, on 26 December. He looked trim and neat in his shirt and jacket, more natural and confident, less 'put on' than on his previous appearance and Letterman invited him over to the couch after his set. Bill talked about giving his girlfriend crotchless pantyhose for Christmas while Letterman looked appropriately flustered. Still, as usual, Bill was just going through the motions. Outrageous was cute, authentic outrage was *verboten*.

Bill began appearing on the program regularly and whenever he did the show, at 12.35 a.m. comedians around town found a TV, in the club or at a diner, to catch Hicks. Once when comedian Tom Hertz's VCR was broken, he brought his Sony Watchman to a club and stood outside on the sidewalk after his own performance just to watch Bill.

In late March, while Bill was away, Pamela packed up and drove home to Houston. She'd had it with freezing New York, Jack Mondrus and Bill's interminable life on the road. 'I had spoken to him on many many occasions; there would have to be more breaks, there would have to be less Jack ... I begged him and he couldn't do it. He just couldn't. So I left.' She knew if she waited until Bill got home, he'd be able to talk her out of it.

Bill was a wreck. He was always calling her from clubs, hotels and airports to check in, argue, flirt with the idea of getting back together, and he couldn't stop talking about her to friends like Peter Casperson and Rose McGathy. Should he fly down to Houston and bring her back? Did he even want her back? He didn't want to marry her but he couldn't imagine not having her in his life. Everyone he talked to got the feeling it was mostly a sex thing; he and Pamela fought constantly but Bill longed to have her next to him in bed.

Rather than go home to his empty apartment on West 44th Street after a set, Bill sometimes drank coffee at the Westway Coffee Shop with two comics he liked, Dan Vitale and Randy Credico. Bill, who normally had no use for impressionists of any stripe, thought the world of Randy. They had first met at Dangerfield's Tropicana in Vegas, where Credico was doing crowd-pleasing impersonations. Bill couldn't believe his eyes when he walked into the Improv and saw Credico doing his real material: radical political satire. 'I can't believe you were doing Popeye and all that shit!' Bill said. 'I had no idea what you really did!' Credico said he did that other stuff just to get through the set. He had gotten kicked off *The Tonight Show* in 1984 for calling Jeanne Kirkpatrick, then ambassador to the UN, a Nazi (suggesting that she was Eva Braun incognito), and had spent most of the eighties as a political activist in Nicaragua.

Credico talked to Bill about politics, schooling him in the industrial-military complex, American policy in Central America and the history of the anti-war movement. They talked about Ed Herman and Noam Chomsky, whose book *Manufacturing Consent* was one of

Bill's bibles ('Noam Chomsky with dick jokes', Bill liked to call himself). As Bill was starting to do more and more overtly political material, he had tons of questions – when he wasn't sneaking off to the payphone to call Pamela.

SEVENTEEN

Beep. *I am* humiliated *to be a part of your personalized message. Oh God. Anyway. This is Willy. I'm between shows.*

Once *Dangerous* was released, in the spring of 1990, Invasion treated it like an indie rock release. The label made up giant posters, and sneaked Bill on to the racks of large retailers by claiming that he was a rock artist. The Recording Industry Association of America had just voluntarily adopted warning labels for records containing 'explicit lyrics' as a defensive conciliatory gesture to Tipper Gore's pet project, the PMRC (Parents Music Resource Center), which had been moving mandatory labeling bills through the legislature. In response, Bill had every *Dangerous* CD slapped with a big sticker that quoted Thomas Jefferson: 'Are we to have a censor whose imprimatur shall say what books shall be sold and what we may buy?'

In fact, most of *Dangerous* was too risqué for radio play and Bill McGathy burned a CD of 'clean' radio edits to take around to morning radio. McGathy had some success with those, but morning show DJs each played their individual favorite cuts for morning such as, 'You know in many parts of our troubled world people are yelling *Revolution! Revolution!* In Tennessee they're yelling *Evolution!*' 'We want our thuummmmbs!' and '*Nonsmokers.* A bunch of whinin' little maggots, aren't they? I'd quit smoking if I didn't think I'd become one of them.' But there was no 'single' to pound home with listeners and often the bit went unaccredited.

In June, Bill did *Late Night,* and Letterman gave the CD a nice plug. Still, sales for *Dangerous* were nothing spectacular, just 2,000 or 3,000 units. Not bad for a comedy CD, but Invasion had been hoping against hope for a breakout.

Jack Mondrus realized Bill wasn't a big enough draw to play

concert venues but he did request that comedy club owners promote Bill's appearances as the 'Dangerous Tour'. He was determined to pull off all the promotion they could, within the confines of where they were making decent money.

Bill was starting to resent his road schedule. A typical itinerary might read Houston 17–22 April, Raleigh 24–28 April, and Dallas 1–6 May. 'My flying saucer tour', he called his constant runs across the Southern club circuit: 'Because I too have been appearing in small Southern towns in front of handfuls of hillbillies and I've been doubting my own existence.'

'How do you do it?' he asked Len Austrevich. 'I work like an animal and I have no money.'

Len was blunt with him. From what he could tell, Mondrus was working Bill way too much. He thought it was unhealthy expending tremendous energy onstage night after night, eating fast food for weeks without a break.

'Man, you gotta slow down,' Len said. 'You're going to kill yourself. Talk to Jack, Bill. You've got to tell him.' Len even offered to pay Bill double one week at the Funny Firm, so he could take the next week off.

And then Jack called with good news. Bill was invited to the Just For Laughs Comedy Festival in Montreal. Held every July, Just For Laughs was a highly influential international comedy festival and featured acts from the UK to China, Australia to South Africa. This year, Bob Newhart, Richard Jeni, Mort Sahl and Weird Al Yankovic were headlining. 'Another first,' Bill told Jack, smiling into the phone.

It would be incredible exposure. Not only did industry from around the world show up to make development deals with ripe young talent, the festival taped several of the events for television. Festival programming director Bruce Hills had asked Bill to play the Nasty Show, the outré late night show, at a comedy room downtown called Club Soda. Bill balked a little at being lumped into a 'nasty' theme but he was also going to get to play the Gala Show, the festival's taped main event at its premium venue, the Théâtre St Denis.

A few days before Bill arrived in Canada, *Montreal Gazette* reporter Bill Brownstein, a long-time Hicks fan, wrote a piece excitedly predicting that Bill's show 'could be the greatest comedy event to occur in Canada since Wayne and Shuster [the iconic Canadian comedy team] gave up full-time performing careers'.

As Hills thought, Bill went over best at the Nasty Show where he got to do a long meandering set, converting swarms of fans as he always did when given time to build. 'He gleefully broke the news to the non-smokers in the audience that they were all going to die, since medical technology aims to keep alive people who screw up on their health, not those who look after it,' Brownstein wrote. 'But Hicks's frustration with the powers that be and with the sad state of rock & roll struck a chord with the young, white middle class audience . . .

'Hicks managed to hijack the Nasty Show.'

One person watching Bill was a British producer named Bruce Hyman. Hyman was at the festival scouting talent for a themed theatrical show he had in mind called 'Stand-Up America'. He was planning to do a six-week run in London's West End using about twenty American stand-ups, three a week. Hyman liked Bill's whole stance – the cocky way he handled the mike, swinging it around, deep-throating it, hitting himself in the head with it. 'He used it as an instrument,' Hyman said. 'There was a lot of rock & roll about it.' Hyman had been thinking about using Denis Leary but as soon as he saw Bill he realized he had to have the genuine article. Meanwhile, HBO asked Bill to tape a half-hour comedy special.

Right away, Jack began to press Bruce Hills about a one-man show for Bill at next year's festival. Standing on the steps of the Hotel Delta, Jack announced that, if Bill came back in 1991, that was the only slot he'd fill. Hills didn't answer him.

Mike Hedge, Invasion's point man in London, managed to have *Dangerous* distributed there in time for Bill's West End date and Hyman saved Bill for the last week of the production, betting that audiences would build over the six weeks. He was right. There wasn't a media buzz yet but Bill was the highlight of that month of shows,' recalled Bob Gold, a concert booking agent Hedge had invited to Bill's performance. 'The buzz was that he was the most intelligent of all the comedians. He was much more biting while the other guys were mainstream. Word of mouth started to spread from the shows and people were going, "Who is this guy?"'

Bill loved the graceful Queen's Theatre on Shaftesbury Avenue in London's West End, a far cry from the strip-mall clubs he played at home, and he thought London was wonderfully civilized. 'This is just unbelievable!' he kept saying. Bruce Hyman, who was pleasantly surprised by how polite and mild-mannered Bill was offstage, drove him around after late post-show suppers, showing him the sights. He found AA meetings within walking distance of his hotel and forsook trolling pubs for the novelty of snooker and Earl Grey tea.

From London, Bill took an eleven-hour flight to Los Angeles to make an appearance on the Comedy Channel show *Comics Only*, hosted by Paul Provenza. Looking slightly worn, he smoked through the whole interview. Provenza, who had worked the road with Bill, loved his impressions of his parents and Bill obliged with two long drawled bits on both of them.

'Have your parents heard *Dangerous?*' Provenza asked Bill.

'They bought it. They said, "Well, we bought your al-bum."' Bill pursed his lips in disapproval and crossed his legs.

'That's all they ever said. My dad does not fully get what I do. "Bill, do you have to use the 'F' wurrd in your act, suun? Bob *Hope* doesn't need to use the 'F' wurrd." Yeah, Dad, well guess what? Bob Hope doesn't play the dives that I play, okay? You put him in some of these joints, he'll have Emmanuel Lewis and Phyllis Diller doing a live sex act. Just to get out of there alive.'

With his CD out, was Bill now working a higher class of gig, Provenza wondered?

'Oh *yeah*, Paul,' Bill said with a laugh. 'Oh yeah. That's the way it works, right?'

At the end of the show, while the cameras continued to roll, Bill walked into the studio audience, bent down and planted a kiss on a pretty girl in the front row. She laughed and Bill gleefully sneered into the camera.

'Sounds like Sam Kinison four years ago,' Bruce Hills scribbled in his notebook as he sat at the Irvine Improv in a strip mall outside Los Angeles in November 1990, watching Bill pace the stage. 'Top-end cutting-edge material. Will offend the average audience.'

Mondrus hadn't let up once in campaigning Hills about a one-man show for Bill at the 1991 Just For Laughs Festival. So when Hills and Duncan Strauss, the festival's US talent consultant, considered various acts in Los Angeles, Jack begged Hills to stay in town an extra day to see Bill play Irvine. It wasn't that anyone had to be sold on Bill's talent. Hills knew that Hicks was the smartest young comedian out there and thirty-two-year-old Strauss, a former *Los Angeles Times* rock and comedy critic, was already a huge Hicks fan who drove hours to see a show whenever Bill came west. But the festival featured just a single one-man show each year and Hills wasn't convinced that Bill was able – or, mostly, willing – to fit into a themed theatrical setting. Nor was he sure Bill could handle doing over eighty minutes.

Bill walked out and ripped the Irvine room apart for almost forty minutes. At one point, he blew the sound system with his sound effects so he just kept going without a microphone for the last twenty, never losing the audience for a second. Hills, who spent the better part of each year traveling all corners of the world looking for comedy, was plainly dumbfounded. 'I just sat there going: "That is the strongest funniest most important stand-up performance I've ever seen. In my whole career." It's the first time that I saw stand-up that I thought sort of bridged rock & roll and comedy. Not because of the bells and whistles and bullshit. Not because he closed with a song. Because of the energy, the passion, the material. That was the first guy that packaged that for me.'

Hills returned to Montreal with a mission. It was up to the festival, he decided, to figure out how to create an outlet for Bill. As soon as he got back, he went to his boss, festival head Andy

Nulman. 'You know what we have to do?' Hills said. 'We have to put the most important act in the one-man show every year if we can. That has to be first.'

In December, Bill spent his twenty-ninth birthday in West Palm Beach, his favorite place to be in the winter. He couldn't get enough of that balmy air. He, Colleen McGarr and her boyfriend, Dave Hogerty, a photographer for the *Miami Herald*, went out for dinner. Since that first booking, Bill and Colleen had been having weekly phone conversations and Bill sent her postcards from the road. Once he gave her a junior high school picture of himself with his bowl haircut. He signed it 'Burl Hicks'.

They had a lot in common: a love of comedy, obviously, and they were both voracious readers. They'd talk tirelessly about their favorites, Tom Robbins and Kurt Vonnegut and John Kennedy Toole. He told her all about his impossible attachment to Pamela and about his brother Steve, whom he still adored. Colleen teased him about his girlfriends, who all seemed to wear cocktail dresses at weird times of the day.

1991 came in with a bang. On 16 January the United States launched twenty-two Cruise missiles on Iraq and heralded the beginning of the Gulf War. That night, Bill was in Austin hanging out in Kevin's living room with David and another Austin friend, Pat Brown. They watched on television the high-tech images of the 'smart bombs' dropping on Baghdad. The guys were trying to record some material for their new band. They were always playing music together when Bill came to town anyway and they figured they might as well record in Kevin's new home studio. Bill said they could even show Invasion a demo tape when they got it together. He had written a bunch of blues songs while he was on the road but Kevin (whose band with Brown, Year Zero, had once had a deal with Chrysalis Records) was into playing straight rock, heavy guitar stuff, and they argued about which way to go. David stayed out of it. He liked hanging out with Bill, writing funny songs, but wasn't even sure he wanted to do the group thing anymore.

They decided to call their band Marblehead Johnson after the biggest fish in the pond at the Booth ranch. (And because it was a good dick joke.) Bill, obsessed with the Kennedy assassination (he watched the Zapruder tape over and over, pausing, rewinding, studying it), thought if they should call themselves the Quiet Loners. Lee on lead guitar, Harvey on bass and Oswald on drums. They could all wear white T-shirts.

The main reason Bill was in town was for the 'world premiere' of *Ninja Bachelor Party*. Almost ten years after they had started the project, they had a half-hour suburban karate epic and were screening it at the Opera House downtown with a special post stand-up performance by Bill. Shot by David, the movie starred Kevin as Clarence, a teenage Robitussin addict, who goes to Korea to kick syrup with a karate guru who accepts credit cards. The warrior training montages were hilarious, and as the 'Ninja Grandmaster' Bill wore a little straw hat and got to say things like, 'Clarence, realize one thing: there are no choices. There is only universal will.'

It had taken David and Kevin months to edit a decade's worth of footage (Bill called in his voice-overs from the road) and with everything Bill had going on he was as excited about showing *Ninja Bachelor Party* as anything else. As superbly stupid as he hoped it would be, *Ninja Bachelor Party* quickly became a cult hit on ACTV and a favorite in gourmet video stores and on the non-stop reels of Hicks footage that played at student parties around Austin.

Ninja Bachelor Party ended with the Grandmaster getting a blow job while declaring, 'Remember: love is all there is. Enough talk of it. Let's show each other: *love.*'

For the first time, the American Comedy Awards nominated Bill for Best Male Stand-up. The way the awards worked, club owners around the country voted to nominate their favorite acts – or at least the ones who were a good draw. Comedy Central showed clips of each nominee and viewers called in to vote for their favorite. In March, Dennis Wolfberg won at a televised ceremony.

In April, while the rest of the country was breathing a sigh of relief that there had been no draft, and declaring its support for the troops, Bill got to broadcast his own response on *Letterman*.

'I was in the unenviable position of being for the war but against the troops,' he said. 'I'm sorry, I just don't like those young people. Don't get me wrong, though – I'm all for the carnage.'

Since the overwhelming success of *Roseanne* in 1988 and the flurry of shows it spawned starring comedians (Seinfeld, Tim Allen on *Home Improvement*, Brett Butler on *Grace Under Fire*), the stand-up business was now almost driven by television. A sitcom was the ultimate post and many performers considered it somewhat amazing that Bill would put his ass on the line like that. As Eric Bogosian later said in the documentary *Totally Bill Hicks* (originally a C4 production, the program aired on Comedy Central in the US under the name *Just a Ride*), 'I had one of the top comedians in the country telling me during the war with Iraq that they were against the war and they wouldn't say anything. Because they basically felt that you watched those little bags of money just fly away. It's like, kiss your career goodbye.' In fact, when Bill did his Gulf War material at the Punch Line in San Francisco, a guy with a shaved head went ballistic on him and the show disintegrated into a screaming match with three-quarters of the audience walking out.

The night before the *Letterman* taping, as Bill and Frank Gannon rode a limo around Manhattan working out the five-minute set at Stand-up New York and Catch, a crew from the CBS program *48 Hours* trailed them. They were doing a special about the lives of struggling comedians. The cameras picked up some of the Frank/Bill dynamic.

'Producer Frank Gannon,' the voice-over intoned, 'decides which comedians will appear on *Late Night with David Letterman*.'

'What qualifies you to know what [viewers] want and what will work?' reporter Harry Dowd asked Gannon.

'Yeaa . . .' added Bill, tapping Dowd's shoulder. 'I've been wondering this, too!'

'Some are born omniscient,' Gannon explained. 'Some achieve it, and some have it thrust upon them. It's a burden.'

Bill burst into laughter.

'Do you trust his judgment?' Dowd asked Bill.

'Uhhhh . . .'

'How does that collaboration work?'

'. . . uhhhh. It's not a matter of trusting his judgment,' Bill said. 'I know that I can't get on without their approval of material. As far as what's funny, *I* know what's funny. Now I also know there are certain parameters when you do network TV. They tell you, "Oh we like you on our show 'cause you're 'edgy' or your 'point of view'. But when you come on our show, could you not do those?" '

Bill's HBO *One-Night Stand* was broadcast on 27 April to favorable, but very limited, notice. With hundreds of cable specials clogging the television schedule, it wasn't like the old days where the whole country talked about what George Carlin had said on *The Tonight Show*. Bill seemed resigned to the state of things. 'What's happened with this plethora of comedy on every channel is that it's totally trivialized what comedy can do and should do,' he later told the *Los Angeles Times*. 'But that's typical of this kind of system we live under. They trivialize everything so that nothing is accomplished.'

EIGHTEEN

Beep. *Roy Gene, where the hell are you at two thirty-fuckin'-five? What in the fuck? All right. I'm goin' to bed.*

Bill spent the summer making meticulous plans for his one-man show at Just For Laughs. The Centaur, where he would perform, was the most prestigious theater in Montreal and, as the festival directors told him and Mondrus, Bill had to deliver more than just 'ranting' in front of a black curtain. Just For Laughs wanted Bill's stuff in 'thematic packaging'.

All he knew, Bill told Hills, was he didn't want to stand there with a library wall behind him. We just need a concept, Hills replied evenly.

Fortunately, Bill hit it off with the festival lighting director, a guy named Spike Lyne. So Hills, sensing Hicks's instinctive loathing of 'suits' telling him how to do his show, suggested Bill and Lyne put their heads together and get back to him.

A few days later, Bill neatly wrote out his vision for the show on lined notebook paper and faxed it to Bruce. At the top he wrote 'The Evolution of Myth'.

'The world appears to us a certain way because we believe it to be that way,' he wrote. 'When we change our beliefs, the world will change as well.' He would look at existing beliefs while, 'in addition, presenting other ways to perceive that will appear "alien" to our unquestioned and accepted myths'.

There was that word again: alien. He and Pamela had looked for UFOs in the Sedona desert, his favorite place to vacation, and he alluded constantly, onstage and off, to the Harmonic Convergence telepathic spacecraft incident.

A few of Bill's friends and fans found his UFO preoccupation hard to stomach ('a complete waste of his time,' said Farneti) but what Bill was interested in, more than the folklorish aspects of the alien, was how it had come to symbolize, in the collective unconscious, the need for mass evolution. 'Let's get on the mother ship and get *out* of here!' he would declare onstage at the end of a show.

He ended his fax to Bruce by describing in detail how he wanted the end of the show to feel. All the lights should go out, he wrote, except for a single beam shining down on his face. As the light faded altogether and Bill disappeared, the Beatles song 'Tomorrow Never Knows' would begin.

Now that he and Spike had hit on the perfect backdrop for Bill's point of view, Bill was as excited as always at the prospect of a group endeavor. He thoroughly enjoyed the production aspects of entertainment, whether it was making up fake promo pictures of Stress in high school, or doing his own comedy video under the aegis of Absolute Creative Entertainment. He sent Spike star-system slides to be projected during the show and an audiotape of one of his shows. 'Feel free to come up with any ideas that we can use to enhance the presentation,' he wrote. 'Let's think big, for after all, Spike, are we not men?'

Bill's work was pulling him out of the clubs, away from the very definition of 'stand-up', and though he wasn't sure what to call himself – satirist? social critic? – he reveled in the transition. In an interview with *Set* magazine in June, as he planned the show, Bill enthused about working in a theater.

'It's the best,' he said. 'Comedy wasn't meant to be in comedy clubs. It's a theatrical performance. That's the angle I take. I'm doing a play. A self-produced, self-written play. It's great to have all these club venues, but ideally I want to work in theaters, because it's a big performance. It's very dramatic. I do lots of dramatic stuff. I do lots of people being shot and murdered and there's mayhem going on. And when you do it after a guy who juggles and a guy who just talks about his ethnicity, people go, "What's this? This isn't the lighthearted jolliness we were just witnessing." To me, real humor is very serious. Mark Twain's humor in *Huckleberry Finn* is funny, but it's about very serious things. It's a deeper, richer laugh for me.'

On Saturday 13 July Bill arrived in Montreal with Jack in tow. The festival had already been under way for two days, and every heavy hitter in comedy entertainment from LA to Australia was packed into the muggy city. Bill, as usual, did his best to stay away from the industry crowds, preferring to hang out with Colleen, who was again there as a talent coordinator, and her good friend Duncan Strauss, with whom Bill had become friendly. Duncan and Colleen came by the beautiful old Centaur Theater both afternoons while he rehearsed. He was in good spirits but he was perspiring profusely. Having imagined a Montreal summer, to be like a Maine summer Bill had arrived with a suitcase of black turtlenecks and jackets for a week of shows in 80-degree weather.

Inside the 255-seat Centaur on Monday evening, the darkened stage was perfectly bare except for a stool and a glass of water. Just as Bill had planned, the star system glowed overhead. At 9.45 p.m., facing a full house, Bill paused for a moment, his hands in his pockets, in the smoky light-filled opening at the back of the stage before walking into the hot glare of a single spotlight. Wearing his customary black, Bill had slicked back his hair and wore small round glasses. The effect was that of an elegant lone assassin, looming rather than lurking against the midnight-blue backdrop.

'It's great to be here,' he said. He joked about how he didn't realize July was summer in the French provinces. He did some friendly amusing bits – stock material he had used when he was twenty – about hating his boss and having an attitude problem. He did a light bulb joke. 'What did moths bump into before electric light bulbs were invented?'

However soft he might have seemed, he was just warming to a slow burn. 'I've greased my hair and I'm a little FUCKIN' poet tonight, all right? I'm a little dark poet, that's who I am,' he said mockingly. With at least three full sets in his arsenal, Hicks had sifted out the very best of his material for Montreal and for the next eighty minutes he prowled the stage under that single light and took clean shots at all the bromides and bullshit soaking America, beginning with the Persian Gulf 'distraction'.

'First off, this needs to be said: *there never was a war.*'

'How can you say that, Bill?'

'Well, a war is when *two* armies are fighting.'

Bill stared blankly at the audience. They began to softly clap.

'So you see right there I think we can all agree ... It wasn't exactly a war,' he said quietly.

He mocked the notion that was crammed down our throats of the Elite Republican Guard. 'Well, after two and a half months of continuous carpet bombing and not *one* reaction at all from these fuckers they became simply: the Republican Guard. Not nearly as elite as we may have led you to believe. After another month of continuous bombing and not one reaction – AT ALL! – they went from the Elite Republican Guard to the Republican Guard to the Republicans Made This Shit Up About There Being a Guard Out There.

'We hope you enjoyed your fireworks show!'

If there had been concerns about Hicks's performing in this context, they soon evaporated as it became clear that he had a graceful presence that filled whatever space he occupied. On this spare stage in front of a quiet intent crowd, he was confident enough to slow his pace, expand on his ideas without the pressure of jumping right in with the punchline. The choreography of his material, sound effects and constant movement were so seamless no one would have believed he had had just one dress rehearsal. Then again, he had been warming up for this show for a decade.

He launched into an extravagant riff on oral sex as a way to broach the absurdity of the Supreme Court's flimsy definition of pornography. It claimed pornography was 'any act that has no artistic merit and causes sexual thought'.

'Hmmm,' Bill said. 'Boy, that sounds like every commercial on television to me ...'

Bill imagined the ultimate commercial of the future. A woman's face. The camera pulls back to reveal naked breasts. Pulls back further, and she's completely naked, legs spread.

Bill sat on his stool and swung his legs in the air.

'Two fingers right here and it just says "Drink Coke".'

'Pornography causes sexual thought. No one asked these four questions: Yeah? And? So? What?'

'I'll tell you this,' he told the *Set* journalist just weeks before the festival. 'It is the "moment" I'm addicted to. That moment is a suspension of time and space when we realize our true selves as timeless. Entertainment is another definition of time and space. If it's scary or funny, if you go, "AHHHHH!", you're entertained! Why? Because you've realized your true self, which is not in a body, not physical, not dying and born to die ... Good God! I'm a pretentious fuck.'

But 'the moment' was exactly what Bill gave the Centaur audience when, for the last ride of the show, he unleashed a torrent of fresh outrage at rock stars who primly decried drug use and were only too happy to link their personas to the highest brand-name bidder. He stuck the mike in his mouth, practically swallowing it, and let forth an amplified snarling snorting wail-moan that sounded something like an angry beast trying to sweat out the devil.

'AHOOOOOHHHHHHHWWWWWWWOOOO-OOO.'

He reserved special contempt for New Kids on the Block. Everyone thought they were such a good image for the children. '*Fuck that!* When did mediocrity and banality become a good image for your children? I want my children to listen to people who fuckin' *ROCKED*!!!'

He began to goose-step up and down the stage. '*We're so clean cut!*' Nazi salute. '*Sieg heil! Heil! Heil!* A good clean country! *HEIL! HEIL! HEIL!*'

'AHOOOOOOWHWOWOAHAHAHAHAHAHA-HAAH!'

'*Fuck that! I WANT MY ROCK STARS DEAD!!!!!!*' Bill put an imaginary gun to his head. 'POOOWWWWWW!'

He jumped up and down, a satisfied concert-goer.

'PLAY FROM YOUR FUCKIN' HEART!!!!!!!!!!!!'

A pause while he adjusted his glasses. 'I am available for children's parties.'

By the third day of the festival the *Gazette*'s Brownstein wrote triumphantly:

> For a brief frightening moment, it looked like Bill Hicks had lost his edge. With a Beatle [sic] tune blaring in the background, the comedian began his one-man show at the Centaur with some placid touchy-feely banter and the spacey, satellite slides of planet earth.
>
> Whoa! Hath the comedy world's angry young man gone mellow? Not quite. It was a classic stand-up set-up, in fact. Hicks, the hit of last year's fest, is back, madder and badder than ever. And funnier, too, it almost goes without saying.
>
> Of course, Hicks is not for all comedy palates. He is abrasive and profane and very nearly over the top. But it's not gratuitous because Hicks has a soul.
>
> And Hicks just may be the closest thing we've got to Lenny Bruce...

Terry DiMonte, then the number one morning DJ in Montreal, caught the show early on, and pronounced himself transformed. He said so every single morning on Mix '96. 'If you see one person this year, you gotta see Bill Hicks,' he told his audience. 'He's a comic genius.'

Bill sold out six shows, and the festival added a seventh. One night a woman named Gillian Strachan sat in the audience. She was a researcher over from London with Tiger Television. Tiger, a small but prominent production company based in London, had a contract with the festival to tape six half-hour specials out of the festival for Britain's Channel Four. Tiger was meant to focus on the big ticket events such as the Gala shows, to create a 'best of' show with that year's hot British and North American comedians. So far the Tiger crew had been pretty disappointed.

'I've just seen something amazing,' Strachan told Tiger producers when she returned to the hotel that night. The British host of the show, Clive Anderson, agreed to check Bill out right away. Anderson returned from the show to report exactly the same thing: Hicks was simply fantastic. As far as he was concerned, they were wasting their time with the rest of it. Anderson returned to the show the very next night with Tiger TV's chairman Charles Brand, director Chris Bould and C4's commissioning editor Seamus Cassidy – instant converts all. They couldn't get over the difference – everything else at the festival was anodyne by comparison. 'I had absolutely no idea what I was going to see and . . . I thought, "Well." Absolutely brilliant,' said Cassidy. 'There was a moral center to all those arguments – which a lot of conspiracy theorists don't have. And I liked the fact that he talked about sex and he did it very well.'

Brand swiftly negotiated with Jack to tape Bill's show in its entirety. Instead of the eight or so standard minutes that Bill, like any festival comic, would have done for the special, they would pull more like fifteen minutes out of Bill's show to intersperse throughout the entire special.

The thing was, they were going to have to do it on a shoestring. They couldn't affect the lighting in the Centaur or the set in any way. Plus, they had only one camera and one cameraman. So Bould, who had never operated a camera before, rented one and manned it himself. They pointed it at Bill and hoped for the best.

Over at the Théâtre St Denis, the Scottish comedian Gerry Sadowitz, who was performing what the papers later called a 'tasteless' show, was attacked by a man who ran onstage and punched him in the head and face. The guy was arrested but Montreal prosecutors declined to pursue the matter. Tiger TV interviewed Bill Hicks and the other featured 'bad boy' of the festival, Denis Leary, on a sidewalk in downtown Montreal about the incident. Did either of the comedians think there was any call for that?

'You should never attack anybody *ever* under any conditions,' Bill replied. 'Okay? How about that?'

'The good thing,' Leary said, 'is if somebody actually takes a shot at me or Hicks it's just gonna be a gunshot from the audience. They won't even bother to come up onstage!'

Bill nodded, laughing. 'We get a different class of hecklers.'

Leary was in Montreal to host the Nasty Show at Club Soda and Colleen was coordinating the talent so she was standing backstage when she heard Leary doing material that was incredibly similar to old Hicks riffs, including his perennial Jim Fixx joke: 'Keith Richards outlived Jim Fixx, the runner and health nut dude. The plot thickens.'

When Leary came offstage, Colleen said, more stunned than angry, 'Hey, you know that's Bill Hicks's material! Do you know that's his material?' Leary stood there, stared at her without saying a word, and briskly left the dressing room.

NINETEEN

Beep. *Blah blah blaaaaaaaaaaaaaah. Blahh blah blah. Blah. I can't think of anything else. I'll talk to you later. Call me if you feel like it. Bill Hicks, your old friend. Remember? Um, Nintendo? Whatever.*

Bill was on a high. Back home, the 29 July edition of *Variety* called his show a 'runaway hit' and the *Hollywood Reporter* noted the 'considerable buzz with his hard-hitting show'. In ten days he was going to perform eleven shows at the Edinburgh Festival in Scotland, the most prestigious and visible performance festival in Europe. Mike Hedge and Bob Gold had gotten Bill the booking and were convinced that it would be the perfect jumping-off point in the UK for Bill after 'Stand-Up America'. Leary had made his name at Edinburgh the year before.

The applause from Montreal followed Bill across the Atlantic and he was a coveted ticket at Edinburgh before he even stepped off the plane. The festival was absolutely wild, way bigger even than Montreal with about one hundred shows a day in all kinds of venues. Jack kept calling it 'Edinberg' which drove Bill crazy.

Jack was beside himself. It was all happening just the way he planned, he said. Now that he had Channel Four on the line, he was going to work on getting Bill his own television special in London. His one concern, shared by Gold and Hedge, was the Edinburgh venue. Called the Dream Tent, it was in fact a circus tent. They had been hoping for bricks and mortar.

Nothing seemed to bother Bill, however. Five minutes to show time on his first night, he stood with Mike Hedge playing at a fairground shooting gallery. And as it turned out, the tent was set up like a cabaret café and wasn't a bad imitation of the smoky club atmosphere Bill was used to at home.

Better still, it was a packed house.

'Good evening, Glasgow!' he yelled.

After the show, more than a few people wanted to take him to dinner. 'When he came off the stage that first night,' Hedge said, 'he was overwhelmed. All sorts of industry were around him. Bill liked to be taken out, he liked a good meal, but he hated all that [show business] forced-ness.' He made his way through the press of people over to Mike and the two ducked out for dinner on their own. Not that he could find anything decent to eat. 'Oh, he wouldn't go near English food. He thought it was shit. He quite liked Indian food. He got quite into that.'

By the weekend, the word on Bill had sold out the tent. He appeared on the stand-up show *STV Funny Farm* and taped a couple of Granada TV spots, *Edinburgh Live* and *Manchester Live*. At the end of the festival, Bill walked off with a Critics Award.

Seamus Cassidy, who had also come to Edinburgh, was feeling very happy to have fifty minutes of Mr Bill Hicks in the can for Channel Four.

Bill hung out in the UK for a few more days, going up to London to play the Hackney Empire, a big cabaret venue in the East End, taping a spot for *London Underground* hosted by Leary, and traveling north to Birmingham for a sold-out show. Bob Gold suggested to Jack that they think about having Bill do a spring tour.

Over at the Tiger TV offices, Brand and Bould were taking a look at what they had. It was frankly magnificent. If the *Relentless* taping wasn't up to industry standard in terms of production value, the lack of fancy cutting perfectly exploited Bill's stark force. They had shot him close-up, drawing back occasionally for a full-body shot (the better to catch him goose-stepping). The camera captured every facial tic and rubbery contortion on Bill's wildly expressive face as he deftly morphed from character to character, contorted and screamed, jumped and danced.

If they hadn't been so British, the two men might not have managed to contain themselves.

Bill returned home in September elated about his success in England. The big news was that Channel Four had decided to air Bill's entire show, separate from festival coverage, as a one-hour special. Meanwhile, plans were in motion for a two-week spring concert tour of the UK. They were really getting him abroad and maybe now was the moment to take things to a higher level at home. Maybe he'd move to Los Angeles. He was definitely going to have to change managers.

Jack had really gotten on Bill's nerves traveling together those past few weeks. Jack had stuck to him like glue, and the tension between them grew by the hour. Bill cringed at his jokes and Jack's bombastic nature was never more glaring than when abroad. Bill kept snapping at him. He couldn't help it. Jack couldn't understand why Bill was subjecting him to 'severe mental anguish', why Bill was holding him at arm's length, why Bill wouldn't sign a new contract with him. The success in England? He'd planned this for Bill all along.

The fact was, all the good news had only exacerbated long-time conflicts between client and manager. Jack was completely dedicated and Bill knew it. But Bill had outgrown him. He was fed up working the road three-quarters of his life. Jack said he was just trying to make Bill – and himself – a living. Bill could turn down anything he wanted! 'Bill always said, "All you do is keep me on the road,"' Mondrus said. 'But I could never make him go anywhere he didn't want to. I could never say, "I'll take this job," if he didn't want to take it. You know, he took the jobs – they were all pretty good jobs.'

Bill held off making any immediate decisions. When he got home, he had a bunch of road dates to do – the Comedy Trap in Buffalo, Giggles in Seattle, the Funny Bone in Philly – and he wanted to get going on his second record. He wasn't crazy about Peter Casperson's production on *Dangerous* and he wanted to record this one on his own and have Kevin produce. In lieu of an advance, Invasion gave Bill a DAT recorder to take on the road with him. In mid-November

he headed down to Austin for a week to start recording material at
the Laff Stop.

The set covered much of the same ground as the Montreal show
but was certainly not identical in the way that the CD title – *Relentless*
– may have suggested. But then there was no such thing as a
verbatim Hicks set. He seemed to have a general outline of a show
in mind but he constantly reshaped material as he went, juggling
ideas and plugging in new connections. There, Bill had condensed
the Gulf War material, done a long bit on the Clarence Thomas
hearings (which he was glued to for those ten televised days in
October 1991) and he laid down a much longer riff on the War on
Drugs.

'I have never heard one reason that rang true why marijuana is
against the law,' Bill said. 'That rang *true* now. I'm not talking about
the reasons that the government tells us 'cause I hope you know this
– I think you do – all governments are *lying* cocksuckers.'

He had tons of great pro-pot material which his fans may have
mistakenly assumed had to do with his own habits. 'To be honest
with you I was never a big pot fan,' he told *High Times* in 1993.
'Which is very ironic, because I always espouse the virtues of
marijuana. My thing was mushrooms.'

The essential message always burned bright. 'About drugs, about
alcohol, about pornography – *whatever that is* – what business is it of
yours what I do, read, buy, see, or take into my body as long as I do
not harm another human being on this planet?'

When Bill played Houston a week later, he arrived at the Comedy
Workshop to see the marquee advertising 'Bill Hicks – X-Rated'.
Jesus Christ. All these years and that's how they thought of him.

'I'm thinking, *man*, what should I do?' he told writer Jack
Boulware in an interview for the San Francisco satire magazine *The
Nose*. 'Should I just go, "You know, I think war is bad and killing
people is wrong" and then like take my dick out and waggle it, and
put it back in? Isn't that weird? Here's the irony of Americans. Adult
humor to me is like childish humor. Adult humor, what they call
adult humor – "Billy talks about this and this and this, pussy and
fucky" – that's childish. That's what children talk about. What should

I do? Should I just start eating pussy while I'm doing my act? In fact, I should do that . . .'

He admitted that his profanity might have something to do with it. 'I read a great thing in a Vonnegut book the other day. The character said, "I don't curse, and I've never cursed, and the reason is, my parents told me that if I curse, it immediately allows people to turn me off, regardless of what I'm saying." I thought that was really interesting. I hear it too, and I listen to tapes of myself, and I go "man". Even I'm getting kind of numbed by it. And my material does not rely on it all. Everything I do can be done on TV except for the more obvious ones, about the actual fucking act, or about drugs . . .'

He bluntly admitted that he was looking for more exposure in the States. 'What kind, I don't know. I'm moving out to LA. What I want is to make a lot of money and get out of the business for ever. I'd like to be more like the J. D. Salinger of comedy. I'd like to produce one book that every year thirty million people buy again.'

Bill sent his Marblehead Johnson tape to Invasion in New York. They'd recorded eight songs. As much as his career was heating up, it was hard to say sometimes what excited Bill most: comedy, music or the movies.

He was too excited, Casperson and Saporta thought. 'Bill's enthusiasm sometimes,' Casperson said, 'it was like, "This is the greatest thing that's ever happened on the planet and it should be more important than my other stuff and I think I'm going to just do this now . . ."'

Saporta said it was the beginning of something, but really he didn't think of Bill as much of a musician. Marblehead sounded like some guys having fun in their bedroom.

'We said no,' Saporta recalled. 'Politely.'

Bill went ahead and put a Marblehead goofabilly song called 'Chicks Dig Jerks' on the new comedy record as a closer. It went: 'Hitler had Eva Braun/Manson had Squeaky Fromme/Ted Bundy got lots of dates/I wonder what I'm doin' wrong.'

The way he looked at his new record, the song was the album and the comedy was the bonus track. 'Okay, it's a fifty-six-minute bonus track . . . The comedy starts to get a little serious after a while. It's so . . . relentless. You need to lighten the mood a little bit.'

Invasion and the McGathys thought including the music track was a good idea: maybe a funny song would get Bill big radio exposure, but Casperson said 'Chicks' needed more work; it seemed to him that Bill had written it in five minutes. The track needed to be juiced and the lyrics, Casperson told Bill, weren't on a par with his comedy prose.

Bill was having none of it. The song was finished and he loved it and it was staying on the album as it was. 'You're wrong,' he told Casperson over lunch. 'I guarantee you this record is going to sell 100,000 units,' he added. Bill wrote the figure out on a napkin and pushed it across the table.

If Invasion had misgivings about the new record, they still believed Bill could be a very big star. They knew Jack was on the way out, and made a strong pitch to take over Bill's management. They wanted to find a downtown venue where Bill could do his one-man show. That way industry could come down and hear him in a tasteful setting. And Bill was signed to William Morris's comedy and acting roster, but Casperson and Saporta felt their friend Johnny Podell, who was head of William Morris's concerts and music department, could do more. They got Podell to agree to get his friend Lorne Michaels down to hear Bill. Casperson and Saporta had an idea about developing a Bill Hicks minute for *Saturday Night Live*. He wouldn't be part of the cast exactly; each week he would do a short rant as himself, the ultimate urban cynic.

Sounds good, Bill said. But first, he told Casperson and Saporta, he wanted to take time off, maybe drive across the country. He talked about spending a few days in his beloved Sedona desert by himself, just chilling out. He scheduled a week-long gig over the holidays in West Palm Beach and planned to spend Christmas Day eating turkey with friends at Colleen's little house.

On 2 January 1992, Channel Four beamed *Relentless* into British homes at 11.35 p.m. In London, sixteen-year-old Chris Lahr switched on the family television. Bill Hicks was just about to rip into the phony

Gulf War. 'Like Iraq was ever, or could ever, under any stretch of the imagination, be any threat to us *whatsoever*...' The teenager watched, captivated, for a few moments. Then he yelled downstairs to his father, John Lahr, theater critic for *The New Yorker*, to come see.

TWENTY

*Beep. Hello? Helloo? Hello? Okay, well, it's me. I'm at home.
I rented three of the newest pornographic epics. 'Cause I, my
friend, have a life. And uh, intend to live it to the fullest here at
thirty-one years of age in my empty apartment, sitting here in the
unholy glow from television.*

Suddenly, Bill was the talk of Britain. *Dangerous* was selling over
there, about double what it had done in the United States.

Bill, meanwhile, was busy moving himself and his Nintendo into
a small apartment on Barrington Street in West Los Angeles. The
place was nothing special but it was right around the corner from
Igby's, his favorite club.

He called back east to tell Casperson and Saporta that he
had just signed with the Hollywood firm Moress Nanas Shea.
They represented Albert Brooks, who was one of Bill's favorites.
Herb Nanas, also a veteran producer, had represented Roseanne
Barr.

Now free of Mondrus, Bill was determined to cut back on road
work. The English tour was coming up, the *Relentless* CD was coming
out and Bill thought he'd settle into Los Angeles life, take some
acting classes and start going to yoga. He would quit smoking once
and for all. It was the last indulgence.

Buzzing from the validation of the last few months, what he
really wanted to do was focus on the whole movie thing – still, as
always, the ultimate dream. Bill felt like he had a hundred scripts in
him. He had one about Elvis that he wanted to give to his new
manager, Bob Shea. It was called 'The King's Last Tour'. Elvis
comes home and is unable to prove his existence among a sea of
impersonators. Colonel Tom Parker, who engineered Elvis's getaway,

is now so rich he has a different house for each month of the year. The slippery manager isn't too happy to see his King.

Shea encouraged Bill to get a laptop computer so he could write while he traveled, but Bill could never get the hang of it. He called it the ten-pound weight. He ended up writing 'The King's Last Tour' longhand on a legal pad and Shea's assistant typed the final draft.

Bill had one other goal: he told Shea that he wanted to get on *The Tonight Show* before Carson retired. With four months of Carson left, all kinds of performers angling for a final appearance, getting booked would be a hat trick.

Casperson and Saporta were a trifle disappointed about Bill's signing with Moress Nanas Shea. Nevertheless they worked with Shea to promote the release of *Relentless*, setting up a bigger marketing budget than they had had for *Dangerous*. Together, they organized a domestic tour to precede the May UK dates, made up new posters and each took out ads in local college papers. Invasion hired people to flyer college campuses at every town he'd been in and the progressive *College Music Journal* (*CMJ*) wrote him up. The McGathys came aboard again and worked the radio stations. Bill McGathy did a special radio edit of 'Chicks Dig Jerks' and got it on some morning radio shows.

Again, Bill put his own warning sticker on the back of the CD, to go with the mandatory parental advisory one. This one said: 'This album contains everything your parents hate, everything the church preaches against, and everything the government fears. Enjoy. Bill Hicks.' Bill joked to Allan Havey on Comedy Central's *Night After Night* that he thought the PMRC warning labels actually helped sales.

'You know, who buys an album that doesn't have a warning on it?'

Comedy albums, Havey noted, weren't that popular anymore. 'Why come out with one?' he asked.

'You're right, it's not like these are giant sellers,' Bill said. This way, though, he could do an idea from beginning to end, and without the watchful eye of television. 'There's stuff on here I'd like to think is fairly realistic beliefs people have, but you don't see elucidated anywhere . . . To me, it's like leaving a body of work.'

The McGathys invited Bill to perform at their annual industry party, an important date in the music business. Every year radio personnel, record label honchos and rock stars showed up to see important new bands play. The McGathys had never had a comedian perform before, but of course they thought Bill was rock incarnate.

Benny Mardones, whose 'Into The Night' was a big hit in the late eighties, introduced him. 'Lenny Bruce died before I had a chance to see him live,' Mardones said. 'Well, I'm going to tell you something. The voice of our generation is here tonight. And as far as I'm concerned first there was Mickey Mantle, then there was Elvis Presley, and now, ladies and gentleman, the one and only Bill Hicks.'

Despite the rousing intro, Bill was half drowned out by the buzz of people busy networking. It pissed him off and the set grew darker and darker.

'These rockers who don't do drugs? ... They suck suck suck suck! Soul-less ball-less pieces of shit! They were made to do fuckin' Pepsi and Taco Bell commercials! ... They suck Satan's cock on a regular fuckin' basis. *AHORRRRRRROOOOOOOOO.* Suck that black wormy jizz down your gullet you soulless piece of shit! You SUCK!!!!'

Half the industry crowd went dead silent and half cheered. Bill spotted Jon Bon Jovi in the audience.

'*And you can take that to the fuckin' bank and you can cash it!* And live the rest of your soulless piece of shit life! And yeah,' he cried, stabbing his finger into the air, 'this does mean you, you *fuckin'* losers!'

For all that attitude and exposure, including a March appearance on *Late Night*, Bill should have been an easy sell that year. Nirvana had just blown up the airwaves with *Nevermind*, knocking Michael Jackson off *Billboard*'s Number One spot the week of 11 January 1992. If Bill's aesthetic wasn't punk, his sensibility was, and if there were a moment for America to embrace his anti-corporate message, it was then.

But a comedy CD just wasn't going to fly off the shelves, and it was as if Montreal and Britain hadn't happened. Even when he did a flurry of interviews to promote *Relentless*, no reporter in the American press, from *Texas Monthly* to the *Contra-Costa Times*, seemed to be at all aware – or they simply didn't report – that Bill had just been recognized, internationally, as an important new voice. They did acknowledge him in *Texas Monthly* as 'the most talented American comedian working the circuit these days' and noted his reputation as 'a comedian of ferocious passion and intellect'. There was nothing about how he had been the breakout star of an international comedy festival, had won the Critics Award at Edinburgh, had his own critically lauded special on Channel Four or that, as they went to press, Bill would be doing a seventeen-date sold-out theatrical tour of the UK. They just dutifully plugged his comedy record.

Not that there weren't pockets of America where Bill was a cult figure. Austin, San Francisco and Chicago were perennial Hicks towns. At Stephens College in Columbia, Missouri, DJ Zoe Taylor played cuts off *Dangerous* on her Saturday morning radio show every chance she got. When she did a long rambling phone interview with Bill in April, what she wanted to straighten out, first and foremost, was the ugly rumors that he was giving up cigarettes.

'You haven't quit smoking.'

'No.'

'Good! I almost lost faith in you.'

'No. Get this. I tried that nicotine gum, right? Smoked while chewing it. And then I ran out of gum. So basically I was getting twice as much nicotine. And then I had to double my cigarettes when I ran out of gum. It horribly backfired on me.'

It was nice to talk to an American fan. They had talked once before, Taylor reminded Bill, and he had promised her he would name his second record after her. Bill apologized profusely and told her he had met a girl named Relentless the following week.

'It's weird that I'm going over to England and I'm playing these colleges,' Bill said. 'Aren't there colleges in America? Aren't there colleges, say, in the surrounding area of my apartment? Why do I have to go to England to do a college?'

'They're waiting for you.'

'Oh, my God. Yeah, waiting for me with their wan, pale skin and their bad teeth. "Bill, you're just brilliant. Brilliant, Bill, just brilliant." Everything's brilliant over there, right? "You're just brilliant. Oh, Bill, it's just absolutely brilliant." And you think, "Cool! Brilliant! All right, I like that!" Then you go out to eat with them. "This tea is just brilliant! Isn't it? Oh, I love this fish! It's brilliant!" Oh, *man . . .*'

Bill said he would perform for his fans at Stephens College if Taylor would put together a gig for him someplace cool in Columbia, a jazz club maybe, and if that didn't work, he would fly his Columbia fan base to Los Angeles. 'You've been very nice to me and I see no reason why you should have to drive to London to see me,' Bill said.

Taylor gave him her number. 'This is great,' he said happily. 'Be my new muse.'

Another Hicks fan, Dennis Miller, had just left his Weekend Update post at *Saturday Night Live* and was now doing a new syndicated show called *The Dennis Miller Show*. They invited Bill on right away.

It turned out to be one of Bill's best TV appearances ever. Miller was so pleased to have Bill on that he immediately dispensed with canned formalities. 'I don't even want to read the intro for this guy 'cause it's all like . . . pap,' he announced. 'I'll just tell you that in my book: one of the best comedians in the world. A discernible point of view, great mind, attitude, the whole bag. He works completely for me, this is Bill Hicks.'

'Bill*ee*!'

Bill looked great, tall and lean with, for once, a good haircut. He did a few minutes of stand-up before crossing to the couch, some funny material about seeing *Basic Instinct* over the weekend: 'A really terrible terrible movie. Really. It's like a bad *Streets of San Francisco* episode, you know?'

'Can I plug something for you?' Miller offered as Bill settled into his chair.

'Yeah. Okay,' Bill replied, laughing. 'I'm going to London on Sunday for a month.'

'London?'

'Yeah. Giggles,' Bill quipped. 'No, I'm going over to the UK for a month.'

'Yeah?' Miller replied. 'Leary's big over there.'

'Yeah.'

'Isn't he? Denis Leary?'

'Oh yeah,' Bill answered. 'It's weird, their comedy scene is, like, where ours was five years ago.'

Bill looked slightly shocked at what had just come out of his mouth – and the two erupted in laughter again.

'Ooh! Sorry, Denis,' Miller said, grinning. 'There's a cold shot!'

On 29 April Bill took off from LAX to London. When he landed at Heathrow eleven hours later, the news was everywhere: while Bill was en route, the four white LAPD officers – Sergeant Stacey Koon, Laurence Powell, Theodore Briseno and Timothy Wind – caught on videotape savagely beating twenty-five-year-old black suspect Rodney King, were acquitted by an all-white jury. Los Angeles had burst into a flame of protest and fury and rioting was spreading from South Central throughout the city. For Bill, who had already started to wish he hadn't left New York, it was one more reason to despise LA.

'Officer *Koon*,' Bill began saying at the top of his shows. 'Is life too fucking weird or what?'

Bob Gold had booked Bill into mostly university theaters throughout the UK, and Channel Four rebroadcast *Relentless* as Bill kicked off his tour. On 1 May, Bill did his first show in Glasgow and then zigzagged all over the country playing Edinburgh, Manchester, Liverpool, Sheffield, Birmingham, Nottingham, Leicester and Leeds. 'It sold out everywhere,' Shea recalled. 'I went on the last four days with Bill and it was wonderful, the response. The English are much more open and have much more respect for performers . . . I think he was fairly overwhelmed. He was gratified that he found a forum for performing that was bigger than the 150-seat comedy club in Columbia, South Carolina.'

He did seventeen dates and on 17 May arrived at the Queen's Theatre. Bill, riding high off weeks of packed houses and thrilled students, pulled off an electrifying show. Shea considered it a complete triumph. 'It was a magical evening. Bill was remarkably relaxed before the show, and took the stage to a wildly enthusiastic reception. He was absolutely electrifying.' Shea turned to Charles Brand and suggested that they think about taping another special of Bill, this time in London. Perhaps Moress Nanas Shea and Tiger could do some kind of co-production.

When Shea returned to LA, he took out a full page in the special comedy issue of the *Hollywood Reporter* touting the success of Bill's first major UK tour and advertising *Relentless* on Invasion Records, available everywhere. He and Herb Nanas began talks with HBO about a one-hour special.

A couple of nights later, on Friday 22 May, Johnny Carson hosted *The Tonight Show* for the last time.

Bill had made enough of an impression on the British as a caustic observer of American life that, as the 1992 presidential race heated up that summer, they wanted his constant commentary on Clinton v. Bush. The BBC's *Jonathan Ross Show* interviewed Bill via satellite from London. With a long time delay, the entire exchange was hilariously awkward.

Ross began by informing Bill it was National Prune Week in Britain and then asked him about the New Hampshire primaries.

'I'm told they are very significant indeed,' Ross ventured. 'Why are they so significant?'

'I have no idea,' Bill deadpanned. 'They're not significant to me.'

Ross asked what was happening with Clinton. 'Because the papers I was reading the other day suggest he is making a bit of a comeback.'

'Not with all these women making allegations about him,' Bill said.

What were Bill's feelings on the electoral system generally?

'Well, I hope to overthrow the American government and replace it with a freely elected democracy.'

It was great that the British press were willing to do a satellite interview with him halfway across the world, but Bill couldn't understand why he couldn't get arrested in Los Angeles. He had moved all the way to this cultural wasteland with its 'hot and sunny

weather every single day' and its 'lizard-skin iguana blondes' and all
he did was go talk to sitcom producers. At first, Bill thought it
would be good to get acquainted with the whole process and he
always came in with lots of ideas, including a nascent proposal for a
salon-type show called *Counts of the Netherworld* that he was working
on with Fallon, but no executive thought his stuff would go over
with the average American.

'Today he would be a mad prophet of the airwaves,' said Jimmy
Miller, who manages Jim Carrey and Gary Shandling. 'He'd be on
HBO, interviewing people, saying whatever's on his mind. But back
then the comedy business just hadn't matured. They didn't know
what to do with him.

'The problem was that what he wanted to say and what people
wanted him to say were two different things,' Shea recalled. 'It's so
funny, I remember meetings and meetings and meetings with production companies like Carsey-Werner and Disney and he would
walk out of the meetings going, '*Ugh*'. It was what was going on at
the time and what still goes on: someone spots a terrific stand-up
comic who could become a comedic actor and they want to plug
him into a sitcom. He didn't want to do that. What he really wanted
to do, and what I wanted him to do, was express his opinions.'

Bill's sour mood was aggravated by quitting smoking (after some
false starts he was on the patch) and, after all this time, still missing
Pamela. He knew it wouldn't work but he couldn't help calling her
up now and then, arranging the occasional weekend rendezvous.
Why wasn't he meeting any decent women? he asked his friends.

'Bill,' Fallon said. 'Look where we work. You don't find your life
partner in a comedy club. And of course you attract psychos. Look
at your act.'

'It's not my act!'

Meanwhile, he boiled over with hatred for LA, but it was okay
because an ode of sorts to that godforsaken place was beginning to
simmer in his head. He liked to fantasize that southern California
would be called 'Arizona Bay' once it finally dropped into the ocean.

The good news was Tiger TV was planning to tape his show at
London's Dominion Theatre in November for another Channel

Four special. With Moress Nanas Shea as co-producers, HBO said they wanted it for a one-hour special but they were being slow to commit. Until then, it was just him in his little apartment, sitting on his futon strumming his beloved Gibson Les Paul guitar, craving a goddamned cigarette.

TWENTY-ONE

Beep. Oh God. *This is just* so *aggravating. Well I'll be in Glasgoo tomorrow and I guess I'll try you then. Oh my* Gooooooooooood. *Madeleine Stowe is the babe of all time, by the way. I saw* Unlawful Entry *and* The Last of the Mohicans. *If this elegant delicate creature does not break your fuckin' heart in a thousand pieces then you apparently have been watching* Reservoir Dogs.

3 November 1992, 8.43 a.m.

Slightly dazed, Bill sat on a pastel couch in London the morning of the American election. Actually, his countrymen were still fast asleep. His first day in Britain, he was appearing on TV-AM alongside Cindy Crawford to talk about the action back home.

'If Bush wins,' Bill ventured, 'I will be "flat" hunting here in London. And if Clinton wins I will return with my return ticket. Yeah, you know it's pretty interesting times in America. Not only are we waking up from the American Dream, we're coming to in the emergency room following a horrible accident. All we can recollect was some guy named Reagan was driving. Margaret Thatcher was in the back seat, telling him which way to turn: "Go right! Go right!"'

The co-hostess told Bill he was 'an extremely naughty man' as she showed a very brief clip of the *Relentless* show, one of few she could air at that hour.

'Did you enjoy that?' the hostess asked Crawford at the end of Bill's segment.

'I think I appreciated the American subtlety of it,' she said.

Bill howled.

The week improved immeasurably as *Scallywag*, a British political

satire magazine, asked Bill to write a regular column and he met
with Charles Brand and Seamus Cassidy about a proposal for *Counts
of the Netherworld*. Over the summer, Bill and Fallon (back in Kansas
City) had prepared a treatment, a 'Counts Manifesto', to give to
Tiger.

The way Bill and Fallon conceived it, in their marathon phone
calls, the *Counts* salon would be comparable to the sixties coffee-
houses or fifties jazz clubs: a safe haven where new ideas, in
opposition to the conventional wisdom, could be explored. The
Counts, 'spokesmen for the damned', would dissect the official story
on gun control, religion, pornography, advertising, consumerism,
imperialism and the mass media. They would have thought-provok-
ing guests come on for 'spontaneous conversation', such as Bill's
champions, Noam Chomsky and Martin Amis. *Money* was one of
Bill's favorite books.

Bill and Fallon saw *Counts* as a panacea to the cultural sludge
spooned out by the mass media. 'For all who've ever asked themselves,' Bill wrote, 'in reference to the world, "Is it just me, or does
this suck?", take heart!'

The demographic? The masses who were seeking 'heroes who
give voice to the decency, commonsense, and love of freedom that
exists in us all'.

Brand and Cassidy very much wanted to produce Bill on a regular
basis. The way they saw it, *Counts* needed a lot of shaping, and
Fallon was an unknown quantity, but if you were so lucky as to have
the John Lennon of comedy walk into your office, you worked with
him.

That Friday, 6 November, Bill started his 'Revelations' tour up
north in Manchester. That time around, Bill's notoriety was enough
that Bob Gold had bumped up the venues to almost double their
size and Bill was playing twenty-three dates, and touring Ireland as
well. 'Bill's posters were all over town and people were stopping him
in the street,' Shea recalled. 'It was really terrific. Bill was a very shy
guy. But I think he enjoyed the attention.'

'He did desperately want to be a star,' Hedge agreed. 'But not in
a wrong way. He wanted to be a star because he wanted his talent

recognized. He realized – which most people with a big talent also realize – that they deserve to have attention paid.'

Bill thanked Mike Hedge and Bob Gold over and over. 'It's just unbelievable, it's great,' he would say.

'Once I mentioned that I liked freesias,' Hedge recalled. 'They're a delicate flower and they're expensive. Not much bigger than a cigarette. Well, he had delivered to my office, it must have been 100 quid's worth of freesias. Stunk the whole office out. That was just a gesture, no occasion.'

Bill was booked on *The Word*, Channel Four's flash and trash Friday night talk show hosted by DJ Terry Christian and aimed at Britain's teens.

Bill winced at the idea but Hedge convinced him. Yes, the show was atrocious but its ratings were huge. 'Until people know who you are, they won't know how talented you are,' Hedge reasoned. 'Even the Beatles had to do crap. Elvis, too.'

When Paul Ross, the producer of *The Word*, popped into the dressing room and asked Bill what kinds of jokes he told, Bill got a little tense. Then Ross popped in a video cassette of pre-taped segments for that night's show. When Bill saw their tribute to Aaron Spelling, creator of *Beverley Hills 90210* and *Charlie's Angels*, he groaned and shot Hedge a look. Ross told him how the show had a great prank that night: producers had brought Britain's favorite drunk, actor Oliver Reed, to a pub before the show and now they were planning to train a secret camera on him in his dressing room.

'I am not doing this show,' Bill announced. The publicist started to tell Bill why he absolutely *had* to go on – he had pulled strings to get Bill booked – and Mike, catching the look on Bill's face, had to ask the guy to leave the room. 'To see this after we'd just talked Bill round! Bill didn't like the idea that Oliver Reed was as drunk as he was,' Hedge said. 'He didn't like that they were exploiting him.'

'Mike,' Bill asked, 'do you honestly think it matters if I do this show? I mean, is it really going to help my career?'

'Probably not,' Hedge answered. 'Not this show. But if we walk out nobody else will touch us.'

Seated on the big red couch next to Christian, Bill managed to smile and cough up witty soundbites when directly questioned. But he looked like he desperately wanted a cigarette. Lillia, the Soviet supermodel (*She left food shortages for shorter hemlines!*), sat next to him and answered Christian's questions about fleeing her country.

'We could trade flats for a summer,' Bill suggested.

A few days before the Dominion show, Bob Shea and Herb Nanas arrived in London. They had flown first class, which pissed Bill off no end. He was already embarrassed that Charles Brand, the guy who had done so much for him (and who was developing a show for him), had been bank-rolling the production alone. HBO's money was critically late to arrive via Moress Nanas Shea (who were the executive producers on the HBO side) and Brand admitted to Hedge that he was feeling financially exposed. When Bill heard that, he was mortified.

Now here they were, Bill hissed into the phone during one of his daily conversations with Colleen, acting like this was Hollywood, asking people to get them coffee. His managers rode in a limo and everybody else involved with the production took the tube. And they were staying at the glitzy new Chelsea Harbour Hotel, while Bill himself stayed in a modest little place elsewhere.

'Yes, they were a wonderful caricature,' Brand said. 'They were in almost matching Armani suits and the beautiful Gucci shoes. I am certain they were doing what is considered right and correct in Los Angeles. But Bill being who he was and knowing the people we had around us at C4, they did stick out like a huge sore thumb.'

Still more tension arose from the fact that Mike Hedge, who had been acting as Bill's de facto manager in the UK, had to take a back seat once Shea and Nanas arrived. 'Here were his managers but they were doing things that Bill felt was the wrong way for here,' Hedge said. 'Because he'd been quite happy with the way it'd been going along. So that was very uneasy.' Having managed Squeeze and stage-managed Pink Floyd and Elvis Costello, Hedge had years of experience setting up live shows. So Bill continued to confide chiefly in him and told Brand and Bob Gold not to go through his American managers, but to speak to him directly.

As if things weren't rocky enough, the night of the show Bill had a bad head cold and it was going to be everything he could do to get through the show. He was also worried that director Chris Bould (who had shot *Relentless* in Montreal) had gone too far with the stage design, a sort of apocalyptic Wild West skyline. He thought the scale of it would dwarf him.

'Chris, I can't come on,' he fretted, looking at the huge black opening upstage that he was to enter through. 'I can't come on. It's too fucking big.' Chris promised him it would look fantastic.

And just an hour or so before show time, John Lahr was coming to see him. Lahr was planning to profile Bill for *The New Yorker*. He felt that Bill was doing something that very few people were capable of doing: thinking against society.

Bill was elated to hear that. He wanted to push this new show, *Revelations*, to yet another level. If his previous work zeroed in on the issues and personalities of the day, with Bush out of the White House Bill was now less interested in the cartoonish villains of the far right. And turning around to hammer the new boy, Clinton, didn't excite him. It was all the Business Party anyway. He was less interested in their personalities than their tools: mind control, propaganda and the struggle it presented to true freedom – and, fundamentally, transcendence. 'My act now is bigger, less specific about personalities and more about attitudes,' he explained to *Time Out*. 'It's only made me get better, actually.'

Bill met Lahr backstage and he invited the writer up to his dressing room. As they walked up the stairs, he told Lahr, 'To me, the comic is the guy who says "Wait a minute" as the consensus forms. He's the antithesis of the mob mentality. The comic is a flame – like Shiva the Destroyer, toppling idols no matter what they are. He keeps cutting everything back to the moment. (The Shiva reference had special meaning to Bill, who had pulled the word out of *William Melvin Hicks* while doodling on a pad during an anagram game.)

Bill paced his dressing room, a funny narrow corridor-like room that looked out over the theater, admitting that he was in a quandary as to whether he should just pull up stakes and move to England or stay in America. He wondered if it would ever happen for him in America. He just couldn't seem to take root there. 'Comedy in the States has been totally gutted,' he told Lahr. 'It's commercialized. They don't have people on TV who have points of view, because that defies the status quo, and we can't have that in the totalitarian mind-control government that runs the fuckin' airwaves.' Lahr thought the big problem was that his ironic voice was alien to the American sensibility. 'The American idiom,' Lahr wrote, 'is optimism.'

A few minutes before he went on, Bill asked Lahr to leave so he could be alone. He liked to say a prayer before he took the stage.

The lights inside the Dominion went down and Bould cued the light on the moon. He started the wind sound. The dogs barked. The bass line of 'Voodoo Child' began to vibrate through the theater. The enormous monolith rose up and Bill, dressed in black jeans, a black cowboy hat and matching duster coat, strutted slowly through the flames to center stage. A silhouette of fiery ruins framed his tall figure. This was theater rock.

'You're in the right place,' he told the audience. 'It's Bill.'

He started out talking about the weather like a nice comic. He did some more stuff about the bombing of Iraq. They loved that. The Kennedy assassination bit went over big. They just adored the rant on Christian fundamentalists. Of course, the 1,500 left-leaning *Guardian* readers were on Bill's side before he even walked out. And to Bill, there was nothing more boring than preaching to the converted.

So he introduced them to Goat Boy. Randy Pan the Goat Boy. More than a new character, Goat Boy was his new onstage alter ego, his unleashed, rampaging libido. Goat Boy eats porn for breakfast. Goat Boy loves young girls. He loves it when they sit on his face. He wants to wear them like a feedbag.

'Why do you like young girls, Goat Boy?'

'Because you are beautiful. There's nothing between your legs. It's like a wisp of cotton candy framing a paper cut. Ha ha ha. Gnorr. And turn you around and open your cheeks, it's like a little pink quivering rabbit nostril.'

Charles Brand listened as the crowd collectively drew its breath.

I remember being aware of how much his material was really quite fiercely anti-PC. Because your initial inclination on Bill's material was how incredibly clever he was at attacking a lot of cultural and political faces of the States. Seeing an American comic do it about America was such a liberation. And when he did this show, there was really quite a long section, a lot of which didn't go to air, which was about sex . . . Not just porn in advertising. It was about twenty minutes and a lot of it was quite favorable to porn. And you could feel this politically left-correct audience go, 'This guy likes pornography! Well, why shouldn't he? He's a libertarian comic. He has very radical views.'

If Bill lost his momentum slightly, those who were still with him at the end of his porntasia probably got that it was all by way of confronting the audience and their middle-class sensibilities in the most immediate way he could think up. Pornography, Bill often said, was in the eye of the beholder.

Brand thought it was bold. He'd have to cut a lot of it, but he thought it was bold.

The second half of the show, Bill turned to talk of evolution and the higher state of consciousness he believed was available to anyone who took advantage of what God left planted for us: mushrooms and marijuana. Bill imagined the Lord's dilemma.

'If I leave pot everywhere, that's going to give humans the impression they're supposed to . . . *use* it.'

Bill sighed. 'Now I have to create Republicans.'

'And God wept.'

He ended on a serious note. The world, he said, is like an amusement-park ride. Our minds are so powerful, it seems real. The people who have been on the ride a very long time begin to question whether it is real or just a ride. 'And other people have remembered, and they come back to us, and they say, "Hey. Don't worry, don't be afraid, ever, because . . . this is just a ride."'

Bill added that we can change the ride any time we want, that it's a choice, right now, between fear and love. He said that we could explore space together, inner and outer, 'forever in peace'.

Right on cue the sound of three 'gunshots' echoed through the theater.

The next morning Bill went to John Lahr's house for tea. They were going to talk some more for the profile. Bill was tired and sort of distracted. He wasn't all that happy with his show. Later he said he was running on two cylinders that night and that he took all the credit for the crowd not laughing. He probably meant the audible gasp at Goat Boy and that's what he mostly wanted to talk about with Lahr. 'He's not Satan,' he told Lahr. 'He's not Evil. He's nature ... There is no America. It's just a big pavement now to him. That's the whole point.'

John's son, Chris, came into the kitchen. 'I don't know how you have the courage to say those things,' he said. Bill smiled.

TWENTY-TWO

Beep. *Hey buddy, it's Willy. I'm at the airport in Raleigh, North Carolina, on my way to West Palm Beach. A little tired. First the good news. It looks like Tiger is going to give us the money to develop* Counts of the Netherworld. *Did you hear that? Okay, well I'll talk to you later. Adieu.*

'I'm over in fuckin' England and Bush fuckin' *loses*!' Bill cried. 'Must have been a Secret Service plot,' he added. 'To protect Bush, you know – his eardrums from shattering when I *shrieked* with fucking laughter: *AAAAAAAAAAAAAAAAAHAAAAAAHAAAAAAAA-AAAA!*'

Bill was performing at the Laff Stop in Austin only a week after he'd returned from the UK in December and his loyal audience screamed with him. Bill was there to record material for his third live CD which he planned to call *Arizona Bay*. He didn't want to lose momentum.

His fans were not so thrilled to hear he had quit smoking.

Booooooo.

'Hey, what is this?' Bill yelled. 'Hey, don't boo me for this. This isn't like Dylan goes electric, you fuckers!' The smoking material was about freedom of choice, he explained. 'That was the *real* routine! C'mon, subtext fans!'

The crowd laughed and screamed for more as he left the stage. The fervent applause refused to let up and Bill came back out as Elvis, resplendent in his white jumpsuit, and sang 'Blue Christmas'.

'Thank ya. You're a beautiful audience. Outside in the parking lot, there's a brand new Cadillac for each and every one of you . . .'

*

'Man, I'm just touring endlessly,' Bill told Stephen Doster over a barbecue lunch the next day. 'I'm really going to have to slow down.'

'You've been saying that forever,' Doster said. 'This has been since you're eighteen years old. You never take any time off.'

Bill was aching to meet someone and he was starting to think about cool towns he might want to live in, maybe Austin or London. At this rate, he said, he couldn't even commit to taking care of a fish. But at least he had a little money now from the HBO deal. He had gone out and bought himself a black Jeep Wrangler. It was the first time Doster had ever seen him buy himself anything nice. And that afternoon, Bill took Doster into a record store and bought him three Nirvana records: *Bleach*, *Nevermind* and *Incesticide*.

In January, the American Comedy Awards again nominated Bill for Best Male Stand-up Comic. His competitors were Will Durst, Richard Jeni, Ritch Shydner and George Wallace. Each nominee got to put his picture and a little quote in the awards ceremony program to be held in March in Los Angeles. Bill wrote:

Pornography is good.
All drugs should be legal.
War is wrong.
The rich get richer.
The poor get poorer.
Thank you I'll be here all week.

Richard Jeni won.

Bill was on the lookout for new management. He was anxious to get *Counts* going with Tiger, and, since he'd returned from the UK, he'd been distancing himself from Moress Nanas Shea. He'd thought seriously about signing with Mike Hedge, who'd essentially been acting as his manager in the UK, but he didn't like the idea of tying up all his interests with Invasion. He was still pissed off about their reaction to Marblehead Johnson. Mainly though, as he explained to Hedge, he needed a manager who lived in the United States, someone who could help him find the recognition that still eluded him there.

'That's my home,' Bill said, 'and that's where I want to be a success.'

Duncan Strauss and Colleen McGarr were now a couple of years into a long-distance relationship and were starting a management company together. Duncan was already an established manager in Los Angeles, representing several stand-ups, and Colleen informally handled a few guys in West Palm Beach for Fantasma. They had often talked about how their dream client would be Bill Hicks and Duncan thought it might be a possibility now.

'You don't understand,' Colleen said. 'One of his managers wears a diamond-lizard brooch.'

Still, when Bill mentioned to Colleen that he had been wanting to get on E! Television's *Stand-Up Sit Down* show, Colleen told him she knew the bookers and offered to work it out for him. Bill wanted to do the show because Robert Klein was the host and there would be an interview afterward.

'Colleen, it tapes at *Disney World*,' the *Stand-Up Sit Down* booker reminded her when she called. Colleen assured her Bill would come with the right set. But when Bill settled into his Disney hotel room with his Mickey sheets and Mickey towels and Mickey toothbrush he began to wonder if he could pull it off.

'Do you think this was a mistake?' he asked Colleen. She had driven up from West Palm Beach to hang out with him and lend some moral support.

'Let's just remember this is Robert Klein,' she said. 'You only have to do seventeen minutes, then there's the interview.'

Bill, in longish hair, a full beard and granny glasses, looked slightly pained as he trudged through the first few minutes of his show at the Pleasure Island comedy club. He said how hard it was to have a relationship and did his joke about how it was either going to take one very special woman or several average ones. 'I'm soliciting sex at Disney World,' he said, shaking his head.

Suddenly the absurdity of the scene clicked for him and the set came alive.

'*Whooo*. I want you to know, folks, there is no weirder booking than me at Disneyland [sic]. Okay? If you notice this sweat coming down my face this is called editing going on in front of your eyes. Massive editing! Like a gardener with hedge clippers. *HARAAAH! HARAAAA! HARAAH!*

Bill ran back and forth across the stage, a crazed gardener whacking away at unruly shrubs.

'There is no weirder booking than me at Disneyland! HAAA-AAAAAAAAA.' He shrieked with laughter and the tourists laughed back with him.

Colleen and Bill went out after for sushi and Bill's favorite, green tea ice cream. The Klein interview had gone well, and Bill let Colleen listen to an early version of *Arizona Bay* in the car. 'Oh, Invasion's going to love this,' she told him. Colleen didn't say anything about the management thing. They were such good friends, she cringed when she thought of how embarrassing it could be for them both. What if he had to say no?

On 6 March, Bill and Kevin drove an hour north from Austin (where they were mixing *Arizona Bay* in Kevin's home studio) to the little town of Waco. They were heading for the Branch Davidian compound to get a look at the FBI stake-out, which had kicked off after a failed raid a week earlier on the 'Ranch Apocalypse' resulted in the death of four ATF agents and six Branch Davidians. As always, Bill was interested in fundamentalism gone awry.

Bill was fascinated by the Branch Davidians' thirty-three-year-old leader, David Koresh. Koresh was born Vernon Wayne Howell in Houston to a fifteen-year-old single mother, had a lonely childhood as a misfit, and headed for Hollywood in the late seventies to become a rock star. When that didn't work out, he moved to Waco in 1981 and joined a splinter group of the Seventh-Day Adventists, the Branch Davidians. By 1990 he was leader of the group and all the women in the compound became his 'spiritual wives', which gave him sole sexual access. He preached to his 130-odd member flock that Armageddon was going to start with a battle at the Branch Davidian compound and he had eleven tons of ammunition, including anti-tank rifles. Bill said Koresh reminded him of himself 'without the guns and pussy'.

With Kevin's video camera turned on, he and Bill got past troopers and sneaked in through some dirt roads closer to the action, but it was hard to see the ranch beyond the mile of satellite trucks. There were groups of bored looking reporters clustered together and a Salvation Army truck dispensing doughnuts and hot dogs to law enforcement and the press. 'The smell is just wafting over the fields,' Bill joked. 'I think that may be part of the strategy to get them out.'

As they drove down I-35 back to Austin, Bill popped in a tape of Denis Leary's new comedy album, *No Cure for Cancer*. As he and Kevin listened, Bill's mouth dropped.

'. . . whinin' fuckin' maggots,' Leary ranted of therapy junkies.

A bunch of whinin' fuckin' maggots. That's what Bill called non-smokers in his audiences.

'. . . We live in a country where John Lennon takes six bullets in the chest,' Leary cried. 'Yoko Ono is standing right next to him. Not one fuckin' bullet!'

We live in a world where John Lennon was murdered yet Barry Manilow cccccccontinues to put out fuckin' albums! Bill had said on *Dangerous* four years ago.

'. . . All these rock stars should have been killed, man,' Leary said. 'Every single goddamn one of 'em. Right after John Lennon died we should have got in the Partridge Family bus and driven around and killed 'em all one by one.'

If you're gonna kill someone, have some fuckin' taste. I'll drive you to Kenny Rogers's house. Get in the car, I know where Wham! lives, Bill had declared on *Dangerous*.

Bill was furious. All these years, aside from the occasional jibe, he'd pretty much shrugged off Leary's lifting. Comedians borrowed, stole stuff and even bought bits from one another. Milton Berle and Robin Williams were famous for it. This was different. Leary had, practically line for line, taken huge chunks of Bill's act and *recorded* it.

Once Bill finished venting his anger to Kevin, he decided to let it go, once again, and focus his energies on finishing *Arizona Bay* with Kevin. They had scored the entire album with dissonant bluesy riffs from Marblehead Johnson. Bill considered it his most innovative work so far. 'It's kind of like New Age music which I play with the band underneath my comedy which is rather ... angry,' he said on Comedy Central's *Short Attention Span Theater*. 'And it has this neat healing effect on the comedy.' It was ironic that Bill even used the phrase 'New Age' considering how he much he hated, and loudly eschewed, the gooey inner child movement so popular in ... Arizona Bay.

When Bill sent the tape to Invasion in New York, their reaction was not exactly what Bill had in mind. As far as Casperson and Saporta were concerned, *Arizona Bay* was too soft and the music didn't work at all. No big surprise considering how they had felt about Marblehead Johnson the year before. Casperson flat out told Bill that he thought *Arizona Bay* was half finished.

'We wanted it sharper, harder, one step more controversial,' Saporta said. 'To me, that's what needed to happen for his career and to start selling records. I felt *Arizona Bay*, interesting as it was, was not executed in a way that we were going to win with it. And we said, "We're not putting it out."'

Bill had no intention of changing a thing. Not 'hard' enough? Considering that *Arizona Bay* opened with Bill's emphatic hope that Los Angeles drop into the ocean and segued into material on the Rodney King beating, the Kennedy assassination and George Bush's glorious defeat – *Call your little Vietnamese pot-belly Rush Limbaugh back to the fold, you demon fuck!* – he didn't know what the hell they were talking about. *Arizona Bay* was exactly what he wanted it to be and, rather than edit it, Bill decided to walk away from the label as per his contract when they refused to release it. Bill figured he'd look for a new label with better distribution.

Despite Bill's promise to Doster that he was going to take a breather, there seemed to be no time. The *Relentless* CD was distributed in Australia through BMG Records, and with a growing legion of fans there, in April 1993 Bill found himself in Australia at the Melbourne Comedy Festival. He was playing sixteen shows in three weeks at the Universal Theater.

Still committed to Bill despite his conflicts with Casperson and Saporta, Mike Hedge had set up the festival date for him. Invasion, oddly enough, still clung to the possibility that Bill would choose them for management. Casperson had met with Bill in New York where he was playing Caroline's the week before Melbourne, and he told him that Bill was the only reason they had bothered to keep Invasion's London office open. Bill promised to get back to him soon and a few days into the Melbourne gig, Casperson faxed Bill's hotel in Melbourne. Since he hadn't heard from Bill, Peter wrote, he would have to shut down London – in other words, Mike Hedge was finished. Bill, meanwhile, had formally asked Colleen and Duncan to manage him. Duncan joked that he'd see if there were room on the roster.

Actually, the last thing Bill felt like dealing with was business. He was spending most of his time between shows in his hotel room stretched out on the bed. He felt really sick and very much alone and was calling Mike in London and Colleen in Florida once, even twice, a day. It was hard to describe what was bothering him – it was a presence, again, but worse this time, a swelling, in his stomach. Every time he had anything to eat it was as if he'd consumed an entire meal. It had to be something in the Chinese food he'd been ordering up to his room every day. It was the 'white mystery gwavy' he joked when he called Johndrow to find out what was going on with the continuing stand-off in Waco. The Australians (who, oddly enough, had a contingent in the Branch Davidian compound) were asking him about Koresh, Bill said.

'Tell them he's like every guy we know in Texas: a frustrated guitarist with a messianic complex,' Johndrow said. Bill got hysterical. That had to go in the act.

One night Hedge's phone rang as he was trying to leave the office. It was almost eight o'clock and he was nursing a hangover from the night before. It was Bill from Melbourne and again he was talking about not feeling right.

'What do you mean you don't feel right?'

'I just don't feel well. Maybe I've picked up a tropical parasite or something.'

'Well, Bill, go see a doctor,' Mike sighed. What the hell could *he* do about it from 6,000 miles away? 'Go get some antibiotics. It's probably a flu or something.'

'Well, I don't think it's that. I feel weird.'

Bill said he might have to cancel his TV appearance on a major talk show in Australia.

'You've *got* to do it,' Mike said. 'It's like canceling on *The Tonight Show.*'

He couldn't believe Bill was being such a nance.

TWENTY-THREE

Beep. Hmmmm. Maybe you did get that gig. Anyway, if you call and get this message I'm going to sleep. I hope, I hope, I hope. I've been sleeping all day and I gotta go to the doctor tomorrow. I've been having just a really kind of quiet night playing guitar. It's just a lot of fun. A lot of fun.

'I want to congratulate you because you were voted by *Rolling Stone* magazine as the Hot Comic of 1993,' Len Belzer told Bill on his syndicated radio show, *The Len Belzer Comedy Hour*, a few days after Bill returned from Australia. 'They've got a Hot Issue which will be on the stands 27 April. They're going to tell America everything that's hot and they've got one comic that's hot and his name is Bill Hicks. So congratulations. And you deserve it.' Bill had met Len Belzer, comedian Richard Belzer's brother, when he moved to New York and Bill had been appearing on his show regularly since *Dangerous*.

'Wow, that's incredible considering the fact that I wasn't in the country at all last year,' Bill said. 'And if this is any hint of how I should conduct my business I will completely disappear and see if I can't be a big star here.'

In fact, Bill was really excited to be home after three weeks on his own in Australia and he was full of energy. The nod from *Rolling Stone* was a real milestone; it was his first national feature, the first major acknowledgment that his star was rising, and Bill didn't want to waste a second. Now that he had new management, he couldn't wait to get to work. He, Colleen and Duncan agreed there were three main priorities: advance the *Counts* deal, find Bill a new record label and get him on to the American theater circuit. Duncan planned to use his press contacts to get serious theater critics out to see him.

Bill and Len Austrevich were working on a movie script together and Bill had enough material – and a title, *Rant in E-Minor* – for another comedy album which he planned to record as soon as possible.

As for the stomach bug he'd picked up, he was hoping it would clear up now that he was back. Mike Hedge called and wanted to know if he had seen a doctor like he promised he would. 'Yeah,' Bill said. 'They did some tests and I'm just waiting for the results.'

Actually, Bill was just putting him off. He hadn't really gone to the doctor. His medical insurance had lapsed and he needed to sort it out, but right now there was so much going on.

He did wonder, as he told Len Belzer on the air, if he would ever really fit in America. 'I really don't know,' Bill mused. 'It's going to take some massive changes in the mentality and the country for me to be an accepted quantity. Because like I said, I don't want to sell tennis shoes on TV. Everything in life doesn't have a price tag on it. It just doesn't. So where does that mentality fit in with what is happening in this world where all there is is talk of "how much it is". *How much is it? How much is he making?*

Not even the angry letters that Channel Four forwarded to Bill on behalf of British viewers, after *Revelations* was broadcast in the UK on 27 May, ruffled him very much. Seamus Cassidy, who was standing by Bill, supposed that the flood of complaints had to do with the show running at 10.35 p.m., an hour earlier than *Relentless* in 1991.

How ironic, Bill thought. He always felt so embraced in the UK and this was the most severe reaction to him on television yet. He read the letters of the indignant clergymen with particular interest. The Reverend Clark of St Leonard's Baptist Church in East Sussex wrote '... my deepest shock, and greatest complaint, was over his disgusting script concerning the basic tenets of Christianity. Whether or not Bill Hicks is a believer, I consider it beneath contempt to curse and swear about the "cross of Jesus" in order to raise cheap laughs. His continued use of the word "fucking" to describe the fundamentals of the Christian faith was dangerous, thoroughly and deliberately disrespectful and obscene.'

Furthermore, the Reverend Clark wrote, if the material had been disrespectful of Islam, they never would have broadcast it: 'Because we all know that Moslem believers are extremely likely to create an explosive reaction that would have deep-seated consequences.'

The Reverend Collins of Christ Church of Harrow found the program 'offensive and blasphemous' on behalf of his 800-odd parishioners and requested that Cassidy send him a copy of the video for review with the leaders of his church, one of whom was a member of the House of Lords.

Bill laughed about it with his friends, but he truly wanted to make the clergymen understand where he was coming from. Gradually he worked up an impassioned response. 'In his rebuttal he said, "This is about freedom and freedom of speech and words can't hurt you",' David Johndrow recalled. 'And then he was saying, "This is my church. I'm not going to show up at your church on a Sunday morning and start complaining that I don't agree with what you're saying. This is what I do and this is what I talk about and it's all freedom." Of course, I can't do it justice because he was a great writer. The letter was very rational and explaining that Bill was coming from a position of truth and understanding, and that he was a religious fellow as well. He was really explaining to the guy what was going on; it was not just a letter saying, "Fuck you."'

When Bill played the Laff Stop on 7 June in Austin, where he was recording material for *Rant*, he called Stephen Doster to meet him for a lunch at their favorite Indian place, Taj Palace. Still irritated by *Invasion*'s rejection, Bill wanted to know what Stephen thought of the tape of *Arizona Bay* he'd sent him. Doster couldn't believe how different the music to *Arizona Bay* was from the furious speed guitar stuff Bill had always liked. But the laid-back sound seemed to match Bill's mood and it was a lunch Doster didn't quickly forget.

'He had this real good vibe about him where he seemed more than ever at peace with himself. He was very focused but he seemed content,' Doster said. Stephen teased him that he wasn't taking off time like he had sworn he would back in January, but Bill just shrugged it off with a laugh. 'He really had his eye on the mark,'

Doster recalled. '"I've gotta get these records out. I got to make two more records, I'm gonna do this." I'm going "Wow, man."'

There was no time to idle. 'We're fighting an art war,' Bill said solemnly as he leaned across the table. His eyes seemed to turn darker and the look on his face was so intense that Doster almost expected him to rise up off his chair.

'And he said to me, "I do what I do so people won't feel alone." But there was none of this kind of self-important "I've got to save the world" type of thing with him. He was more like the little soldier fighting the good fight.'

As they walked out to the parking lot, Bill grabbed his side.

'You better have that checked out,' Stephen said.

'Oh, I have. I'm just fine,' Bill replied.

When Stephen got home, he tried to explain about the lunch to his wife, Melinda.

'I don't know where Bill can go from here,' he said.

'What do you mean?' she asked.

Stephen couldn't explain it.

'Thank you very much! Thank you! Goodnight.' Bill bent over slightly and pressed his hand into his stomach as he walked offstage at the Comedy Corner. It was Tuesday 15 June, the first night of a week-long gig in West Palm Beach. Colleen had scheduled a physical for him with her physician, Dr Donovan, on Thursday, but now she called him and said that the pain in Bill's side was becoming severe. Dr Donovan said he'd meet them at his office in the morning. It sounded like his gall bladder.

Upon examining Bill, Donovan detected a mass and immediately sent him for an ultrasound of his appendix and gall bladder. Both were clear. The doctor admitted Bill to the Good Samaritan Hospital next door for further tests.

'I've never seen anyone check into a hospital in such a good mood,' Colleen said. 'He'd been on the road non-stop and he was so happy to have no pandemonium, no suitcases. He had his little toys – Gameboy, pads of paper, books – and he could finally rest.'

For two days the doctors ran tests but came up with nothing. Finally on Thursday, Donovan ordered a liver biopsy. Bill said Colleen was his wife so that she could come in and hold his hand during the procedure. 'This looks really bad,' the technician said quietly to Colleen. She decided to try not to worry about it. He was just the technician.

Six o'clock Saturday morning, the phone rang next to Colleen's bed. It was Dr Donovan. Could Colleen meet him at the hospital?

William Donovan, an older man with four sons, had known Colleen a long time and he sounded heartbroken. Oncology had been his specialty for nearly thirty years, but, because of Bill's age, cancer had never occurred to him. Certainly not cancer of the pancreas, almost unheard of in people under fifty.

'Colleen,' Donovan said, 'this is the worst news I could give anybody.'

They decided to let Bill sleep.

A few hours later he woke up, the sun streaming in through his window, and saw Colleen tentatively put her head around the door. She walked in followed by Dr Donovan, and sat down next to Bill on his bed. Dr Donovan stood by and told Bill, in honest certain terms, the diagnosis. He had late stage pancreatic cancer, one of the most furtive lethal cancers, and it had spread to his liver. Bill shifted around in his white bedsheets, squirming, trying to absorb what the doctor was telling him. To Donovan, he looked like he'd been shot. Bill obviously didn't need anyone to explain his prognosis further. Dwight's mother had died of pancreatic cancer a few years ago and he knew that survival was, to put it mildly, highly unlikely.

Bill sat up. 'Okay. What's the battle plan?'

Donovan answered that they could start chemo immediately, and Bill could check out as soon as he signed the paperwork.

Bill and Colleen left the hospital at noon. They got into her car and Bill looked at her solemnly.

'Cigarette,' he said.

Colleen began to protest, realized how ridiculous she sounded, and handed him a Marlboro Light. He tore off the filter and lit up.

TWENTY-FOUR

Beep. God, I just love your cute messages so much. It just never gets old. Uh, it's Willy. I don't know where you've been at. We have some breaking news. Which I think you'll find interesting.

Colleen left Bill alone at her house so he could have some privacy while he called his brother. She drove to a payphone down the block and called Duncan, who was in Toronto at the People's Comedy Festival and staying with Colleen's mother, Elizabeth. Colleen had been keeping it together for Bill's sake but now she couldn't stop crying. It was surreal, as if she had woken that morning into a nightmare. Duncan was stunned and in tears when he heard Colleen choke out the words 'pancreatic cancer' but it wasn't until he talked to his parents a few hours later that he understood it was fatal.

Later that night, when Bill was in his suite at the Hilton, he called Fallon. 'Bad news,' Bill announced. But the cancer was just a detour, he assured Fallon; they were still going to plunge ahead with *Counts*. 'I guess now we need to pitch it as a cross between *Brian's Song* and *The Dick Cavett Show*,' he said.

The only other friend Bill called was Bob Fiorella, a comedian he had met a few years before at the Comedy Trap during a weekend engagement in Buffalo. They'd only hung out that one time in person but Bob was one of the phone buddies. He considered Bill his best friend. 'He wanted to talk to someone who had beaten something, I imagine,' said Fiorella, who had been on a terminal ward in Cleveland for two years and survived osteomyelitis. 'First, he wanted me to know that they told him he had cancer. He was selectively listening [to his doctor's prognosis] which was really good because he protected himself from hearing a lot of things they were saying.'

Bill wasn't planning on telling anyone else outside his immediate family, though there were sometimes little hints when he talked to one of his close friends. 'Right after he was diagnosed we were on the phone and he said something about, "I've got a tumor the size of a baseball and it's got Pamela's name on it" and I didn't say anything,' Farneti recalled. 'It just sounded like a routine. He talked about tumors onstage constantly. Big tumors on his aunt's nose and does his mother know *anyone* who doesn't have a tumor . . . tumors tumors tumors. So I didn't take it seriously at all. Later I realized, my God, he said that in July.'

The next day, Sunday, Bill insisted on playing his scheduled show at the Comedy Corner and informed Colleen of a few decisions he'd made. On Monday he was starting chemotherapy and since he liked Dr Donovan, who had recently set up a cancer institute with Duke University, Bill planned to base his therapy in West Palm Beach. Los Angeles certainly held no allure. 'He wanted to be here, near the ocean,' Colleen said. 'He loved to swim in the ocean. He hadn't done that in a long time but he did it here. The water was so warm here in the summer, it was unbelievable. He would just float.'

Bill didn't want to be alone in a hotel and he asked Colleen if he could stay with her for a while. Colleen cleared out a room for him, dug up some of his favorite Miles Davis CDs and asked him what he liked to eat. Bill asked if she would buy him some instant coffee and Ragú spaghetti sauce. Colleen informed him that she didn't allow bottled sauce in the house and that she would make her own. It took four hours, not five minutes. She hadn't known that he liked nice soap, candles, a heavy blanket. 'He loved his little things, his books, a nice pressed shirt. He was very genteel.'

Bill was scheduled to play Len Austrevich's club in Chicago the following weekend. Colleen had planned to clear his schedule but, having done three rounds of chemo, Bill saw no reason he shouldn't go. He felt fine. Ironically, he hadn't had any stomach pain since diagnosis and he was handling chemo with flying colors. Besides, it probably felt good to go onstage, the one place where he was in control. And he was galvanizing that trip.

Onstage at the Firm, he appeared his usual robust self, energized and, if anything, in unusually high spirits. The second night a group of deaf people sat up in front and he lost no time in making the most of the sign-language interpreter who stood a few feet from him. 'I'm used to this right here,' he said. 'We once had a table of people in a coma and we had a guy right next to me with a megaphone.'

Better yet, the interpreter wore a green dress that perfectly matched his green silk shirt. He kept calling her Priscilla.

He had an answer to the recent fuss over gays in the military, after President Clinton and the Joint Chiefs of Staff had reached a compromise with the infamous and asinine, 'don't ask, don't tell' policy.

'Here's what I think,' he said cupping the mike with his hands and pressing it to his mouth. 'ANYONE *DUMB* ENOUGH TO WANT TO JOIN THE MILITARY SHOULD BE ALLOWED IN. CASE FUCKING CLOSED.'

He couldn't believe 'hired thugs' in the military had the balls to get pious about homosexuality. '. . . Tell me about your morality, *motherfucker*.' He glanced over at the interpreter. 'Fuck the military, fuck the FBI, fuck the ATF, fuck President Clinton, fuck George Bush, fuck Ronald Reagan—'

The interpreter's hands flew.

'Keep up!' he yelled, grinning.

The crowd roared. Even 'Priscilla' had to laugh.

'Just trying to give her a workout, that's all. This isn't coming out of my pay, is it?'

Most nights at sunset that summer, Bill and Colleen took long walks along the oceanside Flagler Drive and sat on the sea wall watching the waves. He couldn't stop talking. He told her how alienated he'd felt as a child and that for many years all he'd felt was anger and pain. He wanted to let go of all that, try to feel more joy. He called cancer his 'wake-up call', his chance to heal inside and out. 'He would just talk about everything and cry and ask me questions about my life,' Colleen said, 'and could I relate to any of this and how come I wasn't fucked up or a drug addict. We would have the deepest conversations I've ever had with anyone, really. But the anguish Bill carried around blew my mind.

'He would say how scared he was. He was very open about that. He would freak sometimes. All the work ahead, all the unknowns.'

Bill began to research pancreatic cancer, poring over medical journals and getting information from the American Cancer Society. What he learned was far from comforting but he tried to figure out what alternative therapies might make him the exception to the rule. He experimented with homeopathy and tried to get on a macrobiotic diet. What he mostly did though was study *A Course in Miracles*, a book of channeled teachings from the mind of Helen Schucman, a professor of medical psychology at Columbia University. Schucman said that she had heard rapidly dictated messages (from a voice she later identified as Jesus) and began taking shorthand notes. *A Course* was a collection of those notes, a book of Christian-based interpretations of the Bible, humanist messages about perception, love and behavior. The book produced hundreds of *Course* study groups and had an international following. It had been one of Bill's favorites over the last few years, which encouraged his belief that he could create the miracle of recovering from cancer. Dr Donovan couldn't believe his attitude. Usually patients exhibited some anger toward the disease or even treatment, but Bill displayed none of that. Donovan found Bill so gentle, he'd tease him that he couldn't really be a comedian.

Bill was working hard to relax, wearing shorts all the time, which for some reason struck his friends as funny. He loved Colleen's black cat, Otis, and liked to sit on the porch and play guitar with Greg, the guy next door. Colleen would zip home from the club a couple of times a day and check on him, bring him to Dr Donovan's a few times a week. 'Guess where I am?' he asked his brother over the phone one day. 'I'm on a beach, I'm reading a book and I'm relaxing! What do you think of that?'

There had been one incident at the beach, he told Steve. Bill thought he saw a shark and began wildly signaling to the lifeguard. When the guy paid Bill no attention, he began screaming and running

down the beach. When he reached the guard, he yelled again. '*Shark!*
There's a shark in the water!'

'That's a dolphin,' the lifeguard informed him.

Try as he might to relax on a beach, he couldn't stand not to
work. Since his mid-twenties Bill had been curiously aware of legacy.
He frequently explained his love of making CDs as 'leaving behind
a body of work' and illness seemed to engender in him an urgency
to produce. Colleen, Duncan and Dr Donovan set up a network of
chemotherapy stops all over the country in Chicago, Little Rock and
Los Angeles so that Bill could keep his club engagements. Bill
continued writing his columns for *Scallywag*, wrote a second draft of
'The King's Last Tour' and worked with Len Austrevich on a script
about a serial killer who murders hack comics. Meanwhile, Bill and
Fallon focused on their number one goal: pulling together a detailed
Counts presentation for Tiger TV and Channel Four in London.

At a show at Caroline's in New York, Bill saw from the stage
that the McGathys were in the audience. After he got offstage, he
grabbed Bill McGathy by the arm and led him and Rose to the green
room. The three were alone.

'I'm in big trouble,' Bill said.

'What's going on?' Bill McGathy asked.

A Caroline's staffer came to the door looking for Hicks.

'I hate comedy,' Bill said. 'I hate performing. I hate traveling.'

'You *are* in big trouble!' McGathy quipped as he and Rose got up
to leave.

John Magnuson, who was a close friend of Lenny Bruce's in the
sixties and the producer of Bruce's films *Thank You, Masked Man* and
The Lenny Bruce Performance Film, got a phone call at his San Francisco
apartment from his friend Jack Boulware at *The Nose*. It was early
July and Jack was suggesting that John check out Bill Hicks when
the comedian came to town later that month. Magnuson cringed: he
had had his fill over the years of people swearing that some new
stand-up was going to remind him of Lenny.

But for some reason he marked the date anyway.

Bill was performing for four nights at Cobb's in downtown San

Francisco and he had asked Kevin to come with him to record more material for *Rant in E-Minor* and make a trailer for *Ninja Bachelor Party*. Kevin wasn't sure what to think. He knew Bill had been in the hospital but since he'd gotten out, he was insisting that he was all better. 'Suddenly, he was acting like everything was fine,' Booth said. 'But something was weird. All his toiletries had changed, it was all this industrial hospital stuff.'

Bill avoided talking about it and Kevin knew not to push him.

Duncan had asked Gerald Nachman, a theater reviewer for the *San Francisco Chronicle*, to attend the Friday show and both he and Magnuson watched from the audience as Bill paced the stage and restlessly chain-smoked. He was talking about Clinton's raid on Iraq a month earlier.

'It was just a little news story for two days. Isn't that interesting?' Bill asked. Clinton had launched twenty-two Cruise missiles against Baghdad in response to the *alleged* assassination attempt against George Bush. As a result, six innocent people in Baghdad were dead and the US had spent upwards of $66 million dollars. Bill suggested that perhaps we had overreacted a tad. What we should have done, he said, was *embarrass* the Iraqis and get rid of Bush ourselves.

'That's how you do it, towelhead. Don't fuck with us.'

The room whooped and cheered.

'And if Bush had died there would have been no loss of innocent life.'

Magnuson was rapt. 'Thirty years before that, in June, I first got to know Lenny Bruce,' he said. 'And these two guys were very different, but they're together on one level in my mind: they're satirists with a strong moral core. But I'll tell you the thing about Bill Hicks that he approached like Lenny did: "I'm gonna have some fun and there's nothing like taking a serious subject and tearing it apart." And doing it with great skill. And both guys did it. They had completely separate styles but they did it in their own way. And that takes more than talent. It takes a lot of courage.'

The next morning's *Chronicle* review by Nachman began, 'Bill Hicks is as American as apple pie *à la* cyanide. Love him or leave him, but listen to him.'

Saturday afternoon Bill and Kevin picked up Magnuson, who had introduced himself after the show the previous night, and they all ran around San Francisco making a goofy trailer for *Ninja Bachelor Party*. They had Kevin's Super 8 and Magnuson guided them to some wonderfully bizarre locations in Fisherman's Wharf. Bill was fascinated by Magnuson, an erudite man with an epic past, and he especially loved hearing his Lenny Bruce stories. The two talked about the possibility of making a live performance film for *Rant in E-Minor*.

'I'm thinking, here's a guy thirty years later who's like [Lenny] and he's only thirty-one years old,' Magnuson said. 'And having been through Lenny, that Saturday the first thing I said to Bill was, "Are you on drugs?" He told me no. I said, "That's so good, man."'

TWENTY-FIVE

Beep. *My mom bought me these new flannel pajamas which I've just – I've never had 'em before in my life. And it's just neat to find another aspect to yourself that you've been missing, and suddenly you're in it. Ah forget it, I'm going on about flannel pajamas.*

By late summer of 1993, Bill was taking the occasional Percoset and he worried constantly about whether it was a violation of his sobriety. His AA sponsor in Los Angeles, a comedian named Tony Visic, was a bit of a hardliner so Bill didn't say anything to him. But he kept asking Fallon what he thought.

'Am I screwing with my sobriety with this Percoset?'

'Bill, you're amazing,' Fallon replied. 'I think you're allowed a little bit of something.'

'But what if I'm enjoying it?'

'Well, enjoy it a little bit. Good Lord, Bill.'

Bob Fiorella realized that using drugs represented a defeat to Bill. He saw Bill in New York for five days and did 'five or six hypnotic inductions with him and gave him all kinds of guided imagery that he could use to relax and go to sleep. I made tapes with him and I gave him a shitload of books on healing yourself and positive thinking.'

During his chemotherapy appointments, Bill kept himself as positively focused as possible. He continued to read inspirational books like Bernie Siegal's *Love Medicine Miracles* and he started working on a proposal for a book called *New Happiness*, which would chronicle his recovery from drugs, alcohol – and ultimately cancer.

On 5 August 1993, as he sat in Donovan's office with a needle in his left arm, he wrote in his journal that his friends were 'seekers one & all' who pushed him to grow creatively. 'The holiness of creating is my joy. Being in the moment – time and space are negated and we know our true self – eternal, joyous and free. There is only love. The feeling comes from *any* type of creation – writing, speaking, performing, playing guitar, sitting quietly and relaxing. I live for this. This *is* Life.'

On 8 August, the *San Francisco Chronicle* ran another, larger piece by Nachman. 'Is Bill Hicks the Voice of 1990s Comedy?' the headline asked.

> You have to go back to Mort Sahl, Lenny Bruce, George Carlin and Richard Pryor to recall such an individual, piercing, idiosyncratic mind. He doesn't just make noise, or trouble, but says something that hasn't been said before, venturing into new areas and taking on riskier issues than Dan Quayle and Madonna, both beneath Hicks's contempt. He saves his bile for worthier topics – Jay Leno, CNN, and childbirth are matters he takes special pleasure in mocking in the most coruscating, often crude, terms. However rough he gets, I felt my head opened up by Hicks. He's not everyone's cup of chicory, and may put off as many people as he entices, but if you like your comic witch's brew strong, black and laced with acid, Bill Hicks is the wit of choice.

With his scheduled commitments fulfilled, Bill slowed down a little in August, working just a handful of clubs, putting his energies into *Counts* and spending as much time as possible with Colleen in West Palm Beach. But then he received an invitation too cool to miss. Ever since the band Tool had called Bill 'an inspiration' on their new album, *Undertow*, Bill and lead singer Maynard Keenan had been corresponding, and now the band wanted Bill to introduce them at Lollapalooza in Los Angeles. Bill had decided it was time to clear out his LA apartment anyway, so he flew out and met Duncan, with whom he rarely got a chance to spend time alone anymore.

'Hey, I think I lost my contact lens in the mosh pit!' he yelled to Tool's audience from the main stage before introducing the band.

Afterward, he and Duncan hung out backstage for a little while with
Maynard and the guys but they got on the road pretty quickly. It was
almost 90 degrees at the Santa Fe Dam and Bill, who had spent a
day getting hydrated for the event, still had to go to his Barrington
Street apartment and pack up his things.

Bill was going to store his stuff in Little Rock for a while and his
brother was flying out to Los Angeles to drive with him to their
parents' house, but he gave away a bunch of his belongings, too – a
big dictionary to Andy Huggins (living in LA again) and a microwave
and some silk shirts to Eppy. 'Thanks, man!' Epstein said. 'But why
are you giving away all this stuff?'

'Well, it's good to get rid of your possessions and start fresh
every once in a while,' he said. 'Don't you think?'

A few days later, Bill dropped his keys with his landlord, went to
his chemo appointment and picked up his brother at LAX. 'We got
in his Jeep and he drove for eight hours,' Steve said months later on
the Texas Radio Show. 'It just never affected him physically. The
treatment didn't.'

For five days the two brothers drove across the Southwest,
having a ball together. 'Every town we were in, even if we had to go
miles out of our way, he insisted on eating at a Luby's Cafeteria.
I finally asked him, I said, "Bill, what is the deal with Luby's
Cafeteria?" And he said, "Well, you know I really love my cracker
roots. I just can't help it." '

Bill's spirits continued to soar. His tumor seemed to be shrinking
quite dramatically. The doctors used tumor markers to measure the
size of a tumor and, four times in a row, Bill's had shrunk.

He was also falling in love with Colleen. All that time together
over the summer, Bill had never felt so tranquil with anyone. She
was vital, tender and funny and through this ordeal she'd been his
light every day. Bill was thinking about marriage and a family –
things he hadn't really thought about before – and with Colleen he
could imagine a future. He didn't feel alone anymore. Bill wanted to
talk to her about all of this, but he also realized she was with
Duncan, and he didn't say anything just yet. He and Colleen were

meeting Fallon and Duncan in New York at the end of August for
a big meeting scheduled with Tribeca Productions.

Tribeca Productions was Robert De Niro's New York production
company. A Tribeca development executive, introduced to Bill
through a mutual friend, had become a real fan. Now there was
some talk of Tribeca co-producing *Counts* with Tiger Television.
Charles Brand and his producer, Elaine Bedell, were flying in to
meet with Tribeca president, Jane Rosenthal.

As it turned out, everyone at the meeting thought *Counts* sounded
like an expensive project because they wanted to shoot the television
show on film. Another problem quickly emerged. Tribeca and Tiger,
both fairly young companies, each wanted the other to provide most
of the funding – without sacrificing creative control, naturally.
Suddenly, it didn't look so promising.

A few nights after Bill and Colleen returned to West Palm Beach,
they walked to their spot at the sea wall and, holding her hand, Bill
told Colleen how he felt about her. 'He said he felt completely loved
for the first time,' Colleen recalled. 'He didn't have to change in any
way. I don't know why. I certainly haven't been that way with other
relationships I've had, but he brought out the best in me.'

Colleen was blown away. Here was the dearest coolest person in
the world, announcing he was in love with her. 'I absolutely adored
him. As soon as anyone mentioned his name to me I just beamed.'
She'd had a little crush on him over the years but nothing she would
have dreamed of pursuing. She didn't think she was his type for one
thing – she'd seen his parade of psycho Goth chicks – and she'd
always had a boyfriend the years they were friends. 'I assumed he
really liked me too [but] I never got the impression that he felt as
intensely as I did about him. But then he didn't know how I felt
about him.'

The moment was quickly interrupted by a maelstrom of emotions.
First of all, though it was long distance, Colleen was deeply committed to her relationship with Duncan. Beyond that, Bill was an
important client and Colleen felt strongly about keeping business in
its place. Most significant, of course, was the overwhelming shadow

of Bill's illness. How could she sort out Bill's feeling from what he was facing? Would this have come up had he not been terminally ill, had they not been facing a surreal journey together? But she was not about to challenge the reality of his feelings at that point. And the truth was, they had a deep bond. They always had.

Bill acknowledged that things were complicated. All he could say was that he loved her very much and needed her more than anyone. He had been putting together a book in a giant three-ring binder that he called The House. It was an elaborate plan for his dream house, the place he was going to build when he finished treatment. His dream towns were West Palm Beach, Key West, Austin and Prescott, Arizona. He drew several pencil sketches of the house, which appeared to be a three-story Victorian with a wrap-around porch, surrounded by big trees. Over the picture, he drew a huge sun. 'Where I will live with my mate Colleen,' he wrote.

In the beginning of September Bill called Kevin and David, who still knew nothing about the illness. He wanted to know if they were up for going to the ranch. 'It's been a while,' Bill said. 'Let's have the all-time epic trip.'

On the drive out to the Booth ranch in the Fredericksburg countryside, Johndrow asked him how he was feeling. 'What happened with your gall bladder, man?'

'Turned out it was just something I ate,' Bill said. 'Everything's fine.'

'But what about the pain in your side?' David persisted.

Bill said he thought he had pulled something doing one of his moves onstage.

'I think he wanted us to have this mushroom trip together where everyone didn't have [his illness] weighing on them,' Johndrow said. 'He wanted to go through his own experience.'

The three sat together out by the pond, 'and it was so beautiful, my God, it was the best trip up to that point,' Johndrow said. 'We had all sort of gotten over our differences [over Marblehead Johnson breaking up] and I felt like we were all sort of connected again ... We lay in the grass and the sunset was just crystalline where you could see little rainbows everywhere.' Eventually Bill and David got up and walked around the grounds 'through some weird astral heaven world together and it was all clear and we saw this amazing light come out of the sky . . .'

Back at the ranch they started plotting out *Ninja Bachelor Party Two*. 'We laughed harder that night than we have ever laughed,' David said. 'It was like puking and laughing at the same time. I felt completely purified.

'The other thing was this. My favorite record at the time was Van Morrison's *Astral Weeks*. His first solo one from 1968. I decided that was the greatest record ever made. I played it for Bill and I said, "This thing goes through the whole movement of life, and the record is a circle so that when you play it you can have it repeat over and over again." The record ended and Bill all of a sudden looked really disturbed, really bummed out. I said, "Well, it ends depressing on this weird note. But then you play it again and it completes the cycle." Because the first verse of the first song is 'To be born again/ to be born again'.

'Bill goes, "Well, start it over." So I did and everything lightened up again. I listened to it later after he died and the last line in the last song is, "I know you're dying and I know you know it, too".'

On Tuesday 14 September 1993 *Revelations* aired on HBO to strong reviews, *The New York Times* calling Bill 'very much one of Lenny Bruce's children' and noting that 'the language is strong, the material provocative and frequently hilarious. Not for ordinary prime time perhaps . . .' What was shown on HBO was a revised version of what aired on Channel Four, specifically without the burning American flag at the end.

The flag-burning controversy, still raging in 1993, first heated up in the summer of 1989 after the Supreme Court upheld the First Amendment rights of a Texas man, Gregory Johnson, who had been convicted of breaking a state law by burning the flag. In response, President Bush announced his support for a constitutional amendment that would prohibit flag desecration. While that was shot down in the Senate, The Flag Protection Act of 1989 was passed in

October. In defiance, Americans from Seattle to the steps of the US
Capitol held rallies and symbolic flag-burnings and, by early 1990,
protesters were being arrested and attorney William Kunstler was
filing motions to dismiss the charges as unconstitutional.

It was one of those hysterical hot-button issues that drove Bill
crazy and that he talked about onstage constantly. One of the bigger
smokescreens to come down the pike, he said. It wasn't that he per-
sonally believed in burning the flag, it was that he couldn't believe
the absurdity of putting people in jail for burning the very symbol of
freedom that gave them the right to burn the flag.

'If you don't want to burn the flag, then *DON'T*!' Bill hollered.
But if you did, you 'perhaps did not need to go to jail for a *year*'.

TWENTY-SIX

Beep. *Hey, man, it's Willy. I just did Letterman's show, it's on tonight. Um, that's about it. I'll give you a call later.*

The *Letterman* producers asked Bill to do a spot on their new 11.30 p.m. *Late Show*, in its fourth week at CBS, on Friday 24 September. Since debuting at the Ed Sullivan Theater, Letterman had been beating the pants off Leno every night and the *Late Show* was under a media microscope.

The morning of his appearance, Bill and Colleen flew to New York and went directly to *Letterman*'s new studio at the recently refurbished Ed Sullivan Theater. There Bill met Mary Connelly, a segment producer (Frank Gannon had left the show several months earlier), and went over his set. Connelly approved his material and then she took Bill on a tour of the theater, where Elvis had famously been shot from the waist up on *The Ed Sullivan Show* in 1956.) Afterward, Bill returned to his room at the Mayflower to run through his set a few times and headed back over to the show around four o'clock. After having his make-up done, Bill and Colleen sat in his dressing room waiting to be called. About halfway through the show, Connelly called the two into the hallway and apologetically informed them that the show was running short of time. Bill was being bumped. They would reschedule him as soon as possible, Connelly promised. Bill was a bit disappointed but he and Colleen managed to bolster their spirits with lobster dinners at the Palm that night. Their relationship had tentatively, quietly advanced.

Just one week later, Bill and Colleen were back in New York for a gig at Caroline's. He checked into the Mayflower under the name Otis Blackwell. Blackwell was the author of some of Elvis Presley's biggest hits, including 'All Shook Up' and 'Don't Be Cruel'. This was a kind of private joke Bill had with himself about Leary getting famous on material Bill had actually written.

Manhattan was in full autumn splendor and Bill had foregone his usual all-black attire for 'delightful fall colors' that reflected his happy mood. He was feeling really good. The tumor was continuing to shrink and Bill believed his amazing mushroom trip with David and Kevin had advanced his path to a miraculous recovery.

On Friday 1 October, Bill relaxed in his room and called a reporter at a Florida paper to do an interview for his next engagement at the Comedy Corner in West Palm Beach. As they wrapped up, the reporter congratulated him.

'Thanks,' Bill said. 'What for?'

'Well, you're doing *Letterman* tonight.'

'What? That's news to me. Man, maybe I should get off the phone and find out what's going on.'

Colleen, meanwhile, was out shopping with her mom, Elizabeth McGarr, who was visiting from Toronto, and had no clue either. Bill finally reached her assistant, Cynthia, in West Palm Beach.

'Where have you been?' she cried. 'The *Letterman* people have been trying to reach you all day! They want you on the show tonight! Some other guest has fallen out.'

Bill hung up the phone and immediately called a frantic Mary Connelly. He sheepishly apologized for being so difficult to find, and told her that, of course, he could go on the show. It was 3.30 p.m.; Connelly told him a car would be by at 4.15 p.m. Bill started pulling together his special 'autumnal' outfit, and the adrenalin started pumping again. Pacing the room, he reviewed his set from the week before over and over. *You know who's bugging me these days? The pro-lifers. You know what bugs me about them — if you're so pro-life, do me a favor — don't lock arms and block medical clinics. Lock arms and block cemeteries.*

Colleen and Elizabeth returned to the hotel just in time and hopped in the Lincoln Town car with him. Colleen's mom, a long-time fan of Letterman, had already attended a taping that week and was thrilled not only to see the show twice in one week but to experience the goings-on backstage. That night also happened to be Letterman's twenty-fifth show on CBS.

As soon as they arrived, Bill got to hear all about the mystery drop-out guest. The former cook of the Gambino crime family, Joseph 'Joe Dogs' Iannuzzi, who was in the Witness Protection Program, had written *The Mafia Cookbook* and was on *Letterman* to promote it. Bill thought this was absolutely hilarious. The guy was willing to hawk his cookbook on national television even if it meant losing his government protection and his $1,200 a month stipend! At any rate, the *Letterman* show had received numerous phone calls that day from strange men wanting to know what time the show was going to tape. After some deliberation, they decided it might be wise to cancel the guy. Unfortunately, the cook, living in a secret New Jersey location, was already en route to the studio.

It had fallen to twenty-four-year-old producer Daniel Kellison to break the news to Ianuzzi, who went berserk. ('He thinks he got a problem with that Margaret Ray showing up in his living room, wait until he gets home one night and finds me waiting for him,' the cook fumed to the *Daily News*.) In the meantime, the producers told Bill, they had been frantically searching for him. A good laugh was had by all and Bill went into make-up. Once in the green room, Bill was so focused on his set that he didn't even notice the beefed-up security, thanks to a death threat against Kellison made by Iannuzzi.

Bill Scheft, one of the show's writers and the audience warm-up comic, stopped off backstage after doing his bit. Scheft, who had known Bill for years and had introduced him on *Dangerous*, was to have been the back-up comic if they had failed to find Hicks in time. He took in Bill's new look: Bill looked just like one of the Harvard guys who wrote on the show.

'What the fuck is this?' he asked.

'It's the new friendlier Hicks,' Bill answered. Standing in the wings, Bill listened intently as Letterman introduced him. He took a final drag off his cigarette and strode out to center stage. It was 6.40 p.m.

'Good evening! I'm very excited to be here tonight, and I'm very excited because I got some great news today. I finally got my own TV show coming as a replacement show this fall . . .'

The set went as smoothly as could be. Finally, he was getting to do material – among other things, critical of pro-life and the Pope – that he felt truly represented him for eight million people in the 11.30 audience.

Before he signed off, he questioned the tradition of wearing crucifixes as a mark of Christianity: 'I think it's interesting how people act on their beliefs. A lot of Christians, for instance, wear crosses around their necks. Nice sentiment, but do you think when Jesus comes back, he's really going to want to look at a cross?' Bill's face crumpled in horror, and the audience burst out laughing.

'Ow! Maybe that's why he hasn't shown up yet . . .'

The audience burst into applause and the band struck up 'Revolution'. Bill crossed the set and took a seat next to Letterman's couch. 'Good set, Bill!' Letterman said. 'Always nice to have you drop by with an uplifting message!'

They cut to a commercial and Dave asked Bill how things were going. Bill said fine, that he had been working on a couple of albums. Letterman then asked if Bill had lost some weight. 'Yeah,' Bill answered. 'I've been drinking about a quart of grapefruit juice a day.'

Then something odd happened. Letterman leaned over and asked Bill if he'd quit drinking. Bill couldn't figure out why Dave would ask that, considering he hadn't touched liquor in over five years. And he could have sworn he had talked to Dave about that before. 'No drinking,' Bill said. 'But I have started smoking cigars. Hey, what kind do you smoke?' Letterman named a brand that Bill didn't recognize and handed him one as they came back from the commercial. With fifteen seconds left, Letterman closed the show with a customary thank you to his guests, Andie MacDowell, Graham Parker and Bill Hicks . . . 'Bill, enjoy answering your mail the next few weeks. Goodnight, everybody!'

As soon as they were off air, Connelly again remarked to Bill that the show had gone great and Bill headed for the green room. He was greeted with a wave of applause. Parker, whom Bill adored, came up to him with a big smile and a handshake. 'Great! Loved it, mate.'

Back in his suite at the Mayflower, Bill stretched out in a hot bath and drew on his new cigar. He had just an hour or so to relax before he was due at Caroline's for an eight-thirty show. As he got out of the tub and wrapped himself in a towel, the phone rang. It was Robert Morton. What follows is Bill's recollection of their conversation a week after it occurred.

'Bill, I've got some bad news.'

'What's going on?'

'Bill, we have to edit your set from tonight's show.'

Bill sat down on the bed, stunned. 'I don't understand. What's the problem? I thought the show went great.'

'It did, Bill. You killed out there. It's just that CBS Standards and Practices felt some of the material was unsuitable for broadcast.'

Bill rubbed his forehead. 'Uh, which material exactly did they find . . . unsuitable?'

'Well,' Morton said, 'almost all of it.

'If I had to edit everything they object to, there'll be nothing left of the set. So we just think it's best to cut you entirely from the show. Bill, we fought tooth and nail to keep the set as is, but Standards and Practices won't back down. David is furious.'

Bill tried to make sense of Morton's words.

'But, Bob, they're so obviously jokes!'

'Bill, I know, I know. Standards and Practices just doesn't find them suitable.'

'But which ones? I mean, I ran this set by my sixty-three-year-old mom in Little Rock, Arkansas. You're not going to find anyone more mainstream than my mom in Little Rock, Arkansas, and she had no problem with the material.'

'Bill, what can I say? We'll try and schedule a different set in a couple of weeks and have you back on.'

Bill wanted to say, 'I don't think I can learn to juggle in that short a time,' but he was, for once, speechless.

'We should have spent more time beforehand working on the set, so Mary or I could have edited out those "hot points" and we wouldn't be having to do this now.'

Bill couldn't believe his ears. 'They're just jokes! I don't want them edited by you or anyone else. Why are people so afraid of jokes?'

'Bill, come on. You have to understand our audiences.'

That was a line Hicks had heard before and it really pissed him off. 'Your audiences! What, do you grow them on farms?'

'Bill . . .'

'Your audience is comprised of people, right? Well, I understand people, being a person myself! People are who I play to every night, Bob, and we get along just fine.'

'Bill, look, it has do with the subject matter you touched on and our new time slot. We're on an hour earlier, you know?'

'So what? We taped the show at 5.30 in the afternoon and your audience had no problem with the material then. What, does the audience become overly sensitive between the hours of 11.30 p.m. and 12.30 a.m.? And by the way, Bob, when I'm not performing on your show, I'm a member of the audience for your show. Are you saying my material is not suitable for me? This doesn't make sense! Why do you underestimate the intelligence of the audience? I think that shows a great deal of contempt on your part—'

'Bill, it's not our decision! We have to answer to the network, and this is the way they want to handle it. Again, I am sorry. You're not at fault. Now let me get to work on editing this show and we'll set another date as soon as possible with different material, okay?'

'What kind of material?' Bill shot back furiously. 'How bad airline food is? Boy, 7-Elevens sure are expensive? Golly, Ross Perot has big ears? Bob, you keep saying you want me on the show, then you don't let me be me. And now you're cutting me out completely! I feel like a beaten wife who keeps coming back for more. I try and write the best material I can for you guys. You're the only show I do because I'm a big fan and I think you're the best talk show on. And this is how you treat me?'

'Bill,' Morton sighed. 'That's just the way it is sometimes. I'm sorry, okay?'

'Well, I'm sorry too, Bob. Now I've gotta call my folks back and tell them not to wait up . . . I gotta call my friends . . .'

'I know, Bill. This is tough on all of us.'

'Well, you gotta do what you gotta do . . . Okay.'

It was 7.30, just one hour until the Caroline's show. Bill slowly started to get dressed and the larger implications of what had just happened began to dawn on him. Just like Elvis in 1956, Bill was being censored – from the neck up. In 1993! In America! For telling some fucking jokes.

He took the elevator upstairs to the room where Colleen was hanging out with her mother. 'My whole set just got killed by *Letterman*,' he said standing in the doorway.

The big exaggerator. 'What?' Colleen asked with a smile. 'What happened?'

'They're cutting out my set. Standards and Practices. They think the material is *unsuitable*.'

'*What?*'

Bill's eyes filled with tears.

'Oh, my God.' Colleen jumped up and went into the bedroom to call Mary Connelly. Bill sat down with Elizabeth and ranted some more. 'They're just jokes,' he kept repeating. Elizabeth began to cry as well, stunned that this could happen and sick for Bill.

'What are they so afraid of?' he yelled. He began to sob again. 'Goddammit! I'm a fan of the show! I'm an audience member! I do my best shit for them! They're just jokes!'

It was all feeling more sinister by the second. Here was this show he loved, Bill thought, that touted itself as cutting edge, trying to silence a comedian. Letterman was a comedian himself. How could this happen? They're so edgy, he thought angrily, but they buckle at the first hint of anything resembling true irreverence.

Colleen came back from talking to Connelly, who had told her exactly what Morton told Bill. Colleen had at least managed to extract a promise to overnight them a tape of the banned set on

Monday, but she was still heartbroken for Bill. She couldn't stand to
see him like that, with everything else he was going through.

Suddenly she looked at her watch. 'Holy shit. We've got to get
over to the club.' Shell-shocked, the three headed off to Caroline's.

Bill sat in the dressing room while Colleen anxiously surveyed the
crowd. She thought she saw Richard Belzer in the audience. Nice
house, except for one thing. There was a table down front, kind of
vertically sticking out, with all these old people sitting around it.
They looked like a touring group. Colleen quietly groaned. With Bill
furious and hurt, feeling totally violated, she wondered what the
evening's performance might hold. 'He was, I swear, surrounded by
a white light. Like white rage. There was literally a glow around him,
he was so freaked and mad.'

'Let me tell you what my life has been like in the last couple of
hours,' he began. As he relived the *Letterman* episode, he grew more
and more angry, just flipping out.

A buzz rippled through the crowd. 'Everybody who was there to
see Bill was laughing their asses off,' Colleen recalled. 'Because they
thought Bill had made this up. You'd hear people whispering, "Is
this true?" He hurled abuse at Letterman and performed a deluxe
expletive-coated version of his now-censored set. He then meandered into a tirade against Jay Leno. Actually, that was prepared
material.

Bill found it entirely revolting that a man who made 'three million
a year', a man who was once the most brilliant, caustic voice in the
country, was using his name to sell snacks to 'bovine America'. In
fact, Leno's *Tonight Show*, like *The PTL Club*, was something of an
obsession with Bill. He loved to watch while hanging out on the
phone with one of the guys – Huggins, Pineapple or Austrevich –
and just rail on how cloying Leno had become. 'Both Bill and I
absolutely adored Leno as a comic,' Huggins explained. 'And what
he became on *The Tonight Show* made him absolutely fascinating to
us. We would watch Arsenio Hall and that show was dreadful but it
was exactly what we expected. But Jay was so good at one time. It's
not like he moved just 3 degrees closer to becoming a hack because
"I'm on TV now." He did a complete 180. Stunning.'

(Ironically, Leno was also known to get on the phone with his friends late at night and dissect late-night television. 'I talk to Garry Shandling late at night, I talk to Judd Apatow late at night, but Jay is more famous for it than anybody,' Jimmy Miller said. 'Leno was one of the first guys to have a satellite dish, he was one of the first to record things. Many nights when I first moved out [to LA] I used to go hang at Jay's house. He would have a group of guys and we'd all be watching late-night TV. Or you could just give him a call on the phone.')

'Here's the deal, folks,' Bill told the Caroline's audience. 'You do a commercial, you're off the artistic roll-call for ever. End of story. Okay? You're another corporate shill, you're another whore at the capitalist gang bang, and if you do a commercial there is a price on your head, everything you say is suspect and every word that comes out of your mouth is like a *turd* falling into my drink. You don't have enough money, you *fuckin'* whore?'

The Bill fans loved it. They paid to see him take things way over the top.

Not so the elderly tourists.

'Potty mouth!' one of them yelled.

Big mistake.

'You're disgusting!' another heckled.

Just asking for it.

'Fuck you, you fat fucking tourists!' he screamed. 'What moron put these fat fucking tourists down in front?'

As the group got up to leave, he began dancing a happy jig, hooting in celebration.

Colleen, on the other hand, was miserable. The set was taking too much out of him. He should be conserving energy, she thought, not freaking out. As it was, any performance required plenty of rest and hydration. But that kind of unfiltered anger was an unthinkable setback.

Back at the hotel, there was a message from Frank DiGiacomo, a reporter for the *New York Observer*. The *Letterman* incident was already leaking.

TWENTY-SEVEN

Beep. *Hey Sundance, this is Butch. Um, I think I gave you the wrong room number. Obviously, you're not there. I'll be in the hospital two more days and I'll talk to you from home. Everything is going great, everything is going phenomenal and I love you, man, and keep it up and I'll see you soon. Bye.*

On Monday, with the Caroline's engagement finished, Bill and Colleen returned to West Palm Beach. Bill, who was booked for five nights at the Comedy Corner, rested up on Colleen's couch during the day while she fielded a constant stream of media calls. Di-Giacomo kept calling and he seemed to know something was amiss. A friend of his had been in the audience at the taping and had seen the set.

'We don't even know what's happening yet!' Colleen told him.

'Look, I'm on deadline,' he pleaded.

'I'm really sorry,' Colleen replied, 'but we're not talking right now.'

There was, for one thing, the small matter of getting the tape of the banned set out of *Letterman*. They wanted the tape as evidence that Bill hadn't done anything wrong. The set had been approved by *Letterman*'s producers *twice*, after all. And though Mary Connelly had promised to overnight the tape to Colleen, Monday brought nothing. Colleen put in another call, was told again there was no problem in sending the tape. Colleen gave them her address and FedEx number. The tape would be overnighted. Duncan told her not to count on it. Why should they send the tape? It would only leave their asses hanging in the breeze.

He was right. When nothing arrived on Wednesday, Duncan called Morton to tell him of several pending articles. For starters, *The*

New Yorker, which had back-burnered Lahr's profile all summer, was now going to press with it immediately. Morton, naturally, was less than thrilled and told Duncan he would take 'a dim view' if the *New Yorker* piece were to include any mention of the *Letterman* incident. Of course it was precisely that incident that had given the piece the news hook *The New Yorker* wanted.

All Bill wanted to do was perform the censored set verbatim for as many live audiences as possible. When he played the Comedy Corner in West Palm Beach that week (wearing a black T-shirt that said 'Honest Engine') the audience went for his banned set all the way, whooping it up especially for the pro-life riff and the bit about gunning down Billy Ray Cyrus. Now he really knew. The set *had* been funny.

'Beautiful,' he said over their applause. 'I appreciate that, folks. I did that set just for you because – and you notice I didn't curse once during it – the reason I did that set is because that's the set I did Friday night on the David Letterman show … that was *canceled* by CBS. And I was completely erased from the show.'

The audience laughed a little. Another joke about network television.

'Because they felt you, the audience, are too stupid to know that these are jokes.'

Now he had their full attention.

'Or to have material on that might have ideas associated with them other than, "Boy, food on airplanes sucks, don't it?" or "Gee, 7-Elevens sure are expensive. Aren't they?" Or any number of other stupid, banal, trite, puerile jokes that we all know by heart so that they can keep you without any kind of social fucking awareness and keep us separated from each other while they hawk their fucking beer commercials.'

The audience burst into cheers and applause again.

'You know what really pisses me off the most? I am a big David Letterman fan and it's almost like finding out there's no Santa Claus. Or your folks are Santa Claus. They said, "Bill we fought with CBS tooth and nail to get the set on but we had to edit so much out that, uh, there'd be nothin' left." And I was like, 'Why do you have to edit anything? You approved the set." They fucking folded like a house of cards. Meanwhile, Bob Saget is on tonight.'

Big laughs on that one.

'So that gives you an idea of the level of comedy they think you can handle. Do you understand how much contempt the networks have for us? They put on that puerile bullshit. And not put me – not just *me* but anyone else with a point of view perhaps, maybe even one you don't agree with – on television. They kowtow to the fucking special interest groups and a couple of deranged motherfucking people who hear the word "Jesus" and think immediately you're making fun of Jesus when *I did not* make fun of Jesus. They hear the word "gay". I did *not* make fun of gay. What I made fun of was a double standard that exists in this fucking country. They think you're too stupid to see through that. And that's exactly what they fucking count on while they fucking sell the number two killer drug in this country, fucking alcohol, and they have the gall to do it in your *fucking* living room with your children there, they don't even lurk around playgrounds! You drug-dealing capitalist *motherfuckers!*

'So, understandably, I'm very hoarse, I've been discussing this and wondering what action to take and I think the action I'm going to take is to repeat what I just did and I'm going to play it for many many people and show them the exact set—'

'YAAAAAAY!'

'—that was canceled and see if you, the audience, were so *offended*, that you felt so *threatened* by my little skit that you went out of your fuckin' minds . . .'

When Bill called David to say that he wanted to meet him at Kevin's, that he had something to tell them, David wasn't surprised, not exactly. 'He was racing through all of these revelations and synchronicities and you know, the big thing is getting ready to break. I almost thought he was going to tell us he'd been contacted by the alien brotherhood and that it's going down and here's the deal. There were always these kinds of feelings [around Bill] of a mission in life or something big about to occur.'

Bill was being kicked hard by the cancer for the first time since diagnosis. After months of remarkable progress the chemo was suddenly having little effect. He was having some rough nights and was allowing himself more and more Percoset, to cope with the acute psychic pain as much as the physical.

When Bill walked in the door, he hugged them both. David could see he was very weepy and Bill said he had a whole lifetime's worth of crying that he had to do all at once. They sat down in Kevin's den and Bill lit up. 'He said, "I have cancer and they told me that I have six months to live but this is all a part of this plan and a miracle is going to occur and the tumor's already receded,"' Johndrow said. 'The cancer was the final test and he was going to come through this to some other place. Which is what happens when you die too, but he wanted a miracle at that point.'

'And then he said, "Well, I may die but that's okay because our work is going to continue on the other plane." And that we were going to talk in our dreams and that we would meet under a tree at Kevin's ranch if we needed a spot – in our dreams, we could actually go there.'

'Colleen, some freak pretending to be Jay Leno is on the phone!' Cynthia, the assistant, yelled.

Colleen took the call.

'Colleen, it's Jay Leno.'

It really was Leno.

'Hi, Jay. What can I do for you?'

'Let me ask you a question. Is Bill on drugs again?'

'No.'

'Well, why is he slamming me on stage?'

'Well, he doesn't like the show. But, Jay, you should talk to Bill about this.'

Leno took her up on her offer and called Bill at the house. They had a long talk and Bill told Jay how much he hated *The Tonight Show* (as if the man were not aware) and how disappointed he was because Leno was one of his comedy heroes. Why was the show so stodgy? Why was he showcasing guys like Carrot Top? Why was he being so . . . unfunny?

Leno digested all that and came up with an idea, one that might possibly resolve the problem. He asked if Bill would like to come on *The Tonight Show* and do the set that *Letterman* had refused to air. (With *The Tonight Show* lagging behind *The Late Show*, it would be quite a coup.)

'Are you serious?' Bill asked. 'You want me to come out there and do the set, sight unseen?'

Jay replied that yes, that was the deal. Bill, somewhat skeptically, agreed to a tentative date. If he could come out and do his exact set, unedited, without having to run it by the producers for approval, he would do it.

Somehow, Colleen couldn't see it happening. After all Bill's material about Leno's *Tonight Show*, she just couldn't envision him walking out in front of that heavy purple curtain and doing his set. (To say nothing of the energy the trip would require.) She started checking flights anyway.

Then Jay called back. Could Colleen send him a tape of the set?

'I can send you the set, but he won't do the show if we send you the set.'

'But I just want to see the set,' Leno explained. 'That's perfectly normal.'

It might be normal, Colleen told him, but that wasn't the deal.

'I can't air it without at least viewing it,' Leno protested.

Colleen apologized. She supposed it wasn't going to work out then.

Next, Arsenio Hall asked Bill to do the censored set on his show. *The love child of Merv Griffin and Little Richard*, Bill called him. Colleen passed on that one immediately.

Meanwhile, requests for interviews continued to pour in. *Charlie Rose* called, *American Journal* called, and so did *Dateline NBC*. *Rose* was particularly tempting, but it would have entailed going to New York and Bill had chemo appointments to keep. Howard Stern, on the other hand, could be done by phone.

It was Bill's first appearance on *Stern* and he and the shock-jock got on famously. Stern commiserated with Bill on the evils of broadcasting, and compared Hicks's situation to that of Lenny Bruce.

BILL: I would like to meet this Standards and Practices guy 'cause I got a right hook I've been saving for somebody for about seven years.

HOWARD: I know all those Standards & Practices guys. When I was at NBC – five of 'em on a couch, they would sit there like robots and read me the riot act every week. There were five of 'em. And you can't outnumber 'em. I mean you can't – if you start to say something they each have a new angle on it.

BILL: Plus, everything they say is insane so there's no way to talk sense.

HOWARD: Oh yeah, oh yeah. None of it makes sense. And then as soon as they run out of arguments because you're ten times smarter than they are they go, 'Look you don't understand who listens.'

BILL: But you know what I've found is that 90 per cent of the people in this country are actually reasonable, very reasonable people. They kowtow to that 10 per cent of—

HOWARD: Yeah. Ten per cent idiots.

BILL: The 10 per cent who are in a trailer with a crayon who write, 'I saw a guy talk about Jesus. I am offended. Signed, X.' And they get that letter and they take the one person in the room who complained over the 250 people who howled with laughter.

HOWARD: Now you understand why I have a million and a half dollars' worth of fines against me.

In San Francisco there was a syndicated radio show on Live 105 KITS-FM called *The Alex Bennett Show*, on which Bill was a frequent guest. *The Alex Bennett Show* taped in front of a live studio audience, and when Bill called in to talk about the now-infamous censorship incident, a man in the audience named Harry Nichandros who owned a local real estate business, became so incensed on Bill's behalf that he fired off an angry fax to CBS Standards and Practices, demanding to know why they had censored Hicks. Within a couple of days, Nichandros received a faxed response from the network, which soon found its way to Bill in West Palm Beach.

'It is true that Bill Hicks was taped that evening and that his performance did not air,' CBS wrote Nichandros. 'What is inaccurate is that the deletion of his routine was required by CBS. In fact, although a CBS Program Practices editor works on that show, the decision was solely that of the producers of the program who decided to substitute his performance with that of another comedian. Therefore, your criticism that CBS censored the program is totally without foundation.'

Bill could hardly believe his eyes.

'Creative judgments must be made in the course of producing and airing any program and, while we regret that you disagreed with this one, the producers felt it necessary and that is not a decision we would override. It is my understanding that Bill Hicks will return to the program at a later date. We hope that you will continue to enjoy *The Late Show*.'

This was exactly the opposite of everything Morton had said to him. And intriguingly, though it may not have been foremost in Bill's mind, the network had broken protocol and hung Letterman out to dry.

On Thursday 7 October, the *New York Post* ran a substantial item on Page Six, its widely read gossip sheet, under the headline 'What You Missed on Letterman'. It quoted an unnamed source saying, 'Letterman's staff is furious with CBS's big footing. His producer, Robert Morton, was screaming.' Rosemary Keenan, meanwhile, the network spokeswoman, was quoted as saying it was the *Letterman* producers who made the call. Somehow, Bill had the feeling that what really worried the show was the thought of pro-life zealots picketing in front of the renovated Ed Sullivan Theater. He'd also heard that in some markets CBS was accepting pro-life advertising spots.

Later that afternoon, Bill called Morton to find out why there was still no tape. Morton explained that he didn't think he was legally allowed to send out a tape of an unaired segment of a show.

'Robert, I just want it for my archives and my parents would love to see it.'

'Okay,' Morton replied. 'I'll see what I can do. Are we okay, Bill?'

'Yeah, I'm just looking forward to seeing my set.'

'I understand. I'll get you the tape. And let's work on another set for a few weeks from now.'

'Great,' Bill replied.

Next, both Bill and Rosemary Keenan went on record with the *Los Angeles Times*. Now she was saying the decision had been a joint one between the show's producers and the network. 'It was just that it didn't fit into the show's set of standards,' she said.

'It's absolutely stunning to me, the contempt in which the network holds the audience,' Bill shot back. 'The idea that these people have standards is laughable.'

He began to compose a handwritten letter to John Lahr in London, who was polishing the profile of him. Since no tape of the set seemed to be forthcoming, Bill wrote, 'This puts me in the awkward position of having to recall these events and commit them to paper – basically to stand up for myself and tell the truth with all the possible information that's at hand at this moment'. With no support from *Letterman* – i.e. no tape – he wrote that he felt he had no choice but to speak out. 'Believe me,' Bill added, 'none of this was planned, expected, nor sought after. I did what I've always done – performed material in a comedic way which I thought was funny.'

> The artist always plays to himself and I believe the audience seeing that one person can be free to express his thoughts, however strange they may seem, inspires the audience to feel that perhaps they too can freely express their innermost thoughts with impunity, joy, and release, and perhaps discover our common bond – unique yet so similar – with each other.

Bill went on to write that his dream as a boy, of being a comedian appreciated and wanted by *The Tonight Show*, had been stamped out by his realization that they didn't want his kind. How many times, he wrote, had he been in a pitch meeting with some network, only to have his idea met with, 'That's very funny, but do you think it will play in the Midwest?'

> ... no wonder there's an ever-growing sense of disenfranchisement, apathy and cynicism in our country. When we're all tuned into the real drug of this country – television – brought to us by an elite class of 'unique' and 'special' people who find the dirty herd beneath contempt, and only there really to buy the useless products created to fill the imaginary 'wants' television really hawks between hours of puerile programming. Every few years, they cart out the old argument regarding television's role in our society. As usual, they pose us divided and keep the problem unresolved, then it's back to 'business as usual'. The herd has been pacified by our charade of concern as we pose the two most idiotic questions imaginable: 'Is TV becoming too violent?' and 'Is TV becoming too promiscuous?' The answer, my friends, is this – TV is too *stupid.*

Bill assured Lahr that he didn't have a chip on his shoulder about every single thing on television. He was a fan of *Northern Exposure, The Simpsons* (he once told Johndrow he wished he could live in Springfield), *The Larry Sanders Show* and *Seinfeld.* These shows, he wrote, treat audiences with the love and respect they deserve. 'And, I'd like to take my hat off to Roseanne Arnold for having balls the size of Montana, and overcoming much more serious odds than I've ever faced, to realize her artistic vision, keeping it pure, and silencing the white male elite ruling class by putting on, again, one of my favorite shows on television.'

When he finished writing, the letter was forty pages long.

Ironically, the *Observer,* a Sunday newspaper, got scooped by the dailies and didn't report its Hicks item until 11 October. But they did have one spin no one else had so far noticed. Just six weeks earlier, on 23 August, *The Larry Sanders Show* had aired an episode called 'The Performance Artist' which was almost an exact model for Hicks's subsequent real-life experience with *Letterman.* On the *Sanders* episode, Larry (Garry Shandling) is tired of having safe guests like George Segal and decides to shake things up by inviting on (real-life) comedian Tim Miller, a gay political activist. After seeing his set, Larry and his executive producer Artie (Rip Torn) get nervous about possible fallout and pull his set from the program. Larry blames it on the network, only to be found out later.

'This may be a first, life-imitates-artwise,' DiGiacomo wrote. 'It is not uncommon for plot situations on *Larry Sanders* to be based directly on real-life incidents behind the scenes at Mr Letterman's show (various *Sanders* writers used to work for the Letterman show). But in this case Mr Shandling's show has, for once, been ahead of the curve.'

Larry Sanders producer Paul Simms gave the *Observer* one comment: 'I don't know anything about this, but I do know that Bill Hicks does a lot of fucking hilarious shit.'

TWENTY-EIGHT

Beep. *Hey, bud. I've decided next year I want you to teach me about football, watching football on TV. Show me the schedule. I want your team to be my team. Next year, teach me all about watchin' football. I want to know about the team. All right, bud, I love you, man.*

'This is the last time I'll be here,' Bill told Steve Epstein (now living in Santa Monica) as they walked up to the door of Igby's about half an hour before show time the evening of Wednesday 17 November 1993. Epstein wondered what he meant, but Bill didn't elaborate. What he had been telling a few friends was that tonight and a show at Caroline's in New York the first week of January (a long-standing commitment) were going to be his last live performances for a long time. He didn't mean it in a morbid way. Of course, with his tumor growing, suddenly undeterred by chemotherapy, the fact that he might have less than a year to live was constantly on Bill's mind, but he very much believed in the possibility of a miracle and he felt pretty good most of the time. No, Bill's 'farewell tour' had to do with his plan to move to London in January if the *Counts* pilot was greenlighted by Channel Four, as Bill was sure it would be. Maybe he'd become a big star over there before he came home again. Just like Jimi Hendrix. Whatever happened, he was finished performing for forty people on the 'Comedy Pouch' club circuit and he was done with network television. If he couldn't do his act even on *Letterman*, where was he supposed to go?

On the heels of John Lahr's profile of Bill, 'Goat Boy Rises', in the 1 November issue of *The New Yorker*, Igby's had sold out fast. Up to the last minute Colleen (back in West Palm Beach catching up on desk work) and Duncan, in Los Angeles, fielded a barrage of

calls from industry insiders begging for a place on the guest list. Old
friends like Epstein and Huggins were coming, and new ones like
Maynard Keenan, plus a couple of guys from A&M Records
interested in signing Bill to a record deal. Bill had spent the day
resting in his room at the West Hollywood Hyatt for tonight's show,
his head propped up on a couple of pillows as he drank several liters
of water, studied *A Course in Miracles* and thought about what he
wanted to say in his last show. The warm-up show the night before
at the Brea Improv had been less than stellar but tonight Bill
intended to go out strong. There was so much to pack in – a life's
work, in fact.

At a few minutes past eight o'clock Bill walked onstage in his
usual way, bobbing his head to the beat of Hendrix blaring from the
speakers. *Let me stand next to your fire!* He sang along, mouthing the
words as he nodded to his fans and placed a small glass of water
next to a black ashtray on a stool in the center of the stage. Hands
free, he strummed an air guitar, rocking out across the stage and
back again. Suddenly he raised his right hand, made a sweeping
gesture and, on cue, the music stopped. He grabbed the mike, swung
its stand to the back of the stage and immediately began to
rhapsodize about another hero: Bob Dylan. 'You know he *sings*?'

All these years Bill had been buying Dylan records and now,
suddenly, he got what everyone was raving about. '. . . There's lyrics!
Some quite profound.'

That was about it for niceties. After shaking everyone up with his
'final show' announcement, he began blasting the mediocrity of
television with the too-hot-for-broadcast Billy Ray Cyrus joke and
he was off. His energy not a bit dulled by the weight loss or
painkillers, he performed with the freedom of a man with nothing
to lose, hitting the audience with a best-of parade of his obsessions:
pro-lifers ('You lose. Shut up. Go home.'), 'fucking phony false cult
religions such as the Inner Child', CNN ('This half-hour: war death
famine AIDS homeless recession depression deficit drought flood
earthquake fire . . .'), Easter, guns, Australia, alien motherships, trailer
parks, the Kennedy assassination, Keith Richards ('All my heroes are
dead'), Satan, the perfection of water, the Branch Davidians, Rush

Limbaugh and fundamentalist Christians (in which he worked in a
now rare Goober Dad impression). He was doing what he did best,
making connections between cultural issues normally perceived as
distinct and spinning a 'web' of consciousness – or at least height-
ening awareness of an existing tangled belief system. At the same
time, in questioning all things, he revealed the fragility of that web.
As he described it to Lahr, he was 'cutting everything back to the
moment', that moment of truth (or at least recognition) that *is*
laughter, and drawing his listeners – their illusions pierced, if not
shattered – to his core message (the point, really, of some 260 shows
a year for the last decade) that our only salvation is to evolve ideas.
True evolution, Bill said, was not physical or genetic but mental and
spiritual. 'It's all we have left,' he said.

And then there was smoking. He never failed to come up with
something new on smoking. Bill removed a pack from the pocket of
his tweed jacket and, with an unlit cigarette dangling from his lips,
he shared his latest theory, one he'd come up with over the summer
– 'a hope, really' – that there will be smoking in heaven. Bill
imagined that when St Peter welcomes you at the gate, the first thing
he'll say is, 'Got a light?'. The clouds, it turns out, are cigarette
smoke and hell is non-smoking. St Peter gives Bill a peek at the
prigs down below still whining to each other about the evils of
cigarettes.

'God, how hellish!' Bill cries.

'No shit,' says St Peter. 'Light up, come on in. Hendrix is on harp
tonight.'

Forays into optimism such as this were brief and the speed with
which Bill careened between sheer exuberance and unmitigated rage
– as he flew from a lyrical fantasy of tripping with his seventy-five-
year-old father to genuine rage over the Waco disaster ('They burned
these people in their homes. That's our government, *okay*?'), from a
gorgeous air guitar tribute to Hendrix to the NAFTA controversy –
was breathtaking. 'There ain't no battle over fucking NAFTA,' he
fumed. 'That's a *fucking* charade, like our elections are a *fucking*
charade and tomorrow, ladies and gentlemen, they're selling your

fucking life out from under you.' Bill stabbed the air with his index finger, his eyes flashing. 'Don't you ever fucking forget it either.'

The crowd sat silently, waiting for the comedy. 'Please relax,' Bill sighed. 'There's dick jokes coming up.' But getting laughs tonight wasn't Bill's top priority. For all his ferocity, he had an unmistakable weariness about him. Laughter was good, being funny mattered, but Bill was wise to its empty promise. Ultimately, in credulous America at least, the punchline, the escape hatch of 'just kidding', had failed him. His ideas were still deemed too 'hot' to air. Bill suffered, as Lenny Bruce did at the end of his career (when he read the transcripts of his bogus obscenity trial onstage), from what the scholar Will Kaufman later identified in his book, *The Comedian as Confidence Man*, as *irony fatigue*: 'the internal conflict between the social critic who demands to be taken seriously and the comedian who never can be'. Still, Bill *was* brutally funny, never more so than when absolutely furious. He had a way of making rage an ideal.

'This is the material, by the way, that's kept me virtually anonymous in America,' Bill said. 'You know, no one fucking knows me. No one gives a fuck. Meanwhile, they're draining the Pacific and putting up bench seats for Carrot Top's next Showtime special. Carrot Top: for people who didn't get Gallagher.'

Gallagher, Bill spat. 'Only America could produce a comic who ends his show by *destroying* good food with a sledgehammer. Gee, I wonder why we're *hated* the world over?'

Bill took a drink of water. 'Folks,' he implored once again, 'it's time to evolve ideas.' Confucius was a perfect example, Bill said. The ancient thinker posed the question, 'What is the sound of one hand clapping?' That, of course, was a clever way to say there would be no sound.

'But you know what I say to that?' Bill asked. He raised his thin hand in front of him and flapped it rapidly so it hit his wrist. It made a soft, but distinct, clapping sound.

'Fuck Confucius,' Bill said, bending toward the audience on one leg, his other raised behind him in an emphatic arabesque. 'Let's move on.'

A few minutes later, when Bill gave the sound guy a cue to start his exit music, Rage Against the Machine's hit, 'Killing In The Name', he knew he'd delivered. He'd done just over an hour and five minutes and said everything he'd come to say. After all the television appearances, radio shows, road tours, development meetings, management dramas, record deals, missed flights and men in gray suits telling him what not to say, it all came down to this: a fleeting moment where Bill stood on a stage with a microphone in his hand and, once more, redefined comic performance.

Fuck you, I won't do what you tell me! Rage's Zach de la Rocha roared over the sound system. Bill blew a kiss to the crowd and, as he walked offstage, he bent toward the front row and began to grab and high-five the outstretched hands.

Fuck you, I won't do what you tell me . . .

With the crowd on its feet applauding, Bill returned for an encore carrying a brown paper bag. He pulled from it a large watermelon, which he placed carefully on the stool. He grabbed the mike stand, raised it high into the air and brought it down, tapping the side of the stool. The melon rolled gently on to the floor where it sat unbroken.

Motherfucker!!!!!!!!! Hicks yelled with de la Rocha. He raised his hands in front of him, curled them, extended his middle fingers and gave everyone a two-fisted 'fuck you'.

Just after midnight, Bill returned with Duncan to his hotel room at the West Hollywood Hyatt and they called Colleen to tell her about the incredible turnout. The show had gone just as Bill wanted and he was delighted when Duncan surprised him with a videotape of it. Later, after Duncan had left, Bill stretched out on the bed and called Fallon. 'I'm not going to be up too much longer,' he said into his friend's machine. 'But I'm just fucking wired, man.' Then he took his sleeping pills and drifted off, as he did so often those days, to Miles Davis's *Kind of Blue*.

'Hicks Vents His Moral Outrage but Needs a Unifying Theme' was the headline in the *Los Angeles Times* arts section the next morning. Bill was livid. The *Times* staff writer, Lawrence Christon, had come to the warm-up show at the Brea Improv, the night before Igby's. It was admittedly not one of the all-time greats but it was the last line of the review that got to Bill. Though Christon had conceded in the beginning that 'Hicks brings a lot of heat in his act, which often takes off in gorgeous verbal riffs . . .' he finished by writing, 'Hicks could just as well be a crackpot as prophetic.'

Bill called Christon's answering machine about twenty times. Colleen and Duncan warned him about reproaching a critic but he wanted to make Christon understand. Why couldn't you discuss it with someone when they publicly denigrated your work?

'From around the country, he'd be calling from airports and hotels, wherever he touched down he'd head straight for the phone apparently,' Christon said. 'His messages weren't angry. They were sort of urgent, I suppose. Solicitous. He wanted to explain himself and talk about the review.'

When they finally connected a few days later, Christon told him frankly, if gently, that he found his delivery somewhat querulous and unpleasant. It was as if Bill were blaming the audience. Bill replied that he was just trying to tell the truth. 'It's not a matter of telling the truth, it's how you tell the truth,' Christon said.

'It was cordial. He wasn't angry. He was just anxious to express himself. Like he couldn't figure out why I didn't get what he was saying.'

TWENTY-NINE

Beep. *Hey buddy, it's Willy. Listen, man, eventually we're going to have to have a conversation. I can't just meet you at Heathrow. They don't let calls come in after eleven but if you call and leave the nurse a message, she'll come get me and I can call you back. All right? I hope you're doing well. Hope life is just extra-ordinary.*

When John Magnuson stopped hearing from Bill, he wondered what was going on. Since that first meeting in San Francisco, they had talked a few more times about doing a film version of the *Rant* set, and they'd even reserved a date at the Punch Line for production. Now plans were increasingly vague. Magnuson wondered if Bill just thought he was too old. In fact, Bill was conserving all his energies for *Counts*.

Bill, Fallon and Colleen were scheduled to fly to London on Thanksgiving Day for the big Channel Four meeting, at which the network would decide whether or not to move forward with the pilot. Duncan was back in Los Angeles trying to run the management business on his own. A naturally mellow guy, well liked by all, he felt himself beginning to crack under the strain, the agony of watching Bill die compounded by the months' long misery of seeing his relationship with Colleen fall apart. As hurt as he was by Colleen's involvement with Bill, Duncan cared deeply about him and was almost as grief-stricken as Colleen. They were both frozen and exhausted, staggering through each day without admitting to each other that the end was coming.

And now, with the dramatic turn in the state of Bill's health, Duncan and Colleen privately began having serious arguments about the wisdom of bringing Bill over to London. Was it ethical to enter into negotiations with, as was becoming starkly clear, a terminally ill client?

There was no release, no one to talk to. Even if they could have disclosed Bill's illness to an outsider, they couldn't think of anyone who would understand. Even George Shapiro, Andy Kaufman's manager, who had seen the thirty-five-year-old performer through stomach cancer ten years before, had dealt with an entirely different set of circumstances.

'Even if we had been managers for thirty years, how would you know how to handle it?' Duncan said. 'The dream was coming true and the nightmare was unfolding. We were all denying the truth because treatment was working for a long time. That's the thing, we've all read stories about someone who beats impossible odds. Why couldn't Bill be that guy? And for a long time Bill was that guy.'

'There was money on the table for production,' Colleen recalled. 'We were really far into this, we're dealing with a huge deal and all I could see was that it was keeping him going, it was something to believe in. As the tumor counts were getting higher we had to let Bill at least live out this thing. Because it was being done. It was exactly how he wanted.'

From the first moment the London trip was more nightmarish than Colleen dreamed it could be. The day of departure, as she and Bill packed up in West Palm Beach, Bill called Little Rock to wish his family a happy Thanksgiving. As usual, Bill and his father got into it. His father had a way of upsetting him, saying exactly what Bill didn't want to hear. Bill didn't like being reminded of how bleak his situation was.

Bill seemed to be cracking. The strain of fighting his illness, the painkillers that wrapped his head in cotton, or probably some unholy combination of both, moved him from laughter to tears within seconds. He would become mean, irrational, at times, but mostly he seemed frightened. He had very little energy and he and Colleen spent most nights curled up together in their hotel room. Bill didn't want to talk to Fallon about how bad things were getting. He just kept saying, 'We need to have a long Fallon and Bill conversation.'

As soon as Charles Brand saw Bill walk into the Tiger offices the day before the Channel Four meeting he knew something wasn't right. Bill's hands were shaking, he was wildly emotional and he kept excusing himself to go to the bathroom.

Bill and Fallon were there to work on their pitch. They had mapped out 'spontaneous dialogue' for the pilot, the theme of which was 'Jazz'. The important thing, again, was to assuage doubts about Fallon and Bill as a team (there were a few parties involved who much preferred a solo Hicks project) and assure Channel Four that *Counts*, even with guests like Chomsky and Terrence McKenna, would be comedy. They rehearsed a strong presentation but Charles was worried that Bill had had some kind of relapse, that he was on drugs again.

At Channel Four the next day, Seamus Cassidy, a Channel Four writer named Paul Mayhew-Archer (who had never met Bill), producer Elaine Bedell, Charles Brand and Colleen sat around the conference table while Bill stood at the head of the table. Fallon sat beside him. Carl Jung had a theory, Bill explained, that all mankind shares a collective unconscious. 'But I don't think it's supposed to be unconscious!' he said, pointing his finger at the executives. 'As the Counts of this Netherworld, we'll be in a Victorian era salon which in my mind's eye is the center of our collective unconscious where ideas are discussed and evolution is discussed and the evolution of ideas is discussed. We'll have on guests who have enlightened us so that we can enlighten the audience so that the unconscious becomes conscious.'

The pitch itself was inspired, exciting and wonderfully passionate. But Bill's presentation, even for him, bordered on the hysterical. It was as if, Charles thought, Bill were addressing Shea Stadium. Everything about him was heightened in this indescribable way, which was as disturbing as it was thrilling. Fielding tough questions from the producers (some of the devil's advocate variety) Bill became irate that they didn't *get* it. A small disagreement could prompt a fifteen-minute diatribe. He went on for an hour and a half and at the end, completely spent, Bill sort of pitched forward and grabbed the desk as though to keep from falling. Then he began to cry.

'My feeling,' Brand said, with regard to the network's reaction, 'was, "Now guys you see it, warts and all." So you are buying something which is completely extraordinary and will divide people like nothing has ever divided them before.'

The one-hour *Counts* special was a go. Both Tiger and Channel Four were, as Brand put it, enough 'evangelical converts to Bill's mission' that they probably would have okayed a puppet show as long as Hicks were on board.

Afterward Brand pulled Colleen aside. Was something wrong? 'He's fine,' she assured him. 'It's just the culmination of a dream for him.'

Later, when Bill said goodbye to Brand, he gripped the producer's arms and looked at him intently. 'I thank you,' he said. He wanted to know when they could get going. Brand thought spring would be good, that way they could iron out some kinks.

'No,' Bill said. 'It's got to be earlier. January.'

THIRTY

Beep. *Dude, surely you've checked your messages. Call me and tell me how big your head is. I have a gift for you and I need the size of your head! Leave a message. I don't care how you do it, just say fourteen and a half, eighteen and a half. Extra large, large. Whatever! I need the size of your head! I want the size of your head on a platter! Bring it to me.*

On Christmas Eve, Bill and his parents drove from Little Rock down to Austin to spend the holiday with Steve, his wife and their two children. Bill had gone to visit his parents for his birthday and stayed two more weeks until the holidays. He was anxious to spend time with them, tie up loose ends in some way and he and Mrs Hicks became closer than they had been in years. Bill began to see his mother as a whole person, not just a parent, and the two drank tea together, burned incense, read *A Course in Miracles* and *The Tibetan Book of Living and Dying*. He turned her on to Jimi Hendrix and Miles Davis, talked to her about his comedy and explained his mission. 'Focus on my message, Mom,' he implored her. 'Not my words.'

It was weird to think of having gone halfway around the world, talked to thousands of strangers from hundreds of stages, only to come home in the end to talk to the original two people whose approval – and conversion – he craved the most.

'You know, you are just *that* far from being a preacher,' Mrs Hicks said.

'I am a preacher,' Bill answered.

Before Bill had left for Little Rock, he and Colleen had decorated her little house, buying a big fresh Christmas tree and covering it with homemade ornaments. Bill made one out of folded paper with a reindeer drawn on it and stuck it on the front of the tree. He told

Colleen to go look at it. She unfolded it and inside it said, 'Will you marry me?'

Unfortunately Bill and Colleen would remain apart for the 25th. With the daily chaos of the situation, and ten days in the UK, Colleen had barely been able to attend to other clients or her responsibilities to Fantasma and now she stayed behind in West Palm Beach trying to pull her life together. Besides, she sensed that for the Hickses Christmas was meant to be a family affair that year.

Bill's sister, Lynn, drove down from Fort Worth, and Kevin and his girlfriend, Jerri, were invited too. For Steve Hicks, it was the first time it really sank in that this was probably Bill's last Christmas. 'He was beating it, the size of the tumor was reducing, everything Bill said was going to happen was happening and Bill was such a strong personality we certainly believed that and obviously we wanted that to happen,' he said on the Texas Radio Show months later. 'And then he came down ... and that's where I noticed the first physical change in Bill ... it began to take its toll very rapidly. There were daily changes that were noticeable.'

In fact, when Kevin and Jerri arrived around eight o'clock, Bill had already been taken to the hospital because of the pain. Kevin and Jerri ate some of Mrs Hicks's turkey dinner while they waited for Bill and when he finally returned he gave Kevin a couple of Percosets, which Kevin washed down with wine before picking up the video camera to record the scene. Bill read aloud to his family from the *Course*, and at one point Steve's seven-year-old daughter, Rachel, cuddled with Bill and her grandmother on the living room couch. The little girl had not been told Bill was gravely ill but, as Steve later recalled, she turned to him and said, 'Uncle Bill, you are going to be our first angel.'

Later, wrung out from the emotion of the evening, Bill excused himself to call Fallon. Bill had found him the perfect Christmas present: a hat with ear flaps just like the one Ignatius J. Reilly wears on the cover of *A Confederacy of Dunces*. He hoped that Fallon had received it, he said on his friend's machine, and that miracles would abound. 'Tonight, I'm praying for the ultimate miracle and you know what it is,' he said.

On 29 December, Colleen and Bill met in Las Vegas. She was there to put out fires on a Fantasma-produced Def Jam show and Bill very much wanted to see Frank Sinatra and Don Rickles play the brand new MGM Grand on the thirtieth. Bill always loved Vegas and they must have looked forward to getting away alone together, without official Hicks business, but Colleen couldn't believe her eyes when she met him at the gate. 'I hadn't seen him in about ten days at that point and I couldn't believe how shitty he looked. I remember him looking really really bad and being really sick basically. I picked him up, got him to the hotel and he crashed for like fifteen hours.'

When Bill had some strength again, they took a joyride down the strip, looking at all the funny little drive-through wedding chapels. But he weakened after just an hour or so and they had to return quickly to the hotel. 'I can't tell you how surreal life was that week. I'm at sound check for a Def Jam show of all things. And I'm running back and forth making sure he's okay and he's *so* sick.'

Despite being spaced out by the medication, Bill's usual single-mindedness reigned when he was determined to do something and he somehow got it together to take Colleen to see Sinatra the next night. Photos from that evening show a happy couple at their table, Bill gaunt but beaming.

When they got back to West Palm Beach on New Year's Day, Bill went straight to the hospital. He was in critical shape, his stomach distended as his body began to produce ascites, the accumulation of toxic fluids symptomatic of late stage cancer. Dr Donovan now prescribed a twelve-hour time-release Fentanyl morphine patch for continuous infusion of the drug. Over the next week or so, Bill slept and tried to rehydrate himself. He told Colleen he wanted to go to New York.

In the two months since the *New Yorker* article, seven book publishers had called Strauss McGarr, wanting to find out how they could sign up America's secret boy genius. Bill was elated. He would show them the *New Happiness* proposal.

Colleen felt like she was going out of her mind with grief and frustration. The idea of going to New York was absurd. The London trip had been harrowing enough and Bill was deteriorating by the second, absolutely wasted from all the morphine. He not only wanted to take pitch meetings for the book, but he planned to play his long scheduled four-night engagement at Caroline's.

Colleen gently asked if they shouldn't wait to go to New York until he had built himself up some more, but Bill wouldn't hear of it. As far as he was concerned, he was just hitting a rough patch. Besides, he had too much to do. People, after all, were finally getting him and he meant to make the most of it.

'The publishers who were lined up to meet with him were top of the line,' Colleen said. 'Physically Bill shouldn't have been going anywhere but there were things he still *absolutely* wanted to accomplish. He constantly referred to his diagnosis as his "wake-up call" that he had things to do, he had to get going.'

So fly to New York they did. In their suite at the Mayflower that first night, Colleen continued to implore him. 'We've got to go home, Bill,' she said. 'You're not up for this.' She said it about a million times but he was intractable. 'No, I'm doing it,' he said shaking his head. 'I've got to do this.'

Bill kept appointments with editors from Dell and Hyperion. It was usually a lunch meeting, or just coffee, where Bill pitched his idea. *New Happiness*, he explained, would be the tale of his triumph over drugs and alcohol and of getting his career started in America. And, he disclosed, he was undergoing another kind of recovery even as they spoke.

The editors were slackjawed at his pitch, and barely managed to get a word in. There was one thing they managed to ask: where was the comedy going to come in? 'Don't worry,' Bill told them, 'comedy is what I do.' Meanwhile, Bill was doped up and Colleen watched nervously as he veered from his crystal-clear self to something less than lucid. He trailed off from time to time, just spacing out. If any of the editors found Bill's behavior strange, they didn't say anything. Colleen figured they didn't have anything to compare it with.

THIRTY-ONE

Beep. *Uh, Fallon, this is Bill. I'm back in Little Rock. Uh, call me up. I'm sorry I haven't been in contact with you. You'll know why when I talk to you. Okay, bye.*

On the evening of 5 January 1994, Bill dressed in his customary meticulous fashion for his eight o'clock show at Caroline's. As he hung the tweed jacket he had bought that afternoon by the door, Colleen made a last-ditch effort to talk him out of the gig. But he was fighting her all the way, and she just couldn't stand to break him. Frantic, she put a call in to Dr Donovan, who was appalled to hear that Bill was still working. He spoke bluntly: 'Colleen, Bill is ready to die. He just won't lie down.' Colleen hung up on him. If there was one part of her heart that wasn't already shredded, that was the last of it.

About an hour before the show, Bill put on his trench coat and ventured out into the freezing cold with Colleen to catch a cab.

'Let's just get on a plane and get the fuck out of here,' she begged.

'Absolutely not,' he answered. 'I gotta do this.'

Colleen knew when she was beaten and resignedly followed him down the stairs into the club, quickly saying hello to Jocelyn Halloran, the club manager, as they walked down the short hall to the green room. As Bill took off his coat, he realized he wasn't wearing his brand new jacket. 'I forgot my jacket!' he cried. 'Why didn't you tell me?'

'I thought you had it,' Colleen explained. 'It's okay, Bill. I'm going to zip back to the hotel and grab it.'

Twenty minutes later, as Bill stood in the wings being introduced,

Colleen made it back to the club. He slipped on his jacket and walked onstage. Len Belzer and Donna Coe, a writer from the *New York Post*, were in the audience. Colleen stood in the dressing room, listening to the applause in the huge packed room and prayed for the best. Then she found a payphone and called Duncan. 'Should I pull him off?' she asked. 'Do I just go up there and get him?' But even as she said it, she knew the night was out of her hands. Finally, she moved to a small table in the back row and watched him, though she could hardly focus on what he was saying.

For the first half-hour things went smoothly enough and for a moment Colleen made a deal with herself: if he got through this first set, she'd pull him off the second show and convince him to get on a plane back to Florida.

Then suddenly Bill stopped talking.

He scanned the crowd. 'Colleen, are you here?' he asked.

'Bill, I'm right here.' As Colleen answered, she prayed to be transported from the moment. Bill always looked so big when he was onstage, but now he actually seemed to shrink before her eyes. Jocelyn Halloran was standing at her side, asking what she wanted to do? Then Colleen thought she heard Bill say, 'I can't do this anymore', and she realized he was asking her for a pill.

Colleen jumped up from her seat and, making sure Bill could see her, made her way up front to the side of the stage. He looked over at her and she beckoned to him. He hesitated a second, put the mike on its stand and gingerly made his way offstage. Colleen bundled him up and made a beeline for the exit, but not before stopping by the soundboard.

She had asked the club to record the show and now she demanded the tape. No way was anyone going to see this set again. Halloran handed it to her right out of the soundboard. Somehow the pair managed to hail a cab on Broadway and make it back to the hotel. While Bill lay in bed, the covers pulled up around him, Colleen booked the next flight to West Palm Beach. She managed to buy three seats together for Bill and he lay stretched across all of them the whole way home.

On 8 January, the *New York Post* ran an unfavorable review of the show. Donna Coe, a Hicks fan, expressed her shock at Bill's performance calling it 'surreal' and comparing it to Lenny Bruce's last days when he read his court transcripts onstage: 'Hicks at times rambled about how terrible the audience was, mercilessly ragged on a table of middle-aged women and referred several times during his abbreviated thirty-five-minute set to not feeling well. In all fairness, the thirty-two-year-old comic looked less than robust.'

Coe nonetheless ended with a plea. 'This guy is completely fearless. We desperately need his voice. Don't leave us now.'

As soon as Colleen and Bill arrived in West Palm Beach, Bill went back into the hospital. Colleen could no longer handle the situation on her own and she called Bill's mother in Little Rock. Mrs Hicks flew down a couple of days later and the two spent the next days trying to figure out what to do. 'He would not go back to Little Rock,' Colleen said. 'He did not want to be around his father who he thought was a giant negative energy source that was only going to suck the life out of him.'

Bill continued to focus on work whenever he wasn't napping. After the *New Yorker* piece, Katrina vanden Heuvel, editor of *The Nation*, had written him a letter asking him to contribute regularly 'his caustic observations on life, culture, and our political scene'. (She enclosed Noam Chomsky's most recent piece.) He had also just received a letter from the New York Public Library for the Performing Arts. They were thrilled that he would be participating in their 4 June panel discussion, 'Choices, Risks and Responsibility in Performance', as part of the library's 1994 'Speaking Out' series. Then Colleen got a call saying Bill had just been nominated for the American Comedy Award for a third time.

While Bill rested in his hospital bed, he composed a lengthy essay called 'Bill Hicks on Television . . . Sometimes'. It was an extension of his long letter to Lahr describing the *Letterman* set. Writing on a yellow legal pad in his very neatest hand, he recorded not only his experiences with CBS and *Letterman* but television's ugly role in society. 'Lucifer's Dream Box', he called it. He now wrote that the *Letterman* experience had, ironically, 'been the best thing that has never happened to me, careerwise, and in my own personal growth as a person and artist, respectively'.

He wrote, once again, with great clarity of his boyhood excitement at watching great comics on *The Tonight Show* and thinking, 'Boy, if they like this guy, they're going to love me,' and of his disgust with the 'Bureaucratic Capitalist Whore cowards that run television' treating middle Americans as though they were a herd of 'bib-wearing' fools who are only good for reflexive consumption.

'The elite ruling class wants us asleep so we'll remain a docile, apathetic herd of passive consumers, and non-participants in the true agenda of our governments – which is to keep us separate, and present an image of a world filled with unresolvable problems, that they, and only they, might one day, somewhere in the never-arriving future, be able to solve. Just stay asleep, America, keep watching TV.'

Bill thought the essay might be perfect for *The Nation*. A waitress at the Comedy Corner had a computer and she offered to type the piece up for him. When it came back – forty-five pages double-spaced – Colleen suggested that he might consider cutting it for submission. He added a few pages.

'Final thoughts,' he wrote. 'Now, it seems, more than ever, our deranged nation staggers aimlessly about, seeking, but it knows not what for.'

His final line was 'Heaven is a win/win situation. There is nothing to fear.'

He underlined the word *nothing*.

THIRTY-TWO

Beep. *Hey buddy, it's Willy. I'm at my folks' house. Colleen flew in tonight and my brother is leaving tomorrow. All right, my friend, I hope you're well. Everything is a-okay here. And I'll talk to you later, I hope. If not tonight, tomorrow, tomorrow, tomorrow, tomorrow. All right. Love you buddy. Bye.*

Once Bill was sufficiently hydrated, he agreed it was time to go to Little Rock. 'Bill told me he wanted to die with his parents,' Colleen said. 'He wanted the circle complete. And Bill was very much into circles complete. Because he had been so estranged, he wanted everything back. So finally a date was set.' They would leave on 26 January.

Before they went, Colleen arranged for Bill and his mother to have a night out together at a Frank Sinatra concert in Fort Lauderdale. Since Colleen could only get two tickets, she hung out backstage; Bill thanked her profusely for giving up her seat to his mother and they agreed that when Sinatra began to sing 'The House I Live In', a sticky patriotic standard, they would meet outside for a cigarette.

In California, things were a mess at the Strauss McGarr office. Duncan had canceled all Bill's engagements and club bookers were furious. There were rumors that Bill was doing drugs. Geof Wills wrote him an angry letter about Bill's canceling, for a second time in a row, his appearance at the Punch Line in San Francisco: now that Bill was hot, he was just going to blow them off?

'I took Bill's last cancellation with a grain of salt and chalked it off to experience,' wrote Wills. 'I can not be this way this time. An excuse of stomach flu nine days prior just doesn't ring true . . .

'I bloodied my knuckles to get Bill Hicks into the San Francisco market. I found him publicity. I worked very fucking hard on his behalf when he needed me. Now he's on to bigger and better things which I always knew would happen . . .'

When they landed in Little Rock, Colleen and Mr and Mrs Hicks took Bill directly to St Vincent's Hospital. Steve came up from Austin and he and Colleen stayed with Bill around the clock. Two days later, on 28 January, Duncan had the brutal task of drafting a press release which officially announced that Bill was 'seriously ill'.

Bill was still planning to go to London in the New Year and spent much of his time calling Fallon to make plans. This was just a rough patch, Bill insisted, and Fallon wanted to believe Bill's hospital stay was just a bad reaction to the painkillers.

After a week at St Vincent's, Bill's doctors told him there was not much more they could do for him. They wanted to send him home with hospice care. Shocked, Bill called Bob Fiorella.

'Louise, my wife, answered the phone and started saying, "Hi, Bill, how are you?" and he was going, "Let me talk to Bob! I gotta talk to Bob!"' Fiorella recalled. 'Just shrieking, she couldn't understand him. And Louise handed me the phone. I said, "What's going on?" He was in the hospital and he was sobbing and I could barely understand him and he was saying, "They're telling me I'm going to die. They're telling me I'm going to die." And I'm saying, "Please, Bill, don't listen to that. There are things you can do. It's not over yet. Just keep your eye on the future. There's stuff you can do. It doesn't necessarily mean anything."'

Whatever his earlier reservations, the move back into his parents' house, where everything was comfortable and familiar, calmed Bill enormously and he summoned enough strength to come to terms and make some decisions. On 1 February, he began to write his will on lined notebook paper. He left his estate to his parents and asked that two of his guitars be given to Kevin and David. To Colleen, 'my love', he bequeathed a plaster set of his hand prints. That way, she could hold his hands whenever she wanted.

Then Bill asked her to go. He had explained that he wanted to die with only his immediate family present. Go out the way he came in, he said.

There was another, unspoken, reason. Bill didn't know what was going to happen beyond that point and he didn't want her to watch him deteriorate further.

'Bill was saying, "I am ready to go and I told you how I want to do this and you need to go home to Otis and your house and your life,"' Colleen said. 'I protested slightly – my first instincts were to refuse to leave – but I knew enough not to go nuts and say, "No, I'm not going," because the time was very near. I also knew I hadn't slept in four days because I was watching him in the middle of the night. He wouldn't lie down, he would only sleep in a chair. He was having dreams of being transported already, he was having those visions. He told me about this burly nurse guy all dressed in white coming to him and saying, "You're not packed yet. You're not packed yet." Which Bill took to mean that there were still a few phone calls to make. A few ends to tie up.'

The night before Colleen left, the Hicks family pastor came to the house. 'I'm going on a great adventure, aren't I?' Bill asked him.

On 13 February, Colleen arrived in Austin bearing a present from Bill for both Kevin and David: a little bag of mushrooms, leftovers from the September trip to the ranch. They thought they would use them later to contact Bill, but they never really worked too well.

Alone with his family, Bill sat on the back deck with his father and looked out at Mr Hicks's lush sloping garden. He talked to his father about mushrooms and gave him Terrence McKenna's book *Food of the Gods* with a letter in the back of it saying how much he wished they could be close. Bill made a $500 bet with his brother that he could get their father to trip. Mr Hicks asked what they tasted like but in the end Steve won.

Several of his close friends asked to visit, but Bill gently refused everyone. He assured them that he wasn't in pain, and insisted 'everything is going great' when they called. As if it were up to him to comfort *them*. Other times, in private, he let go a little. 'I've worked my whole life to get here and told a million jokes along the way,' he told Steve one day. 'And now I realize the joke's on me.'

It was time to call Dwight.

'I didn't want to tell anybody,' he explained when he got his old friend on the phone. 'Because I got so many things going on. But I just had to tell you finally.'

Bill began to cry.

'I don't fucking believe this,' Dwight said softly.

'I'm okay now. I'm at my folks'. I've been undergoing treatment for the last, whatever, eight months and I just got out of the hospital again. There's not much more they can do. Anyway, how are you?'

'Well, I suck now, man.'

'I know it's pretty weird news. Much weirder for me, my friend.'

They staggered through for a few more minutes, Bill explaining what had been happening since June. He told Dwight about him and Colleen: 'She's been through thick and thin with me.'

'Well, I just wanted to tell you and stay in touch with you while I could,' Bill said finally. 'And just . . . tell you I love you, man.'

'Bill, I'm just so sorry, and I'm going to do everything I can to help you.'

'That's okay. Everyone is doing everything they can, Dwight. What you can do is take care of yourself, take care of your family. Okay?'

'Yeah.'

'Promise me that?'

'I will do it, my friend.'

'Because life is really precious,' Bill said.

On Valentine's Day, Bill called Laurie Mango. He lay down on the couch in the family room and they had a long conversation. She had last seen him in October in New York, and, thinking back, she realized he was saying goodbye even then. Please could she come see him? she asked. It was really too late, he said. Laurie told Bill she had always loved him and would always love him. After talking to her, Bill announced he didn't want to speak anymore. He would just nod in reply or ask for some water but that was about it.

In Houston, Jimmy Pineapple was doing a Valentine's Day show at the Laff Stop called 'Songs of Love'. Bill spoke with him shortly before the show and told him and Huggins they could tell everyone.

Riley Barber flew in from California just an hour or so before stage time. Andy and Jimmy grabbed him and brought him to a back office to break the news. He thought they were going to tell him that the club didn't want him on the show.

Pamela was in the audience that night and when she heard about Bill from someone there, she broke down in shock. Bill had called her once, left a message saying he needed to talk and would call again, but he never did. At the end of the show, in which Jimmy played Sinatra standards and bitterly ruminated on love, he dedicated the evening to Bill 'because he is an inspiration to me'. He asked everyone to vote for Bill Hicks at the American Comedy Awards.

Colleen was in agony in West Palm Beach without news of what was happening with Bill. She was desperate to see him once more, just to say goodbye. She called Mrs Hicks but she felt coming back wouldn't be a good idea. Finally, Colleen's mother got on the phone and begged Mrs Hicks to let Colleen return, just for an hour or so. Colleen deserves at least that much, Elizabeth McGarr said.

Mrs Hicks relented, and Colleen flew in to Little Rock on Friday 25 February. When she arrived at the Hicks home, she went straight upstairs to join Steve at Bill's bedside. He was unconscious then, but had not been all the time. He had been getting up and pacing around the house almost every night. 'Like a wounded animal,' his mother told Colleen. Steve left the room so Colleen and Bill could be alone. Bill didn't open his eyes but she thought he could hear her when she told him she loved him. She kissed his cheek, went downstairs and called a cab.

At 11.20 on Saturday night, 26 February 1994, Bill Hicks died with his parents at his bedside. The laminated memorial card Mrs Hicks handed out to his friends said he was thirty-two years, two months and ten days old.

That Tuesday, 1 March, Bill's parents held a service for him at 10 a.m. at the Griffin Leggett Funeral Home. Friends, comedians and musicians from both coasts and everywhere in between arrived. The next day he was buried, as he wished, at the Hicks family plot in the Leakesville, Mississippi.

Four days later, on 6 March, Carrot Top won the American Comedy Award.

EPILOGUE

In the last year of his life, Bill wrote a script with Len Austrevich about a serial killer who goes around murdering hack comics. When the police finally catch the killer – Bill's character – he tries to explain. '*Why?* You have the gall to stand here and ask me why? Let me ask you what answer must a surgeon give for cutting from the body cancers that threaten its very existence? For verily I say unto thee my mission was no less holy, my intent no less pure. A changing moment in my life came the day I first laughed. That was when life took a new form and my sad visions were cleansed by humor and from that day on I paid homage to comedy. From that day on I studied with the zeal of monks lost in religious rapture, the works of the comedy masters. For I loved comedy and I loved those who loved it. I loved those who gave their lives to find the perfect laugh, the real laugh, the gut laugh, the healing laugh. For love, I killed those comedians.'